Handwoven Fabrics of India

Ed. by Jasleen Dhamija
and
Jyotindra Jain

Mapin Publishing Pvt. Ltd., Ahmedabad

First published in the United States of America in 1989
by Grantha Corporation, 80 Cliffedgeway,
Middletown, NJ 07701

in association with
Mapin Publishing Pvt. Ltd.
Chidambaram, Ahmedabad 380 013 India

ISBN : 0-944 142-26-5
LC : 88-82476

Editors : Jasleen Dhamija and Jyotindra Jain
Editorial Adviser : Mallika Sarabhai
Designer : Bijoy Shivram

Typeset in Benguiat 10/12
by Fotocomp Systems, Bombay
Printed and bound by
Toppan Printing Co. (S) Pvt. Ltd.

CONTENTS

PREFACE

Scholars from all over the world have been drawn to research different aspects of Indian textiles. This volume puts together some important writing on handwoven and handworked textiles. Many of the papers reprinted in this volume are out of print, have appeared in obscure journals or have never been translated. Dr. Rau's research on the terminology for weaving found in early Sanskrit texts, originally published in German, has been specially translated for this volume. Dr. Moti Chandra's remarkable study of Kashmir shawls published in the *Bulletin of the Prince of Wales Museum* and Dr. Stella Kramrisch's article on *kantha,* a landmark in the study of symbolism in textiles, have both been out of print. Pupul Jayakar's article on *jamdani* is the first detailed study of this ancient technique and her findings on brocades could lead to interesting hypothesis. Françoise Cousin's study of *ajrakh* in Sindh is an excellent source material relating to this technique which is also practised in Dhamardka and Khavda in Kutch, and retains many of the features which link it directly with the cloth fragments sound in Fostat. The article by Jasleen Dhamija making a comparative study of Persian and Indian shawls was printed in Iran and never distributed. Her study of velvets, hitherto unpublished, is a subject on which little work has been done. Dr. Geijer's research on Indian textiles draws from sources which are well recorded but to which no Indian scholar has had access.

Many of these articles appear for the first time in a publication which will be widely distributed and it is hoped that this will lead to further research. Contribution from other authors such as Dr. Matibelle Gittinger and Dr. Lotika Varadarajan were received but could not be included because of problems of space. Permission for the reproduction of John Irwin's article could not be obtained. However the contribution of these authors is well-known.

The regional survey at the end of the volume looks at the current situation of the industry in India and pin-points major developments. Varanasi has emerged as an important production centre and has influenced the designs and techniques of other areas. It has also absorbed a number of techniques which adversely affected other centres. There has been a prodigious development in the *ikat* techniques. Poochampalli and Nalgonda district as a whole have developed, while the old centres of Chirala and Pirala have been lost. In Patan the number of practitioners of *patola* weaving have fallen, while Rajkot, with its single *ikat* continues to have a number of weavers. In Orissa, the *bandha* technique dominates while the technique of extra weft weaving is becoming rare and the quality has deteriorated. The traditional South Indian silks in Tamilnadu and Mysore are all influenced by the designs of Kanchipuram, and the distinctive patterns of Molkalmurru have more or less been lost. Strangely, the splendid extra weft designs of Orissa have been revived in Dharmavaram. Andhra Pradesh's famous *Armoori* sarees, with their gold *pallus* combined with silk and silver patterns, are not to be seen any more. These changes are important to record, for the situation will once again change and some of the important techniques may be lost.

This volume has been made possible because of the support given for this work by the Association of Corporations and Apex Societies of Handloom, Handloom Pavilion, Pragati Maidan, Bhairon Marg, New Delhi 110 001.

While it has not been possible to cover all the important contributions made to the study of Indian textiles, the aspects covered will be of interest to art historians, students of design and textiles, and to connoisseurs of art.

Jasleen Dhamija   Jyotindra Jain

Major Centers of Handloom Production

Delhi

Uttar Pradesh
- Lucknow
1. Varanasi
2. Agra
3. Fatehpur Sikri
4. Tanda

Bihar
- Patna
5. Bhagalpur
6. Ranchi
7. Darbhanga

Punjab
- Chandigarh
8. Jullunder
9. Pathankot

Haryana
10. Rohtak
11. Panipat

Himachal Pradesh
- Simla
12. Kulu
13. Manali
14. Bilaspur
15. Kangra
16. Chamba

Gujarat
- Ahmedabad
17. Surat
18. Patan
19. Rajkot
20. Jamnagar
21. Bhuj
22. Dhamadka
23. Chota Udaipur
24. Khambhat

Rajasthan
- Jaipur
25. Kota
26. Chitorgarh

Madhya Pradesh
- Bhopal
27. Chanderi
28. Maheshwar
29. Bastar
30. Jagdalpur

Maharashtra
- Bombay
31. Kolhapur
32. Paithan
33. Aurangabad

Bengal
- Calcutta
34. Murshidabad
35. Baluchar
36. Shantipur

Tripura
- Agartala

Assam
- Gauhati

Nagaland
37. Kohima

Manipur
38. Imphal
39. Moirang
40. Urkul

Orrisa
- Bhubaneshwar
41. Cuttack
42. Sambalpur
43. Naupatna

Jammu & Kashmir
- Srinagar
44. Jammu

Ladakh
45. Leh
46. Kargil

Andhra Pradesh
- Hyderabad
47. Gadwal
48. Armur
49. Poochampalli
50. Chirala
51. Sangareddy
52. Narayanpett
53. Venkatagiri
54. Siddipet
55. Peddapuram
56. Kalahasti
57. Machilipatnam
58. Dharmavaram

Tamilnadu
- Madras
59. Kumbhakonam
60. Puddukottai
61. Kanchipuram
62. Coimbatore
63. Shankaranayankovil
64. Tanjavur
65. Madurai
66. Kodalikuppur
67. Ootacamund

Kerala
- Trivandrum
68. Trichur
69. Cochin
70. Calicut

Karnataka
- Bangalore
71. Mysore
72. Dharmavaram
73. Karwar
74. Ilkal
75. Dharwar
76. Hubli

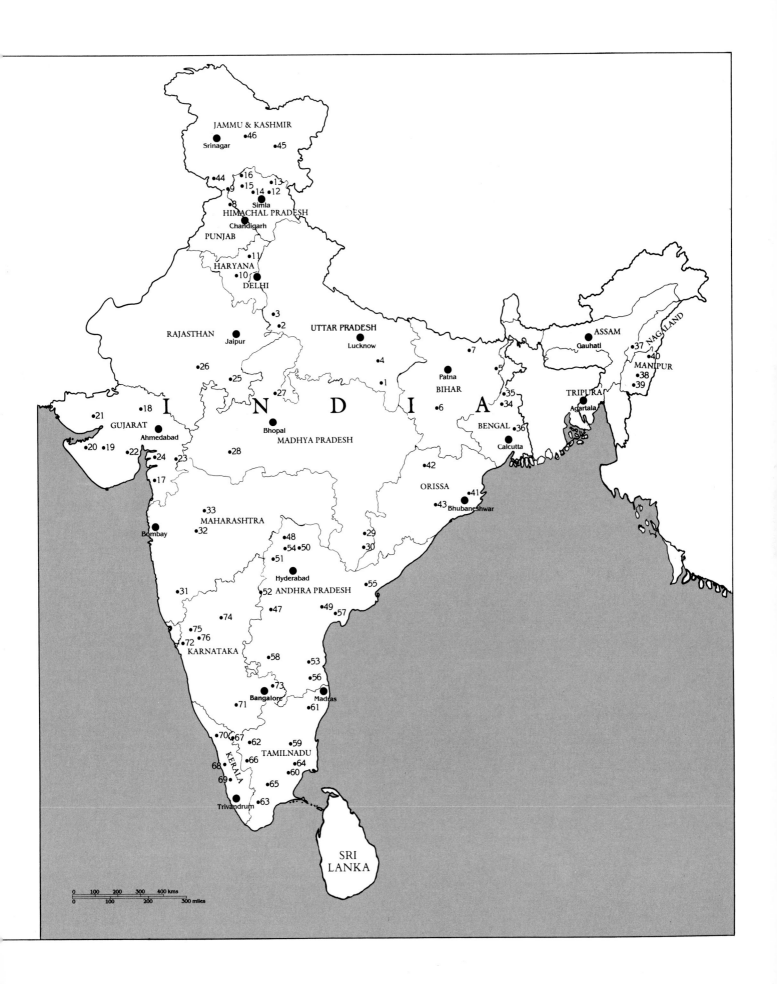

INDIA

JAMMU & KASHMIR
•46
Srinagar •45

•44 •16
•15 •13
•9 •14 •12
•8 Simla
HIMACHAL PRADESH
Chandigarh
PUNJAB

•11
HARYANA
•10
DELHI

•3
•2
RAJASTHAN UTTAR PRADESH
Jaipur Lucknow •7

•4
•26 •1 Patna
•25 BIHAR
•27 •6

•21 •18 I N D I A
GUJARAT
Ahmedabad Bhopal
•20 •19 •22 MADHYA PRADESH
•24 •23
•17 •28 ORISSA
•42
•43 •41
•33 BhubaneShwar
MAHARASHTRA
•32 •29
Bombay •30
•48
•54 •50
•51
•55
Hyderabad
•31 •52 ANDHRA PRADESH
•47 •49
•74 •57
•75 •76
•72
KARNATAKA
•58 •53
•56
•73
Bangalore Madras
•71 •61

•70 •67
•62 •59
KERALA •66 TAMILNADU •64
•68 •60
•69 •65
•63
Trivandrum

ASSAM
Gauhati
•37 NAGALAND
•40
MANIPUR
•38
•39
•35 TRIPURA
•34 Agartala
BENGAL •36
Calcutta

SRI
LANKA

0 100 200 300 400 kms
0   100   200   300 miles

Handwoven and Handworked Textiles of India

Jasleen Dhamija

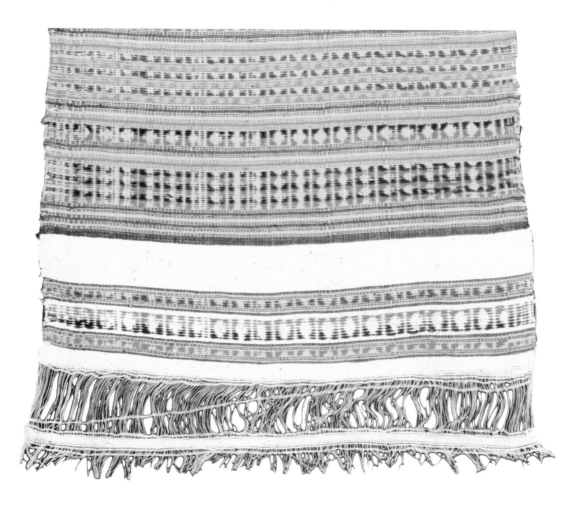

The weaving together of the warp and weft into a fabric has been a source of wonder for the human mind. Many mystic concepts and abstract ideas have taken their imagery from weaving and dyeing technology. The word Tantra is derived from *tanttu,* the cotton thread, and so is the Buddhist term *sutra.* Often the rich imagery of Vedantic thought, of the *bhakti margis* and the *sufis,* is derived from weaving and dyeing.

The wrapping of a thread around the trunk of a sacred tree for wish fulfillment is seen even today in cities. In Tripura the ritual of enclosing a village by wrapping a continuous thread, so as to contain the virtue and cleanse the evil that may exist, is still practised. In many parts of the country the first cotton warp from newly harvested cotton is

blessed by the local priest. The wonder of creating a thread out of the cotton pod and then weaving it together, got carried to the product of the loom; some of the specialised woven fabrics became associated with rituals and imbibed magical qualities. The Patan *patola* became associated with the magic that protects, and rags of the *patola* were placed under the bridegroom's saddle when he rode out to get his bride. Women celebrating the seventh month of pregnancy wore a *patola* on the occasion to protect and bless the unborn child.

The woven fabric has always been of great importance as an expression of the tradition and culture of the people. It not only protects the wearer from the elements, adorns them and enhances their personality, but is also seen as protecting them from negative forces.

The dress of a person designates his status and identifies him with a group, thus giving him a sense of belonging. It is also an extremely personal form of expression and becomes an extension of the wearer's personality, conveying a number of signals which are part of the non-verbal vocabulary of a people.

From being an essential part of the personality of an individual, a group, or a whole society, the use

Paithani *shalu*, late 19th century

Detail from a cotton Paithani *shalu* used as a cover by upper class Maharashtrian women has a rich mat border and good Paithani *pallu*. The body carries *ashrefi* gold coin *butis,* all over the body.

Opposite Page

Rathwa loincloth, Chhota Udaipur

The narrow width loincloth with an elaborate pattern at both ends is woven by the local weavers on a narrow pit loom. The Rathwas of Gujarat and the Bhilalas of the adjoining area of Madhya Pradesh traditionally wear the loincloth and on special occasions drape themselves with cotton *chadars.*

Baluchar saree, Varanasi, contemporary

The Baluchar saree was revived during the '60s by the Handicrafts Board in Varanasi, after the traditional weavers of Bengal had discontinued weaving them.

Opposite Page

Chanderi sarees, Madhya Pradesh, contemporary

These very fine silk warp-cotton weft sarees use bright but subtle colours and rich gold borders making them quite distinctive. These sarees used to be worn by the royal families and the well-to-do families of north-western India.

of fabrics was extended to decorating the home and also for festive occasions. The wealth of a person, as well as the cultural traditions of a country were conveyed through its textiles. Textiles thus became an essential decoration for the home, whether a simple mud hut or a palace.

The use of sumptuous textiles for decorating palaces and even encampments of rulers to convey their power and wealth, is an ancient practice. The description of the personal tent of Chengis Khan given by travellers is like a list of rich textiles prepared in different techniques and designs and gathered from all over the world. Fabrics being easy to transport, as well as highly valued, travelled long distances. Egyptian, Chinese, Indian, Persian and Coptic textiles were found all over the world and the distinct styles of different countries were known from ancient times. Often the conquerors captured not only the woven treasures but also the master weavers of the countries they conquered. Tributes paid to powerful rulers were not only in precious metals and jewels, but also in the form of special textiles from different countries. Aurangzeb's tax levied on Bengal had a list of Dacca muslins and *jamdanis*. Maharaja Ranjit Singh received shawls from Kashmir as part of a treaty. In Tripura a rebellious tribe was punished

Karalkuddi saree, Kerala

This saree is woven in fine quality
unbleached cotton and uses a range
of textures of gold to create subtle
varying effects.

by being forbidden to use colour in weaving and certain designs were reserved for royalty or religious leaders since that gave a recognition of their privileged position.

India has one of the richest traditions of woven textiles made from different materials and using a variety of techniques for the processing of materials, for weaving and for embellishing. Each region has its distinctive style and technique. Even within the region there are variations in styles of weaving and designs, which have been retained because of distinct cultural traditions expressed through their ceremonies and rituals. The Salvis of Patan wove different styles of sarees for their Gujarati clients, preparing auspicious motifs on the body of the saree for the Hindu communities and geometric designs for the Voras. For the Maharashtrians of the Deccan, they wove the nine-yard saree with a plain striped body carrying a rich border and *pallu*. Those woven for export to the Far East had different motifs yet again.

Cotton cultivation and its use in weaving originated in India[1]. The very nature of the cotton fibre led to the development of a highly refined technique of spinning fine yarn with which superfine cotton fabrics were woven. India became known for its gossamer weaves and decorations which went with this technique of weaving. The dyeing of the fabrics, the printing and painting of patterns were highly developed from ancient times and India became synonymous with dyed and painted fabrics. The distribution all over Europe of painted and printed cotton from India through Fostat, old Cairo, gave the name Fustian to printed cottons.[2] Resist-printed cotton of fine quality became known as *sarasa* or *serassah*, a trade name used in the invoices of printed piece-goods of the East India Company during the 16th and 17th centuries. The term is used even today in the Far East for printed goods and was possibly derived from the term *sareiso* for a skirt worn in South India.[3] The brilliant colours of the dyed cotton were long lasting and had the reputation of glowing with use. According to reports a fragment of cotton fabric dyed with the use of mordants was discovered in one of the Harappan excavations adhering to a silver jar. Chemists who analysed the cotton fibres found the presence of madder which necessitated the use of mordants.[4] The Greek physician Ktesas (fifth century B.C.) mentions in his *De Animalium Natura IV* the popularity of the bright coloured Indian textiles among the Persians. It is also believed that the art of dyeing with the use of mordants was developed in India and was taken from here to Egypt.[5]

The popularity of Indian textiles, specially hand printed textiles, was so great that from ancient times it caused controversies. The Roman Senate, in its proceedings, blamed the vanity of Roman women for pouring out Roman gold for Indian hand printed cottons, to an extent that the Roman economy was adversely affected.[6]

Anglo-Saxon records mention that in the eighth century the Synod of Calcyth discouraged priests from wearing garments with Indian colours.[7] In the 17th and 18th centuries, France and later England prohibited the use of Indian cottons as it was adversely affecting the silk industry of Europe and of England. An interesting example of Persian *kalamkari sofre* of the late 19th century with verses inscribed on it, claims that the Persian printing industry was doing very well until the Indian craftsmen's products adversely affected their market.[8]

Besides cotton dyed fabrics, the other technique developed in India and expressive of the properties of finely spun and woven cotton, was that of the *jamdani* inlay technique, where fine patterns were woven all over the body along with the weft and in the same count. This technique suited the quality of the fabric, for the pattern was like the working in of a shadow, discernible only when held against the light. The gossamer quality of the cotton weave was accentuated by the *jamdani* patterns, and the flowing unstitched garments, given a light weight at the borders, draped better.

A range of checks woven with the use of dyed yarn and in varying counts must also have been woven, for fragments of these materials have been found in Fostat and other recent excavations at Red Sea ports. Early murals also show the use of checked patterns and stripes for the garments worn by women and men. Embroidered garments however were known from ancient times. The discovery of needles from the Chalcolithic period indicates that stitching of cloth and consequently embroidery must have been known from very early times.

Perhaps the oldest samples of Indian cloth are the fragments of printed fabrics found at Fostat, the old Egyptian site. The samples are supposed to date from the 8th to the 16th century A.D.; examples seen in different collections range from the 13th to 16th century A.D. Recent excavations at the Red Sea port of Qaiser-al Qada have also brought to light a range of Islamic fabrics which are typical of Indian cottons with dyed and resist printed patterns.* The Islamic fabrics which were seen by the author at the University of Chicago are very similar to the fragments found at Fostat. The Roman textiles discovered at this site are yet to be examined. The preliminary report however indicates that the greater number of these fabrics are in cotton, rather than flax. This is an indication that the fragments may be of the early styles of weaving, dyeing and designing of Indian cottons. Publication of this material will certainly give an indication of the early styles of weaving, dyeing and printing of Indian textiles.

After the Fostat fragments the earliest available dated textiles are embroidered silk *puthias* of the 15th century found in Jain *bhandars*. Well-known examples are in the Calico Museum of Textiles and in the Mittal collection. Though a range of techniques was known in India in the pre-Mughal period, few examples have survived. Kashmir shawls of fine quality must have been woven as a number of literary references describe the technique in detail. It is likely that the technique of 2 × 2 twill tapestry-weaving of non-continuous weft threads, which distinguishes the Kashmir shawl, may be derived from the *soumak* technique of Central Asia, which in turn had led to the development of the Iranian *termeh*. The *kani* shawl of Kashmir however, far surpassed the Persian *termeh* because of the availability of fine quality wool, and the mastery of Kashmir weavers over the spinning and weaving of *pashmina*.

The earliest known examples of silk brocade shawls and carpets are from the Mughal period. Even here the study of Indian textiles has been difficult as most of the dated examples are in collections abroad and are often classified as Islamic, Near Eastern or Persian. There has been a tendency to label all fine quality silk textiles as Persian. Recent research by experts in weaving techniques has, however, effectively questioned this approach. Mughal period textiles, nurtured by discerning patronage, display a remarkable mastery of techniques, of design and a consummate use of colours. The finest velvet brocaded silks, sashes, shawls, hangings and carpets were woven from the period of Akbar's reign to the time of Aurangzeb.

A weakening Mughal empire, an impoverished court, and political instablity led to the dispersal of master craftsmen to provincial courts. The patronage changed but the crafts survived. The new patrons however were smaller principalities with limited revenues, or traders making products for export or local sales. Budgetary restraints meant that superfine quality products could no longer be manufactured. But traditional centres catering to local needs continued, serving different communities, as they had done for centuries before.

The Indian craftsman's skill to adapt a range of techniques and develop them to perfection in a short period of time continued through the centuries and even until the beginning of this century; when Persian craftsmen were brought to Masulipatnam at the turn of this century, to introduce the *kalamkari* designs of Ispahan, the local craftsmen soon mastered the technique. In a short time, the Ispahani craftsmen found it difficult to compete with them.

Even in recent years the capacity of the weavers to meet the challenge of the market shows their mastery over the technique. In 1947 when the country became independent, the handwoven textile industry was in disarray. A number of traditional techniques were virtually lost because of a lack of design assistance, an intermittent supply of raw materials and a lack of access to markets. Today with the support of the government and a growing demand for fine quality goods in the country and abroad, most of the traditional techniques have been revived and some of the finest textiles are once again being woven in India.

FOOTNOTES

1. Agnes Geijer: *A History of Textile Art*, Sotheby Parke Bernet Publications, London, 1979.

2. Agnes Geijer: Ibid

3. Lotika Varadarajan: *South Indian Traditions of Kalamkari*, The Perennial Press, Bombay, 1982.

4. A.N. Gulati and A.J. Turner: "*The Note on the Early History of Cotton*", Bulletin No.17, Technique Sr. No.10, Indian Central Cotton Committee 1928.

5. Catherine B. Brett and John Irwin: "*Origins of Chintz*", Victoria and Albert Museum, Royal Ontario Museum, London, 1970

6. Jasleen Dhamija: *Indian Folk Arts and Crafts*, National Book Trust, New Delhi, 1970.

7. Catherine B. Brett and John Irwin: Ibid

8. Collection of Ali Afshar, Chicago, USA.

Weaving in Vedic India

Wilhelm Rau

With growing knowledge, a scholar of *Vedic* studies is able to support the prehistoric archaeologist. A number of sites from *Vedic* times are being discovered in Northern India which can be linked with the literary tradition thus identified. Pottery and metallurgy have a number of references here. However, material on textiles, weaving and braiding, collected from the oldest Indian texts, is presented.

Editorial Note: This is an abbreviated version of "Wilhelm Rau, Weben and Flechten im Vedischen Indien, Akademie der Wissenschaften und der Literatur zu Mainz Abhandlungen der Geistes und Sozialwis-senschaftlichen Klasse, Jahrgang 1970, Nr. 11¹¹. Circumstances did not permit the author to read proofs. This article has been translated by Jutta Jain-Neubauer.

Unfortunately, not much is known of the general living conditions of the *Vedic* people and hardly anything about their craft traditions. *Vedic* texts contain only a few and widely dispersed notes about the daily life of the people.[1] Secondly, the scholars' interest was nearly exclusively directed towards the linguistic, philological and philosophical aspects of the *Vedas.*

Because of the limitations of source material, mention of my book[2] may be made, as the following lines are an elaboration of what has been indicated earlier.[3] In this case, however, additionally, the *mantras* are taken into account, while the *sutras,* except for a few exceptions, remain outside the lower time limit. Our sources, *Samhitas* and *Brahmanas,* bear testimony for the region of western and central part of Northern India during the first half of the last millenium B.C.

Raw Materials

In the texts available to us, the grass *Eragrostis cynosuroides* R. & S. = *kuśá* or *darbhá*[4], is mentioned as one kind of plant that is used for the manufacture of textiles: both these terms are synonymous.[5] The plant supplies the fibres[6] *(kuśornāḥ)*[7]. Then there are a few references to *kṣaúma* garments,[8] which were whitish. Most of the scholars identify it with linen material but the equation of the term *kṣumá* or *kṣoma* with a kind of *Linum.,* probably *Linum usitatissimim Linn.,*[9] is not certain. The plant name *úmāḥ* (pl. f.) which appears together with *śanāḥ* (pl. m.) = *Crotalaria juncea Linn*[10] is supposed to describe a kind of flax. The fibres of the latter are described to be soft and stinking.[11] It is not sure whether hemp was also used for manufacturing textiles: our texts do not give any clue to this. During the period of the Pali canon, it was in general practice.[12]

More important than plant fibres has probably been sheep wool. One type of wild sheep[13] was known; however it is possible that three[14] kinds of domestic sheep[15] were used for this purpose. There are only a few indications for identifying them more clearly: their colour was described as

Previous Page

Weaver, Saurashtra

The weaver is weaving the traditional *dhabla* in wool on his pit loom. The blanket is woven in two pieces and joined together in the middle to obtain the required width.

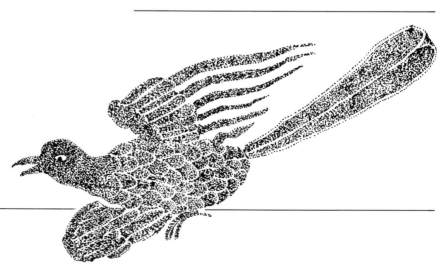

black,[16] whitish-grey[17] or reddish;[18] the horns of the ram were called either *śṛṅga*[19] or *viṣāna*[20]. Mention is also made of a sheep, *avir malhā*,[21] that has small pendants on its throat.

Animal husbandry had developed to such an extent that there were professional shepherds.[22] The area of their rearing is indicated as being in the North,[23] with a special mention to the area of Gandhara.[24]

Wool is called *ūrṇā(ḥ)* and *stukā*. The latter term, according to K.F. Geldner[25], describes the "sleek-haired sheep which is suitable for the production of wool", and according to H. Oldenberg,[26] "carded wool". Wool was an item for bartering in a raw condition as well as in the form of spun yarn.[27]

Processing

As evident from the term *alūnaḥ ... pétvaḥ*,[28] the root *lū*[29] is used for indicating the removing of hair from the animal's body, probably more as "pulling out" rather than "shearing".[30] The Vedic sources unfortunately do not clarify the further processing of wool until the spinning stage. More detailed information is available from the later texts. Two references are mentioned here, although these describe the processing of cotton rather than sheep wool.

Milindapañho mentions:[31] "Is it true, venerable Nāgasena, the Tathāgata is not more important, more worthy, more dignified, to receive presents as the jewel of the monks' congregation, that he had ordered to present the coat for the rainy season, which was loosened, teased, carded, spun and woven by her own hands by his aunt, to the monks' congregation?"

The reference in *Bhikṣuṇī-Vinaya* of the *Mahāsāṅghika-Lokottarayādins* is also as follows:[32] "These (nuns) went up to the terrace (of the house) and took up cotton: by one it was cleaned, by another, batted; by another one loosened, by another one carded, by the other one it was spun. (Then) they took up a ball of yarn and went to the householder lady: 'Householder sister, (we have done you) a favour!', (She) said: 'This is not an obligation to me that you venerable ones have loosened or carded or combed or spun the cotton'."

There is no doubt that in both the references the procedure[33] is enumerated in chronological sequence.

Spinning

Spinning[34] was exclusively the occupation of women: "That is verily the product of women, that woollen yarn"[35]. A priest who has received a garment as recompense, takes it with the following words: "Women have spun you; industrious ones have stretched you (on the loom); weaving women have woven (you)".[36] Nevertheless spinning and weaving women were considered to be impure[37] probably because all handicrafts were despised.[38]

Weaving

For weaving,[39] firstly, a certain number of threads are to be stretched parallel to each other, i.e. a warp has to be prepared. This activity in Vedic language is known by the verbal root *tan*,[40] the warp is called *tatá* or *tántu*(sg.) the warp-threads *tántavaḥ* (pl.)

"The sacrifice which is stretched with warp-threads in all directions, which is stretched with one hundred and one divine actions, that one these fathers who have approached are weaving. Sitting at the warp, they say: 'Weave back, and weave forth'!"[41]

From this reference, it is evident that the language makes a difference between weaving forth *(pra-ve)* or back *(apa-ve)*. Usually the same is expressed by *pra-ve*: *ā-ve*.[42] In case the direction is not taken into account, the weft is simply called *ótu* as opposed to *tántu* and the weft-yarns *ótavaḥ* as opposed to the warp-threads *tántavaḥ*.[43] In another reference, *ótu* stands in contrast to *prácínatāná*.[44]

Prányā tántūṃs tiráte is clearly to be translated as: "the one extends the warp-threads", and *dhatté anyā* is complimentary to this portion; it is obvious that the verbal root *dhā* means "to do the weft". In my view, H. Zimmer translates rightly: "the one continues to stretch the warp-threads, the other one throws in the weft-threads".[45] *Nāpa vṛñjāte* can be amended without doubt to *nāva pṛjyāte* which occurs as follows:

"These are the same dawns which flicker as first ones. These goddesses create the five colours. Coming again and again, they do not bring to an end. They never come to an end."

"Two girls of different colours (i.e. day and night) are weaving a textile having six sticks (i.e. time), while appearing one by one after the other (*éke*). The one extends the warp-threads, the other one throws in the weft-thread. They do not make an end. They do not come to an end."[46] The sticks mentioned in the text (*mayūkha*) are also referred to in the following:

K.F. Geldner translates: "The man stretches it, draws out the thread, the man has fixed it firmly to this firmament. These are the poles. They have taken their seats at the respective places: melodies they have made into shuttles in order to weave."

W.D. Whitney translates: "A man (*pumáns*) weaves it, ties (it) up; a man hath borne it about upon the firmament (*nāka*). These pegs propped up the sky; the chants they made shuttles for weaving."

In spite of Geldner's and Whitney's efforts, some portions remain unclear, but one can assume that the procedures of the first lines follow the later one chronologically.

At first the warp is stretched (*tan*) i.e. the work of weaving started (*ve*). Then follows *út kṛṇatti — ud gṛṇatti* the first word a *hapax legomenon*, the second one certainly corrupted. Here *kṛt* "to spin" is closely connected with *ve* "to weave". Since *ud-ve* is used in the sense of "to fix above", [47] *ut-kṛt* could mean something like "to draw upwards". This assumption could be confirmed by *ud gṛṇatti*, corrupted from *úd gṛhnāti*, "he draws upwards". In this case, the drawing up of the heddle-rod is referred to, by which the second counter-shed is created. The end is indicated by *vi-tan* (RV) — *vi-bhṛ* (AV), probably referring to the stretching of the pulled cloth.

Even if the sources are rather scanty, they correspond to the description of a loom by Walter Hirschberg and Alfred Janata:[48] "In the looms the warp is stretched between breast-beam and warp-beam, upper and lower threads are kept apart by the shed-stick. The heddle-rod having the heddles is placed crosswise between shed-stick and breast-beam above the upper threads. These heddles pass in between the upper threads and take up the one lying below it. By pulling the shed-stick towards the heddle-rod the upper and lower threads are placed parallel (shed). By pushing away the shed-stick (in the direction of the warp-beam) and pulling up of the heddle-rod, the upper and lower threads cross each other (counter-shed).

After the formation of such a shed, the weft is passed through as a ball or wound around a rod (shuttle). In order to bring the weft-threads as close as possible to the preceding one, a sword or beater-in is used. This beater-in has the second function of widening the shed: by placing it on edge, the shuttle glides through easily. Additional tools prevent the entangling of the warp (warp-spacer or weaver's reed) or serve to keep the width of the web even (temple or stretcher)."

Is it too bold to identify the "six" mentioned above as

(1) warp-beam   (4) heddle-rod
(2) breast-beam   (5) beater-in
(3) shed-stick   (6) warp spacer or temple

It is possible that the entire implement was called "*paridhí*"[49]. Which was the measuring rod, the pattern, which was the basis? Which was the lard, which was the loom? Which was the metrum, the *Praugasastra*, when all the gods offered to the God?'[50]

In his notes to this reference, K.F. Geldner translates *paridhí* in the sense of "loom" — whereas "the entire equipment for weaving" is preferable.

We again come back to the term *tásara*[51] mentioned above which was translated by K.F. Geldner as "Webschiffchen" (shuttle) and by W.D. Whitney as "shuttles"[52]. It appears again in *Āpastambaśrautasūtra* which W. Caland translates as follows : "After having purchased (from an eunuch) rice, barley and fennel for (a piece of) black metal (iron) and a black pillow and a black *tasara*-thread and after having bound these objects (separately) into a linen dress, the rice is kept for sprouting and the barley is slightly roasted."[53]

Another reference appears in four texts of the *Yajurveda*: "Together with both the *Nāsatya*, *Sarasvatī* weaves by thinking (for *Indra*) a coloured (i.e. black-white)[54] object, (namely) a handsome body. The skilful fermentation (weaves for *Indra*) a sap, (as) red as (sap) of *Arrak* (i.e. blood), like the shuttle (weaves) (red) yarn (into the black-white warp)."

The exact meaning of *véman* (neutr.) however remains unclear. Possibly it is "yarn", since some words ending in "-man" denominate at least secondary terms for substances:[55] *ádman* (n.) food, *áśman* (n.) stone, *ūṣmán* (m.) steam, *pākṣman* (n.) animal hair, *bhásman* (n.) ashes, *róman* (n.) short body hair, *śleṣman* (m.) slime, *stárīman* straw, etc.

Finally, a small error of the venerable H. Zimmer is also to be rectified. He writes, "*Mayūkha* means a wooden peg for drawing up the textile; as weight for stretching lead was used (*sīsa*)[56]. The translation should be as follows: "For the cost of lead, wool and yarn, the excited seers weave by thinking a texture (namely) the sacrifice: both the *Asvin, Savitṛ, Sarasvatī, Varuṇa* — healing the body of Indra."

If this interpretation is accepted, then there is no reason to understand lead (*sīsa* sg.) as lead-weights (plural) for stretching the warp-threads, which would mean a demand for a vertical loom (with vertical warp) during Vedic times, of which there is no trace at all.

Weaving was done mainly at home and preferably by women: the mother,[57] the houseladies,[58] or by servant women.[59] A garment woven at home [60] was considered purer than the one woven somewhere else[61] i.e. given as gift or bartered. The weaving woman is called *vayanti*,[62] also *vayitrī*,[63] and for the weaver the term *vāsovāyá*[64] is used.

If we have understood the above text[65] of the *Yajurveda* correctly, then we can assume that during that time the skill to weave three-coloured fabrics had been developed; while two coloured ones were often woven, though the usual fabric must have been the single coloured. It is conjectured that besides the term *pesas (pesa)* and its derivatives[66], the sources mention words from this word-group seven times in connection with textiles, and everywhere the meaning of 'colourful' i.e. 'of mixed colours', maybe only "black-white, yarn or texture".

"The colourful (strip) of verses are those which are invitation verses.[67] If these are placed during the morning pressing *before* the verses, then it is as if a man weaves in the beginning of the textile something multicoloured. If they are placed, during the noon, pressing in the middle, then it is as if one has woven something colourful at the end of a textile."

"These two, dawn and night, who grew big for us in earlier times, like two swift weaving women (weave) their products, (namely) the colourful (thing) at a sacrifice, while weaving the stretched warp jointly (black and white), both these (cows) giving good and plenty of milk."

"Morning dawn and night, both these (cows) giving good and plenty of milk, both these beautifully decorated ones, offer a sacrifice to the mighty hero *Indra*, the God of gods, while weaving the stretched warp jointly with colourful things (white and black)."

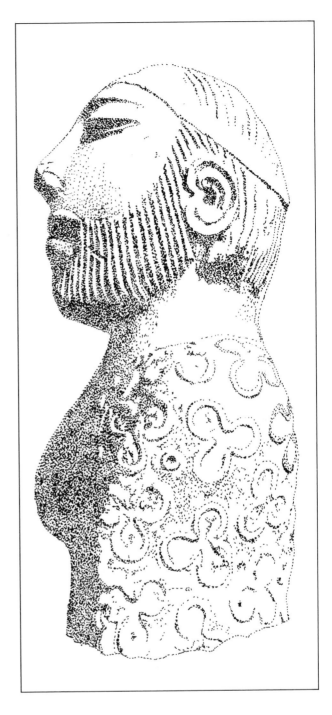

"The two *Aśvins*, the physicians (weave) this following the tracks of *Rudra* — *Sarasvatī* weaves the inner colourful part (i.e. black-white, at Indra's body), by putting *māsara* as leg and marrow into the hide of the cows like a strainer."

"The immortal face (*Indra's*) was woven by both the *Aśvins* with two mugs, with the goat (and) the cooked rice-offering (his) sharpness, with wheat corns (and) *kuvala*[69] fruits (his) eye-lashes. As if into a colourful (one), both (the *Aśvins*) dress in white and black (of the eyes)."

"You *Agni*, who are dressed now in colourful (i.e. black-white namely consisting of smoke and flames) garments at the navel of the world, born reddish at the place of comfort, as authorised agent, O King, sacrifice here to the gods!"

If we neglect *pesas* and turn now to the terms which are certain, then proof could be furnished for greyish-white,[70] black,[71] red[72] and yellow[73] fabrics in our sources. It seems most likely that for *ksauma*-textiles the first,[74] and for woollen textiles, the first three colours[75] were natural, because only for the dying of yellow is a dying agent mentioned — *Carthamus tinctorius Linné.*[76] The dying woman is called *rajayitrī*.[77]

Names for Garments

There are *Vedic* words (listed here according to the Sanskrit alphabet) which certainly determine woven objects. Except one word for "pillow" all these are for garments. Those terms are excluded which identify pieces made of fur, pelt, leather, felt, raffia or are braided, etc.[78]: *ákṣu, átka, apaśrayá, astárana, upadhāna, upavāsana, upaśraya, upastúrana, upastír, opaśá, kambalá, kurira, drāpi, nirṇíj, paladá, pavásta, vásman, veṣyá* and *śamulyà; adhivāsa*[79] or *adhivasá*[80] shoulder cloth for men, besides *vasas*[81] *tārpyá*,[82] *pāṇḍyà* and *uṣṇíṣa*[83] worn over *tārpyá* and *pāṇḍya. Upabárhana* pillow on the throne,[84] and probably a pillow for sitting, rather than in a backrest,[85] although this word surely identifies a pillow for the head and *upabárhaṇī* probably the entire bedstead. Sometimes, this consisted completely of threads[86] and evidently had a colourful design.[87] *Uṣṇíṣa* (m.)[88] and (n.)[89] means firstly a cloth or strip of cloth in general;[90] secondly, besides *vāsas*,[91] *tārpyá*,[92] *pāṇḍara*,[93] *krṣṇaśa*,[94] it probably[95] means a turban for priests;[96] arrangers of the sacrifice;[97] drivers of chariots;[98] runners[99] and *vrātyas*[100]; it also may mean — besides *tārpyá, pāṇḍya, adhivāsá* — a turban for a king.[101] This garment is also for gods,[102] even goddesses.[103] *krṣṇaśa* blackish garment for men,[104] besides *uṣṇíṣa*.[105] *Cándātaka* short skirt for women, made of *kuśa (Poa cynosuroides, Retz.)* fibres, worn instead of a garment (*vāsas*) made of the same material as a consecration garment (*dīkṣitavásana*).[106] In fairy tales, heavenly girls wear golden *candātaka*,[107] *tārpyá*,[108] a certain kind of *vāsas*,[109] besides *pāṇḍara*,[110] *pāṇḍya*,[111] *adhīvāsá*[112] and *uṣṇíśa*.[113] It therefore is a lower garment for men[114] that could have been made of *darbha (Poa cynosuroides Retz.)* fibres.[115] If we interpret verses from *Satapatha Brahmana*[116] correctly, then certain de-

signs could be embroidered or appliqúed thereon.[117] Unfortunately only this much can be said with certainty:[118] *nīví* is the loincloth, the lower garment in contrast to *paridhāna.*[119] This garment covered the central part of the body and the upper thighs. The series of terms: *upapakṣá* (armpit) — *kaṇṭhá (upper part of chest) — ūrú* (upper thigh) — *jānu* (knee) — *kulphá* (ankle)[120], corresponds somewhere else with *upakakṣa* (armpit) — *kaṇṭhá* (upper part of chest) — *nīvi* (loincloth) — *jānu* (knee) — *kulpha (ankle)*[121], respectively. *Śiras* (head) — *grīvāh* (neck) — *nīvi* (loincloth)[122] — *kulpha* (ankle) and *pāda* (foot),[123] are the other terms. There is reference to a simple cloth that was wound around the hips from the right direction[124] and was worn tightly bound[125] or loose[126], similar to the present-day *dhoti* "a cloth worn round the waist, passing between the legs and tucked in behind."[127] The loincloth could also be used for keeping small objects.[128]

Three close references[129] refer to the term *nīvi* as a certain part of any textiles — may be the selvage[130] or the thrum resp. selvage[131] — *paridhāna* or upper garment for men, besides *nīvi* and *pravará*,[132] possibly dyed yellow with *Carthamus tinctorius Linn.*[133] *Pāṇḍará*[134], is an upper garment for men, besides *tārpyá* and *uṣṇíṣa*,[135] made of whitish-yellow wool. *Pāṇḍvá*, is same as *pāṇḍará*, besides *tārpyá, adhivāsa* and *uṣṇíṣa*,[136] *pravará*,[137] *pravāra*[138] and possibly *prāvaráṇa*,[139] a shoulder cloth for men in contrast to the upper garment.[140]

Barāsi,[141] is a garment for men.[142] With lace trimming, it becomes *akṣāvana* or the *govyaccha*.[143] *Vāsana*,[144] and *dīkṣitávasana*, a garment for the consecration during the sacrifice[145] is worn not only by the arranger of the sacrifice but also by his wife;[146] a kind of *vāsas*.[147] *Vástra:* is the fabric on the loom[148] or one which is pre-

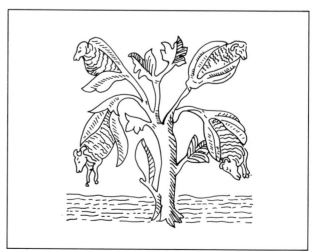

pared by the fuller.[149] This is a valuable object that is mentioned as gift,[150] as tribute,[151] as barter[152] or as a booty in theft.[153] Also a garment of a woman,[154] and of a bride, in addition to vāsas.[155]

Vāsas is on one hand a cloth or garment in general,[156] and on the other hand the upper garment, in contrast to adhīvāsa, to uṣṇīṣa,[157] to vástra.[158] It is also used during a sacrifice (= sacrificial garment)[159] and for women.[160] Made of darbha — (Eragrostis cynosuroides, Retz), fibres[161] or of flax[162] provided that ksumā is identified rightly, it has unravelled borders,[163] fringes[164] (woven) braid[165] or applique.[166] It is not sure, whether these four terms are identified correctly.

Among the colours we learn about black,[167] yellow[168] and red.[169]

There is no doubt that garments were held in high esteem and considered to be precious; wherever there is a mention of wealth, they are never omitted.[170] They are used as barter,[171] and were most often the items that a priest would demand as a gift for performing a ritual.[172] Because of the fear that they could be stolen or robbed, they were kept in safety by precautions[173] and care was taken that repetitive washing[174] or mending[175] did not harm the fabric too much.

It can be concluded that Vedic garments for men consisted of four pieces: lower garment (tārpyá, nīvī), upper garment (pāṇḍará, pāṇḍyà, paridhāna, vāsas, strictly speaking), shoulder-cloth (adhivāsa, pravara, pravāra, prāvaraṇa) and turban (uṣṇīṣa). It is not possible to put kṛṣṇása, barāsī, vasana and vastra into this classification with certainty. Garments for women consisted of two pieces: under-skirt (cáṇḍātaka, vástra) and upper garment (vásana, vāsas, strictly speaking); uṣṇīṣa is only mentioned for goddesses.[176]

The main point of interest in these investigations was concerned with weaving and their products. If however the same material is scrutinised from the point of view of the philosophical approach, it is interesting to observe that the technical terminology is closely linked with philosophical thought. It is not by chance that technical terms play a basic role in early philosophy (for example, guṇá, tarka, nidāna, bándhu) and to a much larger extent such terms which designate scientific works (for example grantha, sūtra, tantra, nibandha originate from textile techniques.) Thinkers of earlier times must have visualised their actions with the following pictures: he, who writes a text, strings something up;[177] he who formulates a sequence of rules (sūtras) is spinning;[178] he who creates a textbook (tántra),[179] is stretching out warp. The whole of ancient Indian scholarship is reflected in the simple but skilled manipulation of the warp and weft of a loom.

FOOTNOTES

1. Exceptions:
   ZIMMER, Heinrich: Altindisches Leben, Die Cultur der vedischen Arier nach den Samhita dargestellt. Berlin 1879, specially pp. 245-255.

   MacDONELL, A.A. and A.H. KEITH: Vedic Index of Names and Subjects, 2 vols., London 1912. (Reprint: Varanasi 1958)

2. RAU, Wilhelm: Staat und Gesellschaft im alten Indien, nach den Brāhmana — Texten dargestellt. Wiesbaden 1957.

3. lcc. cit., pp.27-28

4. MS 1, 11, 8 (100, 10); KS 14, 7 (206, 13); TB1, 3, 7, 1; SB 5, 2, 1, 8.

5. JB 2, 100 (201, 21)

6. Cf. WATT, vol. III, pp.253 sqq.

7. SB 2, 5, 2, 15

8. MS 1, 6, 4 (54, 16); 2, 6, 1 (144, 2); 3, 6, 7 (254, 11); 3, 7, 4 (261, 17 sqq.); 4, 3, 1 (353, 8); 353, 8); KS 15, 1 (210, 8); TS 6, 1, 1, 3.

9. TA 1, 32, 3 (116, 11)

10. SB 6, 6, 1, 24

11. SB 3, 2, 1, 11 and 6, 6, 1, 24

12. Cf. The Pali Text Society's Pali-English Dictionary, s.v. cīvara. — Compare also Heredot IV, 74

13. mesa...āranya MS 2, 7, 17 (169, 12); 3, 14, 11 (317, 3); KS 16, 17 (241, 13-14); VS 24, 30, 38

14. avi, mesa and edaka. JB 1, 51 (22, 22) = aidaka SB 2, 5, 2, 15; 12, 4, 4 = bhavedaka TA 4, 31, 1 (337, 3)

15. avi sheep in general; aidaka mesa ursni ursnihulu: JB 3, 328 (488, 30) ram; petva: weather; mesi avika: ewe; uran: lamb, cf. K. HOFFMANN, Munchener Studien zur Sprachwissenschaft, part 1 (1952), revised reprint 1956, pp. 61-62

16. asita: AV 12, 2, 20: — krsna: AV 12, 2, 53; MS 2, 5, 2 (134, 8); 2, 5, 6 (138, 4, 10); 4, 5, 7 (374, 7); KS 12, 13 (175, 2 sqq.); 13, 1 (180, 1); 13, 2 (180, 15; 181, 7); VS8, 3 (182, 5); TS 2, 1, 2, 2); 5, 5, 21; VS 29, 58; —rāma: AV 12, 2, 19.

17. balaksa: MS 2, 5, 2 (134, 8); 2, 5, 11 (142, 16); 4, 5, 7 (374, 8); KS 12, 13 (175, 2 sqq.); v. 8, 1 (182, 1); TS 2, 1.

2, 2; 5, 5, 23; —
aveta: KS 13, 1, (179, 11); JB 2, 371 (320, 8)

18. *phalgu:* KS 12, 13 (175, 2 sqq.); — *phalguna:* TS 2, 1, 2, 2; — *lohita:* 4, 5, 7 (371, 8)

19. KS 25, 6 (110, 20); TS 6, 2, 8, 4.

20. SB 3, 5, 2, 18

21. 'One other feature of the sheep of many parts of India must be omitted, for, although never satisfactorily explained, it is too frequent to be devoid of significance. From the throat dangle "two long rounded pendulous lobules from two to three inches in length", much after the same fashion as has been noticed regarding certain goats. So far as the author can discover these (externally) goitre-like excrescences have never been investigated. They do not appear to be indicative of peculiar breeds, though they are more frequent in the sheep of certain tracts of country than others.' WATT vol. VI, part KK, p.568 sqq.

22. *avipāla* VS 30, 11; TB 3, 4, 9, 1; SB 4, 1, 5, 4; JB 3, 121 (405, 16, 20).

23. SB 7, 5, 2, 15

24. RV 1, 126, 7

25. Note to translation of RV 9, 97 (809), 17

26. *Rgveda.* Critical and exegetical notes. 7th to 10th vol. Berlin 1912, p.187. # AKGWG Phil. — hist. Section, new series, vol. XIII, No.3

27. SB 12, 7, 2, 10: *sīsena saspāni krīnāti ūrnābhis tokmāni sātrair vrihin. — -ūrna sūtrena krīnāti...* — 'With lead he barters for malted rice, with wool malted barley, with yarn (roasted) rice. ... He barters (for this) with woollen yarn. ...' JB 2, 257 (271, 3 sqq.): *gaur itarā gaur itarornāe trayasyaivainām* (read: *itarornāsūtrasyaivainām) āvikasya yāvad arhantīm manyeta tāvatā niskrīniyād iti — ūrnāsūtram u vai gob kim cid iva —* 'One cow is like this, the other one like that (i.e. the cows are of different value). Therefore he should redeem her with as much yarn of sheep-wool, as he feels, she has the value of. Woollen yarn namely is, as it were, something from a cow.'

28. MS 2, 5, 11 (142, 18); cf. also *vrsnir alūnapurvah* Mānava Srauta sutra 1, 7, 3, 35.

29. P(āninīya-) Dh (ātupātha) 9, 13; *lūnñ chedane.*

30. BLUMMER, p.102. According to Kautilya's Arthasāstra 2, 29, 41 the 'shearing' took place every half-a-year.

31. ed. V. TRENCKNER, London 1880 (reprint: London 1962). p.240, 4 sqq.

32. *vikaddhesur* HS

33. Cf. WATT, vol. VI, part II, p.625.

34. The best description is in W. LA BAUME: *Das Spinnen mit der Handspindel in vorgeschichtlicher Zeit.* (The spinning with the hand-spindle in prehistoric times). Blatter fur deutsche vorgeschichte, Zeitschrift des WestpreuBischen Geschichtsvereins, Fachgruppe fur Vorgeschichte, heft 6, 1929, pp.1-9. The term for spindle, *tarku,* occurs — surely by chance — first in *sūtra*-texts.

35. SB 12, 7, 2, 11. J. EGGELING translates differently: '-this, to wit, wool and thread, is women's work' with the note: "Thus '*ūrnā sūtram'* is to be resolved, according to Kāty. XIX, 1, 18; the wool being used for buying malted barley, and the thread for buying fried rice.' comp. above, p.14, note 8.

36. PVB 1, 8, 9; similar MS 1, 9, 4 (78, 14); KS 9, 9 (111, 12). W. CALAND translates: 'The women have cut thee (viz. the fleece for the cloth), the industrious ones (viz. the fingers of the women) have stretched (thee on the loom), the weaving females have woven (thee)'. In this the translation of the first sentence is surely wrong, as already shown in the translation of W.D. WHITNEY's of AV 14, 1, 45:
yā akrntann avayan yās ca tatnire
yā devīr antām abhito'dadanta
tās tvā jarase sam vyayanty
āyusmatīdam pari dhatsva vāsah

"They (f.) who spun, wove, and who stretched (the web), what divine ones (f.) gave the ends about, let them wrap thee in order to old age; (as) one long-lived put about thee this garment".

37. TS 2, 5, 1, 7; SB 3, 1, 2, 19; text below p.24, note 4.

38. Cf. RAU, p.28.

39. PDH 1, 1055; *ven tantusamtāne.*

40. PDh 8, 1; *tanu vistāre*

41. RV 10, 130 (956), 1; translation according to K.F. GELD-NER.

42. see VS 32, 8; SB 14, 6, 6, 1 sqq.; 14, 6, 8, 3 sqq.; *pra-ve* could also mean 'to place on (to)'; with *sūle* 'fence in': Mahābhārata I, 57, 77:
sūle protah purānarsir acoras corasankayā —
animāndavya iti vai vikhyātah sumahāyasāh ——

43. RV 6, 9 (450), 2, 3; AV 14, 2, 51; KS 23, 1 (73, 6)

44. TS 6, 1, 1, 3-4. Unclear is SB 3, 1, 2, 18: below note 190.

45. AIL, p.254

46. This reference is from AV 10, 7, 42. A similar verse is found in Mahabharata 1, 3, 151:
krsnān sitāma caiva vivartayantyau
bhutani ajasram bhuvanani caiva ——
'And this multicoloured fabric two virgins are weaving, while they continuously let the yarn roll, unwinding black as well as white: without fatigue, the creatures as well as the worlds.'

47. KS 33, 6 (31, 21); T8 1, 2, 4, 2; AB 4, 19, 3; AA 5, 1, 3 (250, 2); SB 5, 5, 4, 28.

48. HIRSCHBERG, p.142.

49. Cf. also RV 7, 33 (549), 9, 12.

50. Translation according to K.F. GELDNER.

51. Cf. text RV 10, 130 (956), above.

52. also J. WACHERNAGEL and A. DERBRUNNER, *Altindische Grammatik,* Gottingen 1896-1964, vol.I, p.8 32; additions to vol.II, 1, p.11, 22; vol.11, 2 p.215, 31 and a number of other authors. Cf. further R.L. TURNER, *A Comparative Dictionary of the Indo-Aryan Languages,* London 1966, lemma No. 5744. — *Divyāvadāna,* ed. E.B. COWELL and R.A. NEIL, Cambridge 1886, p.83, 24 means *tasarikā* 'work with the bobbin.'

53. *Das Srautasūtra des Āpastamba. Sechszehntes bis vierungzwanzigstes und einunddreiBigstes Buch aus dem Sanskrit ubersetzt,* by W. CALAND, Amsterdam 1928, (= Verhandelingen der Koninklijke Akademie van Wetensbhappen te Amsterdam, Afdeeling Letterkunde, Nieuwe Reeks, Deel XXVI, no. 41, p.173.

54. see p.23

55. *Die Altindische Grammatik* (-cf. p.22, note 2) mentions in vol.II, 2, p.756, 21: "From later texts VS. *veman* — 'loom' (or 'shuttle'); lat. *vimen* 'wickerwork' (!), newir. *fiamh* 'warp' to v. *va* — *vay* — 'to weave, to weave a basket.' From the Latin and Celtic term it becomes evident that the *material,* not the *instrument* is meant.

56. AIL, p.254

57. RV 5, 47 (401), 60

58. AV 14, 2, 51

59. SB 3, 1, 2, 19: *tad vai nispestavai brūyād yad evāsyātrāmedhyā krnatti vā vayati vā tad asya medhyam asad iti* 'He verily ought to give instructions to wash this (garment), (thinking); what an impure one is spinning and weaving there, should then become pure!'

60. *amotam vāsah* AV 9, 5, 14; 12, 3, 51.

61. *anyatrota* MS 4, 5, 7 (374, 10)

62. RV 2, 38 (229), 4a.

63. PVB 1, 8, 9. — Unclear is *vayieva,* may-be nom. dual. fem., B.V. 2,3 (194), 6b, cf. below text (8) — and *savātarau* VS 28, 6 = TB 2, 6, 7, 3, a term that is translated according to RV 2, 3 (194) 6b by J. HERTEL with 'two jointly working weaving ladies': Das indogermanische Neujahrsopfer im

Veda, Leipzig 1938, p.157, 17 with note 5. (= BVSAW, Phil. hist. Kl. 90th vol., 1938, 1st fasc.)

64. RV 10, 26 (852), 6c.

65. Cf. above previous page.

66. The latest research according to my knowledge RENOU, Louis: *Studes aus le vocabulaire du Rgveda. (Premiere Serie)*, Pondichery, 1958, p.25-27 — Publications de l'Institut Francais d'Indologie, No.5.

67. Cf. THIEME, Paul: *Untersuchungen sur Wortkunde und Auslegung des Rigveda*. Halls 1949 (Hallische Monographien, ed. by Otto EISSFELDT, no.7), p.33.

68. RV 2, 3 (194), 6. AUFRECHT has *Vavyeva* for *vayieva*.

69. *Zyzyphus jujuba* MILL.

70. *pāndara* MS 4, 4, 3 (360, 17); *pāndya* SB 5, 3, 5, 21; *sukla* SVB 3, 1, 2; 3, 9, 3; TA 1, 32, 3 (116, 11)

71. *krsna* MS 2, 1, 2 (104, 6); 2, 6, 1 (143, 19); 4, 3, 1 (352, 7); KS 11, 10 (156, 16); TS 1, 8, 1, 1; 2, 4, 9, 1; 5, 7, 5, 1; TB 1, 6, 1, 4; SB 5, 2, 5, 17; *krsnasa* PVB 17, 1, 14; AB 5, 14, 6; *krsnatusa* having black tassels TS 1, 8, 1, 1; 2, 4, 9, 1; TB 1, 6, 1, 4.

72. *lohita* SB 5, 3, 1, 11; SVB 3, 8, 22; *valūka* (according to Sāyana) PVB 17, 1, 15.

73. *māhārajana* SB 14, 5, 3, 10; *Kausumbha* SA 11, 4 (40, 19).

74. above, footnote 10; TA 1, 32, 3 (116, 11).

75. above, footnotes 17-19

76. *kusumbha* or *mahārajana*: safflower (*Carthamus tinctorious*).

77. VS 30, 12; TB 3, 4, 7, 1; *prakāmāya rajayitrim* 'by the desire of a dyer's lady'.

78. Already in Vedic times a difference was made between garments having (*tantava*: GB 1, 2, 4 (35, 16 sqq.), cf. below footnote 189) and those not having it (*nistantava*: SVB 2, 4, 9).

79. SB 15, 2, 8, 1; = 13, 5, 2, 2.

80. RV 1, 162, 16 = MS 3, 16, 1 (322, 1) = KS v, 6, 5 (178, 9); d TS 4, 6, 9, 2 = VS 25, 39; MS 2, 5, 1 (133, 17); KS 13, 1 (180, 9); SB 5, 3, 4, 22.

81. RV 1, 162, 16 = MS 3, 16, 1 (322, 1) = KS v, 6, 5 (178, 9) = TS 4, 6, 9, 2 = VS 25, 39; SB 13, 2, 8, 1 = 13, 5, 2, 1.

82. MS 2, 5, 1 (133, 17); KS 13, 1 (180, 9); SB 5, 3, 5, 20-24.

83. SB 5, 3, 5, 20-24.

84. JB 2, 25 (164, 27); AB 8, 12, 3; 8, 17, 2; SA 3, 5 (12, 23)

85. SB 13, 8, 4, 10 is translated by J. EGGELING *purāny āsandī sopabarhanā* with 'an old arm-chair with head-cushion'.

86. *sarvasūtra* MS 1, 6, 4 (54, 11).

87. TB 1, 1, 6, 10: *upabarhanam dadāti — rūpānām avaruddyai— Sayana's tasmai yad deyam upabarhanam sirasah prsthasya vādhārabhūtam tasya kārpāsasānornādhimayaih suklanila -pītādivarnaih sarvaih sūtrair nispannatvāt tena rūpānām prāptih —*.

88. masc. MS 4, 4, 3 (360, 17); VS 38, 3; SB 3, 3, 2, 4; 5, 3, 1, 11; 14, 2, 1, 8; JB 3, 199 (437, 22).

89. neutr. AV 15, 2, 1, 2, 3, 4; MS 4, 9, 7 (406, 4); PVB 17, 1, 14; TA 4, 8, 2 (279, 5); 5, 7, 2 (384, 17)

90. e.g. MS 2, 3, 1 (119, 19); *yathā salyam nihrtyosnisena vestayanty evam tat* 'This is as if people tear out the arrow (from the wound) and bind a bandage (around it).' Similar: KS 13, 10 (192, 8); TS 3, 4, 1, 4; AB 6, 1, 4; AB 6, 1, 4; KB 29, 1 (151, 9); SB 3, 3, 2, 3-4; 3, 3, 2, 18; 4, 5, 2, 2; 4, 5, 2, 7; 4, 5, 2, 17.

91. AV 15, 2, 1, 2, 3, 4; SVB 3, 8, 22.

92. MS 4, 4, 3 (360, 17); TB 1, 7, 6, 4.

93. MS 4, 4, 3 (360, 17).

94. PVB 17, 1, 14.

95. The only certain reference: JB 3, 199 (437, 21 sqq.)

96. TB 1, 7, 6, 4; SB 5, 3, 1, 11; *red*: SVB 3, 8, 22: red.

97. PVB 16, 6, 13

98. JB 3, 199 (437, 21 sqq.)

99. SB 5, 3, 1, 11; *red*.

100. AV 15', 2, 1, 2, 3, 4: PVB 17, 1, 14.

101. SB 5, 3, 5, 20-24.

102. Rudra MS 2, 9, 3 (180, 22) = KS 17, 12 (256, 2) = RS 4, 5, 3, 1 = VS 16, 22 — Indra GB 1, 2, 19 (53, 16)

103. Aditi MS 4, 9, 7 (406, 4) = TA 4, 8, 2 (279, 5) = 5, 7, 2 (384, 17). — Indrani VS 38,3 = SB 14, 2, 1, 8.

104. PVB 17, 1, 14; AB 5, 14, 6.

105. PVB 17, 1, 14.

106. SB 5, 2, 1, 8.

107. JB 3, 235 (152, 7)

108. AV 18, 4, 31d; *tārpya*

109. AV 18, 4, 31; MS 2, 4, 5 (131, 1); KS 12, 4 (166, 4 Sqq.); SB 5, 3, 5, 20-25.

110. MS 4, 4, 3 (360, 17)

111. SB 5, 3, 5, 20-25.

112. MS 2, 5, 1 (133, 17); KS 13, 1 (180, 9); SB 5, 3, 5, 20-25; *krttyadhivāsa*: TB 3, 9, 20, 1-2.

113. MS 4, 4, 3 (360, 17); TB 1, 7, 6, 4; SB 5, 3, 5, 20-25.

114. TB 4, 3, 7, 1; *tārpya* of the arranger of the sacrifice corresponds with *candātaka* of his wife: SB 5, 2, 1, 8.

115. TB 1, 3, 7, 4.

116. *Tat tārpyam iti raso bhavati tasmint sarvāni yajnarūpani nisyūtāni bhavanti* 'With this there is the garment *tārpya*: onto this all forms of the sacrifice are fixed.' Cf. SB 6, 7, 1, 6-7; *(rukmah) krsnājine nisyūto bhavati* 'The golden plate is fixed onto the fur of the black buck.'

117. Here it is reminded of *vadhūdukūlam kalahamsalaksanam* Kumarasambhava, 5, 67, *hamsacihnadukūlavān* Raghuvamsa 17, 25, and *rājahamsa samithunalaksmani sadrse dugūle* Harsacarita (ed. A.A. FUHRER, Bombay 1909) p.274,2.

118. Some more, but contradictory presumptions are found in *Katyananasrautasutra* 15, 5, 7-11; in Sāyana comm. to SB 5, 3, 5, 20 (ed. A. WEBER), p.491, 2 sqq.; J. EGGELING, SBE 41, p.85, no.1; W. CALAND, note to *Āpastambasrautasūtra* 18, 5, 7 (German translation); see above note 72.

119. AV 8, 2, 16.

120. SB 12, 2, 1, 3.

121. GB 1, 5, 2 (114, 6, 10)

122. W. CALAND, selection p.207, note 13: 'loincloth as garment in the centre.'

123. JB 2, 369 (318, 30)

124. MS 4, 1, 13 (339, 10) and KS 31, 10 (12, 17): *daksinato nivih*.

125. *udguhya*: SB 3, 2, 1, 15.

126. *udyrhya*: SB 2, 4, 2, 14; 2, 6, 1, 42.

127. PLATTS, J.T.: *A Dictionary of Urdu, Classical Hindi and English*, 5th impression, Oxford 1930, p.550 s.v.

128. RV 6,32 (473), 4 and AV 8, 6, 20.

129. KS 23, 1 (73, 5); TS 6, 1, 1, 3; SB 3, 1, 2, 18: text below note 190.

130. 'unwoven fringe (thrum)' A.B. KEITH for TS 6, 1, 1, 3.

131. 'unwoven fringe (thrum)' J. EGGELING for SB 3, 1, 2, 18.

132. So SB 14, 9, 1, 18 = BAU (M) 6, 1, 10; BAU (K) 6, 2, 7; *pravāra*.

133. SA 11,4 (40,19)

134. MS 4, 4, 3 (360, 17); SB 14, 5, 1, 3, 15.

135. MS 4, 4, 3 (360, 17)

136. SB 5, 3, 5, 21

137. SB 14, 9, 1, 10 = BAU (M) 6, 1, 10

138. BAU (K) 6, 2, 7.

139. SB 14, 6, 11, 3 the coat is used as blanket.

140. SB 14, 9, 1, 10

141. *barasī* — *Altindische Grammatik* (cf. note 70), vol.II, 2 p.386, 39 might be a printing mistake. — KS 9, 14 (115, 21) and PVB 18, 9, 16; *varāsī*.

142. MS 1, 9, 6 (80, 4); KS 9, 14 (115, 21); PVB 18, 9, 16; 21, 3, 4

143. KS 15, 4 (212, 3); *barāsī dāmabhūsā*, comparable PVB 17, 1, 15: *valūkāntāni dāmatūsani*.

144. SVB 1, 5, 15 (71, 1); SVB 4, 4, 14; SA 4, 15 (18, 19); CHU 8, 8, 5

145. KS 23, 2 (74, 18); 23, 3 (77, 21 and 78, 1); SB 3, 1, 2, 18; 3, 2, 1, 11.

146. SB 5, 2, 1, 8.

147. SB 3, 1, 2, 18; 3, 2, 1, 11.

148. RV 10, 106 (932), 1; mothers weave *vastrā* for the son: RV 5, 47 (401), 6.

149. AV 12, 3, 21; *grāvā sumbhāti malaga iva vastrā*

150. RV 5, 42 (396), 8; 6, 47 (488), 23.

151. AV 5, 1, 3.

152. SB 3, 3, 3, 4; KB 7, 12 (35, 7)

153. RV 4, 38 (334), 5

154. RV 8, 26 (646), 13

155. AV 14, 2, 41-42: *vādhūyam vāso vadhvas ca vastram*. May be in the sense of dowry.

156. *vāsāṃsi* are *tārpya, pāndya, adhivāsa, usnīsa*: SB 5, 3, 5, 20-25; *vāsa = tārpya*: AV 18, 4, 31: = *tārpya*: MS 2, 4, 5 (131, 1); KS 12, 4 (166, 4 sqq.); = *paridhāna*: AV 8, 2, 16; = *pāndara*: SB 14, 5, 1, 3, 15; = *vasana*: SB 3, 1, 2, 18; 3, 2, 1, 11.

157. RV 1, 162, 16 = MS 3, 16, 1 (322, 1) = KS v, 6, 5 (178, 9) = TS 4, 6, 9, 0 2 = VS 25, 39; SB 13, 2, 8, 1 = 13, 5, 2, 1.

158. AV 15, 2, 1, 2, 3, 4; SVB 3, 8, 22

159. AV 14, 2, 41-42

1Z60. MS 3, 6, 7 (254, 14)

161. AV 14, 2, 41-42; SB 1, 3, 1, 14

162. MS 1, 11, 8 (100, 10); KS 14, 7 (206, 13)

163. MS 2, 6, 1 (144, 2); 3, 6, 7 (254, 11); 3, 7, 4 (261, 17 sqq.); 4, 3, 1 (353, 8); KS 15, 1 (210, 8); TA 1 32, 3 (116, 11).

164. *bhinnānta* MS 2, 6, 1 (143, 19); 4, 3, 1 (352, 7); KS 15, 1 (210, 2).

165. *dasā* SB 3, 3, 2, 9; 4, 3, 4, 6.

166. *tūsa* KS 23, 1 (73, 5); *tūsadhāna* TS 6, 1, 1, 3; *krsnatūsa* TS 1, 8, 1, 1; 2, 4, 9, 1; TB 1, 6, 1, 4; *dāmatūsa* PVB 17, 1, 15.

167. *upādhyāyapūrvaya* TS 2, 2, 11, 4. Compare also Baudhayanasrautasutra 26, 5: *upādhāyyapūrvayam vāso daksineti — pravenato vāntato vā tāmrāni vā nilāni vā sūtrāny upahitāni bhavanty api vopadhānarajjur evaisoktā bhavati* 'It is said: "The reward for the sacrifice is an appliqued garment." — at the beginning or the end of the fabric red or blue threads are affixed: or here braiding with cord is meant.' — SB 1, 2, 4 (35, 15); *dhāyaiva pratidhīyate svarge loke pitrn nidadhāti tāntavam na vasīta yas tāntavam vaste ksatram vardhate na brahma tasmāt tātavam na vasīta brahma vardhatām mā ksatram iti* 'A braiding is affixed: (with this) he puts the ancestors into the heavenly abode. He should not wear a garment which has a decorative edging. If he wears a garment which has a decorative edging, then the nobility grows, not the priesthood. Therefore he should not wear a garment that has a decorative edging (thinking); the priesthood should grow, not the nobility.

168. KS 23, 1 (73, 5): *vāsah paridhatte 'gnes tūsah pitrnām nīvir osadhīnām praghāto vāyor vātapā visvesām devānām otavas ca tantavas ca naksatrānām atirokāh* — TS 6, 1, 1, 3-4: *rāsasā diksavati saumyam vai ksaumam devataya ... agnee tūsādhānam vāyor vāyor vātapānam pitrnām nīvir osadhīnām praghāta* (3) *adityānām prācīnatāno visvesām devānām otur naksatrānām atikāsāh* — SB 3, 1, 2, 18; *tasya vā etasya vāsasah — agneh paryāso bhavati vāyor anuchādo nīvih pitrnām sarpānām praghāto vesvesām devānām tantava ārokā naksatrānām* —

169. MS 2, 1, 2 (104, 6); 2, 6, 1 (143, 19); KS 11, 10 (156, 16); TS 1, 8, 1, 1; 2, 4, 9, 1; 5, 7, 5, 1; TS 1, 6, 1, 4; SB 5, 2, 5, 17; PVB 17, 1, 14.

170. SB 14, 5, 3, 10.

171. AB 6, 27, 2 may serve as one example out of many: *hastī kamso vaso hiranyam asvatarīrathah silpam* 'Magnificence, — that is an elephant, bronze (objects), garments, gold, a chariot drawn by hinnies.'

172. TS 6, 1, 10, 2; SB 3, 3, 3, 18.

173. SB 4, 3, 4, 7: *catasro vai daksināh — hiranyam gaur vāso 'svah* 'there are verily many rewards for sacrifice: gold, cow, *garment*, cow, horse, slave, bed, chariot. — SVB 5, 10, 7: food, gold, cow, *garment*, horse, land. — More references are not necessary: whenever there is a reference to garments in our sources, these are gifts for the priests.

174. SB 5, 2, 3, 5.

175. root *han, ahata* = not yet washed = new; SB 3, 1, 2, 19 and more; root *nis-pis* SB 3, 1, 2, 19; root *palyūlay* TS 2, 5, 5, 6; SB 3, 1, 2, 19. We prefer *this* form with PDh 10, 335 and Ksīrasvāmin's Ksīratanginī ad loc. The texts mention *palpūlap* — or *palpūlav*. VS 30, 12 and TB 3, 4, 7, 1.

medhāya vāsahpalpūlīm.

176. AB 3, 1, 8, 6: *syūma haitad yajnasya yad dhāyyās tad yathā sūcyā vāsah samdadhad iyād evam evaitābhir yajnasya chhidram samdadhad eti ya evam veda* 'Concerning the inserted (verses), these are the seam of the sacrifice. As one mends the garment if need be with the needle, like this the one who knows mends the crack of the sacrifice with these (i.e. the inserted verses)'. 'mended or patched up' is *punarutsyūta*: MS 1, 7, 2 (64, 5); KS 8, 15 (98, 19); TS 1, 5, 2, 4.

177. Cf. note 123.

178. E.g. the term *kalāpaka* means 'ornament (of four precious stones or pearls)' in poetic language the group of four closely connected verses; cf. e.g. Raghuvamsa 13, 54-57; Kirātārjunīya 3, 1-4; 4, 27-30; Sisupālavadha 7, 53-56; 12, 67-70; 16, 72-75; 19, 26-29.

179. Could it not be possible that the term *sutra* originates in the fact that in all ancient works of this literary form a number of rules, having different lengths and being complimentary to each other, are twisted into a thread of equal thickness — as it were like longer or shorter fibres — ? OLZ 1957, Sp. 536. I may mention that Bhartrhari uses the term *anutantra* in the sense of *vārttika*. *nityāh sabdārthasambandhās tatra†mnātā maharsibhih* —

sūtrānām bhāsyānām bhāsyānām ca pranetrbhih —— *Vākyapadīya* I, 23. This term does not occur in the dictionaries.

Translator's remarks on the raw materials (this information was kindly compiled by noted botanist and expert on Oriental flora, Prof. Dr. H.F. Neubauer): grass similar to millet.

— *Linum usitatissimum Linn.* = flax

— *Crotalaria juncea Linn.* (skt. *sanah*) = a fibrous plant belonging to the group of Papilianaceae.

State Weaving-Shops of the Mauryan period

Romila Thapar

The date of the *Arthāsastra* has been the cause of considerable arguments among scholars of Indian history. Suggested dates range from the Mauryan period (third century B.C.) to the Gupta period (fourth century A.D.)[1] Majority opinion is now coming round to the view that the text was originally written during the Mauryan period, but was edited with interpolations of various kinds in the centuries following. The original text was written by Kautilya[2] or Cānakya as he is sometimes called, who was the minister of the first Mauryan emperor, Chandragupta. It was expanded and

First published in the *Journal of Indian Textile History*, Vol. 1, 1955, Calico Museum of Textiles, Ahmedabad. Reprinted with kind permission of the Calico Museum.

edited by various writers, until it was rewritten in *sūtra* from by Visnugupta in the fourth century A.D.[3] This is the form with which we are familiar today.[4]

The *Arthāsastra* is not, as is often mistakenly believed, a text on Hindu political thought. It does not concern itself with the development of political ideas or discussions on the validity of various political institutions. It assumes that monarchy is the most superior form of government and proceeds to explain how best a monarchy can govern. It is in fact a text-book on administration in a monarchical system. The work is divided into fifteen sections, of which the most detailed is the second, which deals with the organisation of various administrative departments. The work as a whole reflects a period of economic development, when the idea of obtaining a national income via taxation from various urban and agrarian sources, had just emerged. Consequently there is an insistence on state supervision of all activities. The purpose of this was both to control production and to derive an income from taxation at various stages. Thus not only had the cultivator to pay a tax on the land he cultivated, and a percentage of the grain he harvested, or the merchant a percentage on the goods he sold, but even prostitutes and the keepers of gambling houses paid a regular part of their income to the treasury.[5]

Activities concerned with spinning and weaving would thus fit into this category of production, whether supervised by the state or carried out privately, which was in both cases taxable. One of the chapters in the second section of the work deals with the duties of the government superintendent *(adhyaksa)* of weaving. His duties consisted of distributing the raw material to qualified weavers and other persons whom he thought suitable, and supervising the work in the government weaving house. Secondly the guild-weavers.[6] Those individually employed were either professional weavers working independently of the guilds, or non-professionals with special permission to work because of hardship or other causes, which will be specified.

References to women who could earn a livelihood through weaving, contain revealing indications of the social relationships between men and women in Mauryan society. It is significant that the profession of weaving was one of the few open to women. Generally, it would seem that a woman who was not respectably married, was regarded with some suspicion, since the only other activities open to her were employment in the palace as a servant of the king, prostitution, joining the flower and perfume trade or belonging to a theatrical troupe. Even in connection with weaving, only women in certain conditions were permitted this activity. These conditions are clearly specified.

Widows were allowed to work. This category included women whose husbands had died, as well as those whose husbands were living or travelling in a distant place. In view of the fact the profession of a merchant or trader was a popular one in urban society, there must have been a fair number of women whose husbands would be away periodically. Owing to the uncertain nature of speculative business at that period, the additional income from occupations such as weaving may have been essential to the livelihood of these women. Young women who were cripples could also support themselves from weaving. Strangely enough women ascetics and nuns were not debarred from this activity. This is surprising, as usually men or women who forsake society and devote themselves fully to a religious life are expected to support themselves through charity or alms. Perhaps it was difficult, if not impossible, for a woman ascetic to wander through the country, begging alms. Women who had committed offences and had therefore to pay fines, could earn the money for the fine by working as weavers. Mothers of prostitutes, retired women servants of the king, and retired temple prostitutes, were all permitted this occupation. Clearly these were women who were too old to continue in their profession and had no means of sustenance. Housewives or women who had decided to remain unmarried, other than those listed above, were not permitted to work.

Furthermore, women were only given that type of work which could be done at home. This could be either the processing of certain types of raw material, or spinning. Any process which required equipment not available to the women in their homes, was prepared by men in the state weaving house, under the supervision of the superintendent. This was no doubt partly to avoid employing women in the weaving house, and partly to keep a check on the material and thus prevent theft.

Instructions on dealings with women workers are very precise. In the case of women who could not leave their homes, each one was to send her maid-servant to collect the raw material or return the completed work, the superintendent thus being unacquainted with the actual person who worked for him. Women in a position to leave their homes had to call at the weaving house early

in the morning at dawn, when the yarn could be exchanged for wages. The author adds that the light in the room should be subdued and only sufficient for the superintendent to examine the work and assess its value. Presumably the subdued lighting prevented the superintendent from recognising the face of the woman concerned. On no account was the superintendent to engage in conversation with the woman on any subject but that concerning the work, otherwise he would be severely punished. This implies rigid segregation between the two sexes, which was not characteristic of social life as described in other contexts in the same work.[7] Perhaps strictness in this case was to ensure honesty amongst the officials.

The raw materials mentioned consisted of wool, cane and bamboo bark, cotton plants and cotton, hemp, and flax. Apart from the weaving of piece-goods, blankets, ropes, armour and girths are also mentioned. The inclusion of armour is puzzling. It is possible that apart from chain-armour, corded armour was used by those who could not afford the former. The reference here may have been to corded armour. The girths were used on domestic animals and those drawing chariots, etc. The cloth girths were probably similar to modern webbing belts, which are used to this day as an essential part of the horse's harness.

The system of wages is explained in great detail. Both guilds and private weavers were given work on the basis of fixed wages. Payment was determined by the quality of the work done and the amount of time taken over it. In the case of the guild-worker, payment was made through the guild. Technical efficiency naturally played an important part in assessing payment. Threads spun from raw material were divided into three categories, fine, medium and coarse. The fine thread was more highly valued. Similarly in the weaving of cloth, the finer weaves fetched a higher wage. A careful check was kept on the raw material provided, which was weighed and recorded. A calculation was made as to how much could be expected in thread or cloth. When the complete work was brought back, it was measured and compared with the calculation. If it was found to be short, then the value of the missing amount was cut from the wages of the weaver. It is stated however that blemishes in the raw material were to be taken into account when the calculation was made. Natural loss of weight or length through processing was also noted. We are told for instance that in woolen threads there is a loss of one-twentieth of the total weight when the hair falls in the process of threshing.[8] Women were paid according to the amount of work completed and payment was to be made only on completion. If any weaver took payment in advance and failed to complete the work commissioned, the punishment was severe.

Encouragement in the way of prizes are suggested for fast workers. These could consist of oil and cakes (the latter were made with dried fruit and were obviously regarded as delicacies). Special rewards of perfumes and garlands of flowers are also mentioned, which could be made to those who worked on holidays.[9] These were in addition to the normal wages. Unfortunately no indication is given of the actual amount paid for a particular piece of work.

Fraudulent practices of various kinds were apparently well known. One section of the work warns the citizen against the trickery of artisans, and weavers are listed as among the more unreliable of artisans.[10] Kautilya advises that wherever possible work should be commissioned through a guild, as the responsibility then lay with a recognised group and not with a single person. Severe penalties are suggested if weavers were caught cheating the superintendent or any person who had commissioned work from them. The usual penalty was a fine and this was cut from the wages. Weavers who defaulted by failing to produce work in the agreed time had to forefeit a quarter of their wages and in addition were fined twice the amount of the commission agreed upon. If goods were damaged by the weavers, then they had to pay compensation. Those who produced what was not asked for, had also to pay a heavy fine and in some cases forfeit their wages. If the length of the cloth was short, then the value of the missing length would be deducted from the wages and a fine would be imposed, equivalent to twice the value of the loss. If the finished article was short in weight, then the fine would be as much as four times the value of the loss. The offence of substituting yarn of inferior quality was to be punished by a fine of twice the value of the original.

One of the better known methods of cheating practised by weavers is described. By soaking yarn in rice-gruel, weavers could increase its weight by ten per cent.[11] In this way, the weight of finished linen or silk cloth would be increased by fifty per cent, and of blankets and woollen garments by one hundred per cent. Such practices were punishable by a fine equivalent to twice the total value of the yarn provided, in addition to forfeiture of any advance payment made.

Strangely enough mutilation of the thumbs is not suggested as punishment in any of these cases. Yet this is regarded as normal punishment in the case of women who have received wages in advance and fail to complete a commission. Generally fines were regarded as the usual form of punishment in any offence. Mutilation is suggested by Kautilya only in the case of serious crimes. He lists three categories of punishment in relation to various types of offences. The first category was always the highest.

The various stages, from raw material to textile, entailed a series of taxes, which were paid by the cultivator, the weaver and the merchant or the textile guild. All cultivators paid a land tax, and a further tax on their produce, irrespective of whether this produce was a food crop or a cash crop.[12] Both these taxes varied according to the quality of the land and the facilities for irrigation, etc. The tax on the produce ranged from a quarter in the more fertile areas to one-eighth or less elsewhere.[13] (The average tax is thought to have been one-sixth.) In a period of emergency an additional one-sixth could be demanded from the cultivator.[14] The weaver, unless he worked in a guild, was taxed for hiring a loom if he worked in the state weaving house. This worked out to 1½ *panas* per loom per annum. The exact value of the *pana* remains uncertain, but some indication of the amount may be arrived at through the fact that artisans were paid a salary of 120 *panas* by the state. This is listed together with the salaries of other state officials. Presumably this was the salary per year.[15] No commodity could be sold other than in a government controlled market. Here toll dues were paid either by the weavers if they were selling the articles or by the merchants. Work commissioned by merchants or citizens was paid for separately to the guild or to the individual weaver. Undoubtedly this too must have been taxed. Toll dues amounted to one tenth or one-fifteenth on the following textiles; linen, cotton, silk, curtains of any kind, carpets and woollen goods. Clothing, cotton yarn and fibre were taxed at the rate of one-twentieth or one-twenty-fifth of their total value.[16] In addition to toll tax dues *(sulka)* there was a gate-tax *(dvārādeya)* of one-fifth of the toll dues.[17] In times of national emergency, weavers could be asked to pay an additional tax of one-sixth and merchants trading in textiles, an additional tax of ten *panas.*[18]

In another section of the work, relating to products from various parts of the country, a fairly detailed mention is made of textiles.[19] However this section refers only to those products which are sent to the state treasury as part of the tax. The list of textiles is as follows.

Blankets

These were generally made of sheep's wool. They could be white or various shades of red. The main techniques are those of *khaticham* (tightly woven woolens), *vānacitra* (loosely woven), *khandsanghātya* (various pieces joined together), and *tantuvicchannam* (woven with uniform threads). Many varieties of blankets are listed: *kambala, kecalakah, kalamitika, sarumitikā, turangastaranam, varnakam, talicchakam, vāravānah, paristomah, samanatabhad.* These are thought to be coarse blankets, such as those used by herdsmen and farmers, blankets spread on the backs of animals such as bullocks, horses, elephants, and woolen material woven to the size of blankets. Of these the best quality blanket is that which is slippery and soft.

Nepal is said to have produced blankets known as *bhingisi* and *apasāraka*, both of which were black in colour and waterproof.

Blankets were also made from wool gathered from other animals and described as *samputika, caturasrika, lamvarā, katmavānaka, prāvaraka,* and *sattalika.*

Other textiles

Vanga (Bengal) produced a soft white bark-cloth called *dukula*. [20] From the Pandya country (the region of Madura) came a smooth black cloth, described as being as smooth as the surface of a gem. *Suvarnakudva*[21] produced a bright golden yellow cloth with a smooth glossy texture, woven while the yarn was damp. Linen *(ksauma)* came from Kāsi (Banaras) and the Pāndya country. Fabrics of bark-fibre were especially woven in Māgadhikā (Magadha), the Pāndya country and Suvarnakudya. The trees giving fibre included the Nāga tree, which produced a yellow fibre; the Likuca *(Artacarpus Lakucha),* the colour of wheat; the Vakula *(Mimusops Elengi),* white; and the Vata *(Ficus Indica),* the colour of butter. Of the cloths made with these fibres, the best came from Suvarnakudya. Silks from China are described as *kauseya* and *cina-patta.* [22]

The finest cotton textiles came from Madhurā (south India), Aparānta (western India), Kalinga (the coastal region between the Mahānadi and Godāvari rivers), Kāsi (the neighbourhood of Banaras), Vanga (Bengal), Vatsa (the region around Kausāmbi, near Allahabad) and Mahisa (the region of the Narmadā).

Summary

The state must have derived a fairly large profit from the manufacture of textiles. This was one of the rare industries which in Mauryan times employed both men and women. The type of work given to both is of some interest. Women were only permitted to do the lighter work, the processes that could be carried out at home, without elaborate equipment. The weaving house, organised by the state or by a guild, where the greater part of the work was done and probably that of a more arduous kind, appears not to have employed women. The average wage of the weaver (120 *panas*) seems small when compared to that of the superintendents which ranged from 4,000 to 12,000 *panas.* The manufacture of textiles was clearly one of the foremost industries. They are mentioned among the more lucrative articles of trade. Textiles were regarded as valuable enough to be stored in the national treasury, and are described in the same section of the *Arthasāstra* as that referring to the various kinds of precious stones and gems.

FOOTNOTES

1. *Arthasāstra*. Preface to Shamasastry's translation (5th Ed.) pp.vii-xxxiii; Jolly, *Kautilyam Arthasāstram*, Panjab S.K. Series, No. IV; Jayaswal, *Hindu Polity*, Appendix C, p.364; D.R. Bhandarkar, *ABORI*, vii, p.80 ff.; Raychaudhuri, (HCIP, i), *The Age of Imperial Unity*, p.285; Kalyanov, *XXIII Orientalists Congress*, Cambridge, August 1954.

2. There has been much discussion on the name of Kautilya and its grammatical derivation. (Jolly, *Arthasāstra of Kautilya*, pp.1-47; and Kane, *JBOR'S*, vii, 1926). I agree with the view that the name was Kautalya and not Kautilya, and that it was derived from its owner's *gotra*, which was Kutala.

3. Book XV, I.

4. I have used the edition of T. Ganapati Sastri, Trivandrum, 1924.

5. II, 24; II, 22; II, 27.

6. II, 23; IV, I. The guild system was by now a regular feature of urban life. It had begun with the large scale development of commerce during the Buddhist period (circa sixth century B.C.). It appears from the *Arthasāstra* that skilled workers generally preferred to work in guilds, since this system had commercial advantages. In certain trades however it was equally lucrative to work as a private individual.

7. For example, the rights and duties of a married woman, laws of inheritance, etc.; III, 2,3,4,5,6.

8. IV, I.

9. The calendar of a working year (from the month of *Āsādha* to *Āsādha*) omitting the intercalary months, was 354 days.

10. IV, I.

11. IV, I.

12. The *bhāga* and the *hiranya* (Ghoshal, *The Agrarian System of Ancient India*, p.6). This is confirmed by the Asokan inscription at Rummindei, Bloch, *Les Inscriptions d'Asoka*, p.157.

13. One-quarter is stated in the account of Megasthenes. Quoted, Strabo, XV, I, 40; Arrian, *Indica*, XI.

14. V, 2

15. V, 3

16. II, 22

17. Ibid.

18. V, 2

19. II, 11

20. A fine quality cloth made from the inner bark of a delicate plant. It should not be confused with linen.

21. The identification of *Suvarnakudya* (literally, "golden wall) is uncertain. *Suvarna* was a fairly common prefix in a number of place names. *Suvarnabhumi* was the name for Burma and at a later period *Suvarnadvipa* was the term used for the South East Asian islands. *Suvarnakudya* may have been on the east coast and connected with the eastern trade, or else it may even have been an alternative name for *Suvarnagiri*, the Mauryan provincial capital in the south (Mysore).

22. The references to *cina-patta* was one of the reasons why the *Arthasāstra* was dated to the early centuries A.D., since there were no contacts with China in the Mauryan period, which would permit the importation of Chinese silk via eastern India. However there is evidence to prove that silk was used in Bactria, which was imported from India in the second century B.C. if not earlier. *(Ssi-ma-ts'ien, Shi-ki*, 123; translated by Hirth. JAOS, xxxvii, 1917, p.89 ff.). Chang K'lien in about 129 B.C. found the Bactrians using Chinese silk, which according to the inhabitants came from India. The interesting point is that it is referred to as silk coming from the province of Szechuan. This province has been known as the area where the silkworm flourished. The implications of this are that there was no silk manufactured in Gilgit. Thus it would appear that Chinese silk was available in India at an early period and that is came from Szechuan.

The identification of China with *cina*, may be a reference to the feudal state of Chin (during the Chou period), before the reign of Shi Hwang Ti (cf. Kosambi, *Introduction to the Study of Indian History*, p.202).

Some Evidence of Indo-European Cotton Trade in Pre-Mughal Times

Agnes Geijer

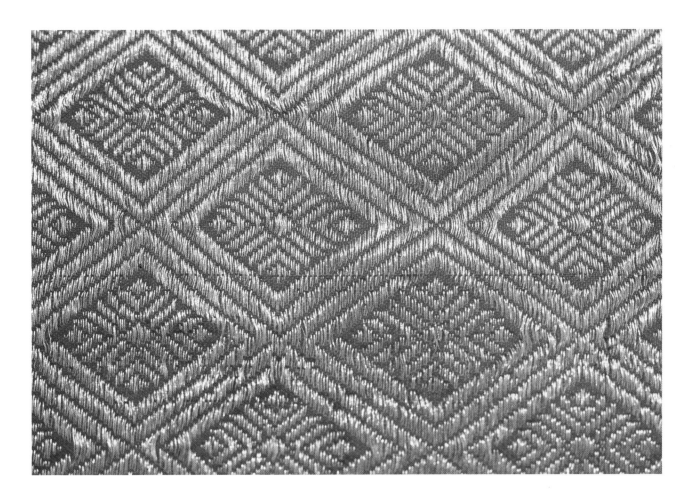

Just over a hundred years have passed since Francisque-Michel, that great scholar of European medieval studies, published his erudite work on medieval textiles as reflected in contemporary literature.[1] In that work, Michel drew attention to certain words which he thought indicated textile fabrics of oriental origin. At the time he wrote, few actual fabrics of the period had been classified or

Editorial Note: *The leading ideas in this article were presented in a Swedish publication in homage to H.M. King Gustav VI Adolf, edited by the Swedish Archaeological Society, Stockholm, 1952.*

This article is an extract of an article published in *Journal of Indian Textile History*, Vol. 1, 1955, and reprinted with the kind permission of the Calico Museum.

even studied, and it is a measure of his brilliance
and foresight that, in spite of great advances since
made in textile research, the questions he raised
are as relevant today as they were then.

The next landmark was reached in 1913 when the
famous German scholar, Otto von Falke, published
his monumental work on silks,[2] which, although
needing revision in some respects, is still unsur-
passed. The new period was to a great extent
dominated by silks, because so many examples
have survived from the medieval period as eccle-
siastical garments in European churches. Nevertheless, other materials, such as woollen, linen
and cotton fabrics were gradually coming to light
in Egypt. One of the richest finding-places was
Fostat, the important medieval harbour-town of
old Cairo.

It was not until later that the cotton fabrics were
made a subject of comprehensive research, and
in this work, a Swedish scholar, C.J. Lamm, a
trained art-historian and orientalist, made a valuable contribution.[3] A catalogue of technical descriptions of different fabrics containing cotton
was paralleled with a series of excerpts from medieval texts, mainly Arabic. The most important
categories among these Fostat textiles were the
Indian resist-dyed cottons, and woven fabrics of
Persian type, made of cotton and wool. The latter
class has been comprehensively studied by Lamm,
in the book already mentioned as well as in special articles. A representative selection of the Indian cottons was published by R. Pfister, most of
them being identified as having been exported
from Gujarat between the fourteenth and sixteenth
centuries.[4]

As part of his thesis, Pfister set out to prove that
until at least as late as the sixteenth century, India
was the *only* country which produced cottons fixed
with non-fugitive dyes. Although, from as early as
the first millennium B.C., men in other countries
had understood how to fix colours in silks and
wool, only India, he claimed, had mastered the
more exacting art of dyeing vegetable fibres with
non-fugitive as opposed to fugitive colours. It is
this mastery which distinguished Indian materials
from cotton or linen fabrics printed in medieval
Europe. For the latter, the colours consisted
merely of pigment, and its application demanded
no great skill: technically speaking, it was on a
level with engraving or primitive book-printing.

The earliest evidence of Indo-European textile
trade belongs to antiquity. The use of the oriental
word *carbasina* (Sanskrit *karpāsa*) for cotton in

the *Pausimachus* of Statius Caecilius suggests that it was reaching the Mediterranean at least as early as 200 B.C. Even before this, Herodotus had referred to the "tree-wool" of India. The Greek word *xylon* gave rise to *xylinum* in medieval Latin, which was defined as *lana de ligno* ("wooden wool"). The German synonym *baumvolle* ("tree-wool") gave in its turn *bomull* to the Swedish languages.

The author of the *Periplus* (A.D. 60-100) gives us valuable evidence of the great importance of Indian cotton goods in Imperial Rome. Although he does not specifically mention dyed cottons, there is little doubt that they were included, for the skill of the Indian dyer was proverbial in Rome itself. This is proved by the interesting reference in St. Jerome's fourth-century Latin translation of the Bible, Job being made to say that wisdom "may not be compared with the dyed colours of India."[5]

With the collapse of the Roman Empire, Indo-European trade appears to have declined, and it is not until the growth of Arab trade that we are able to pick up the threads again.

The Arabic word *qutn, qoton* was the name by which medieval Europe came to know cotton (It. *cottone,* Fra. *cotton,* Spa. *algodon,* Germ. *kattun).* The Arabic form with the definite article *(al-quton)* gave the French *boqueton, anqueton,* in the sense of a vest of cotton padding to be worn under the armour. The same word may also have given rise to *gudbvefr* in Icelandic literature. Hjalmar Falk, the Norwegian philologist, in his extensive work concerning textile terms in Icelandic and other Northern literature and written documents from about A.D. 1100-1350[6] has suggested this derivation, and says that the word is common to all Germanic languages (Anglo-Saxon, *godwebb,* Early Saxon, *godowebbi,* Early High German, *gotaweppi)*[7].

Cotton fabrics, dyed and undyed, were known to medieval Europe from the names of three of the important emporiums from which they were obtained: Fostat, in Egypt; Bokhara, in Central Asia; and Calicut, on the Malabar coast of India.

Fostat probably gave rise to the vulgar Latin *fustana.*[8] On the other hand, there can be no doubt that Bokhara gave rise to *boceranum, bogranum* (Fra. *bougrain, boquerant;* Eng. *buckram).* The third, Calicut, gave rise to the better known *calico.*

The word *chintz* (from Hindi *chint,* 'variegated', Sanskrit *chitra)* did not, at least in unaltered form, reach Europe until the opening of the sea route to India by the Portuguese. Now as commonly known, it has universal currency in the sense of white figured cotton, painted or printed.

However, when hunting for traces of Indian cottons in Europe before 1500, there is one kind of source which only recently has been observed: Scandinavian documents. In the Swedish and Norwegian records from the fourteenth and fifteenth centuries, occurs a word, alternatingly spelled *seter, setar, sather,* which, according to linguists consulted, is of the same derivation as *chint.*[9] According to the well-known German dictionary of Schiller-Lubber, it also frequently occurs in medieval German texts (up to the seventeenth century) under various spellings: *zeter, tzeter, zitter, czeter,* etc. It is also interesting to learn the related Turkish word for fine cotton: *cit,* even *citary,* from which the Rumanian *citares* was derived.[10]

The medieval Latin word *cottonum* seems generally to have been used to denote the raw material, used as ticking for mattresses or other padded fabrics as well as for spinning and for lamp-wicks, which became very important in the late Middle Ages. It was seldom employed to describe a woven material, although in the list of the fourteenth century Papal treasures of Avignon there appears the following sentence: *parvus pannus de cotoni tincto, diversis coloribus cum aliquibus vetis filis aureis* ("small cloth of dyed cotton in various colours with some threads of old gold"). The quotation reminds us of the fine Indian muslins with interwoven gold threads so often spoken of in travellers' stories.

Michel gave many quotations from early French literature to show that *bougran* was a rare fabric. He stated that it was either monochrome, meaning that it was printed by the resist method, so that the pattern would be standing out in white on a coloured ground, or that it was decorated with a hand-painted or printed pattern on a white ground. The following passage from Charles V's Inventory (King of France 1337-80) seems to suggest the latter method: *"coultepointe de bougran blancbe pointee bien menuement et a plusieurs bestes de poincture de mesme."* Towards the end of the Middle Ages (about 1500) the word lost its meaning as a costly stuff, and instead came to mean a special woven material of linen or hemp similar to buckram, which is now used for bookbinding. The meaning, however, did not everywhere change so quickly: an item in the list of Henry VIII — for the purchase of a mantle and nightdress for Anne Boleyn (c. 1530) — shows that in England in the sixteenth century the world still preserved its original meaning.

In fourteenth century Avignon the word *bougran* occurs roughly in the same context as *fustian* but it is hard to understand what was the difference. In one case it was used for a chequered stuff; many times it is specifically described as white, which notice seems to state that this was not a matter of course.

In the inventories of Angers cathedral, *bougran* is often mentioned as lining for church vestments, particularly when dealing with the fourteenth-century garments. A *capella*, (the name of a whole set of vestments used in the Mass) of red velvet with golden flowers was described, in 1390, as *"dupplicate bougrana perseo"* (the letter word meaning at this time "blue"). A large number of copes made of various kinds of precious silk (described in 1418 as already old or much repaired), are said to have been lined with *bougran* in blue, green, (viridis) or "adureus" — an objective which cannot be explained so far.

Michel did not actually mention *fustian* in his researches, which is surprising when we consider its importance in Spain and Italy. The word occurs only once in the Angers inventories, in 1467, where it is described as *"gallic"* — i.e. indigenous. In the Avignon lists, the word occurs with a similar meaning to *bougran* — i.e. fabric for cushions and mattresses, for dalmatics and mitres adorned with gold bands, which later also were made of white *disasper* (a patterned silk of special type). There is no other description of the colour, but it is obvious that they did not mean a monochrome fabric. The kinds of articles show that the stuffs must have been of decorative character, patterned in one way or another.

Referring back to the quotation already given from Charles V's fourteenth century inventory, we might hazard the conclusion that white *fustian* or *bougran* was synonymous with chintz, a fabric decorated with coloured ornament on a white ground. It may be noticed that chintzes, in that special meaning, although recognizable in Gujarati miniature painting before the sixteenth century, have not hitherto been discovered among the medieval Indian cottons found in Egypt.

The earliest reference to fustian in Nordic literature dates from the Egil's Saga of A.D. 960; *"Egil bafdi fustans kyrtill raudan"* ("Egil had a skirt of red *fustan")*. Since the Saga was not actually committed to paper until the thirteenth century, the

earlier dating should be regarded with reserve. Another reference dates from 1179: *"Erlingir Jarl Hafdi raudan kyrtill of fustani ok silkihufu"*. ("Erlingir the Earl had a red skirt of *fustian*, and hood of silk").

Icelandic chronicles mention *fustan* in red, white and blue. In 1321, a Norwegian church was to possess five chasubles, including one of *baldakin*, one of *pell*, and three of *fustan*, red, white and "and old one".[12] In the Icelandic church inventories (the "Maldagar", XII-XIV centuries) liturgical vestments of red, white and blue *fustan* are frequently mentioned. A Norwegian church in 1321 owned five chasubles: two were made of different kinds of precious silks, *pell* and *baldachin*) and three of *fustan*: one was red, one blue and the third was only described as old.

With regard to the word *gudhvefr* (earlier mentioned as a possible derivative of the Arabic *goton*), Falk gives various references to suggest that it was two-coloured. Thus a temple had a "tjald av tvilitudum gudbvefr". (Wall curtains of two-coloured godwebb). The literal sense of the word *tvilitadhr* is "two-dyed".

The first time we know the word *seter* is from the inventories of Queen Blanche, a French princess who married Magnus Erikson, king of Sweden and Norway. The inventory, made in 1365, lists a number of precious fabrics among which "a piece of red seter" appears. The personal estate of a Norwegian bishop, enlisted in 1429, contained a "big cover of *saian* (a silk fabric)" embroidered with white herons and lined with yellow *saeter,"* and another cover "of *bedinstycke*[13] framed by a border of cloth of gold *(drap d'or)"* and a lining of red *saeter*. "Red *saeter*" was further mentioned in 1489 for solemn use as covering the interior of the shrine of Sainte Catherine.

These extracts suggest the following conclusions. Dyed or painted cottons, almost certainly of Indian origin, were by no means rare in Europe before the sea-trade period, i.e. before c. 1500. Resist-dyed cottons dyed with one colour (red or blue) forming the ground, the pattern remaining white, or dyed twice, the two colours and the tone of the fabric itself giving a joint effect, were known in Northern Europe probably as early as A.D. 1000, certainly from the twelfth century, and were in use throughout the Middle Ages. Chintz — i.e. patterned cottons on white ground — were known in Avignon by the mid-fourteenth century and were mentioned in Norway as early as 1321. Even plain coloured cottons were apparently imported.

In this connection, attention is drawn to two points which may raise doubt about Indian origin: the "yellow-*saeter*" from Norway (1429) and the green *fustan* from Angers (fourteenth century). The latter presumably derived from a combination of yellow and blue eyes. The blue and red colour and scheme is, no doubt, an exclusive criterion for the Indian cottons from Fostat as well as, to a large extent, the large stock of Indian printed and painted cottons. The yellow colour does not appear until late. The question is, how early does it begin? When describing the Indian cotton printing methods, which he had studied during his sojourn at the French missionary school at Pondicherry in 1742, Father Coeurdoux complains that it was very difficult to dye yellow as a fast colour (nota bene!)[14] That must mean that the Indian liked yellow and also dyed this colour! Since how long ago? The fact that nowadays there is no yellow to be seen on the flowered chintzes, dominated by the clear (i.e. fast) blue and red shades does not necessarily deny that it was used. Analogous colour-alterations have very often taken place in textiles, much more than what might be imagined. Further, there is no indication of the fastness of the yellow fabric mentioned in the quotation. When new they certainly all looked the same. On the other hand, it is of course possible that plain cotton fabrics were imported from India and dyed in Europe.

Lastly, there is one quotation which suggests that Indian dyed cottons were known in England as early as the eighth century A.D. The Venerable Bede wrote in his *Life of St. Cuthbert* that the synod of Cloveshoe forbade priests to wear clothes *tinota India coloribus* ('dyed with Indian colours').

FOOTNOTES

1. Francisque-Michel, *Recherches sur le commerce, la fabrication at l'usage des etoffes de soie, d'or et d'argent,* 2 vols, Paris, 1852-4.

2. Otto von Falke, *Kunstgeschichte der seidenweberei,* Berlin, 1913; translated into English under the title *Decorative Silks,* London, 1936.

3. Carl Johan Lamm, *Cotton in medieval textiles of the Near East,* Paris (Libraire orientaliste, Paul Geuthner), 1937.

4. R. Pfister, *Les toiles imprimees de Fostat et de l'Hindoustan,* Paris, 1938.

5. For an explanation as to how this interesting analogy came to be made, see John Irwin's detailed note in *The Art of India and Pakistan,* edited by Sir Leigh Ashton, London, 1950, p.203.
   I should like to take this opportunity of acknowledging John Irwin's valuable suggestions and other friendly help in connection with the preparation of this paper.

6. Hjalmar Flak, *Altwestnordiscbe Kleiderkunde mit besonderer Berucksichtigung der Terminologie,* Kristiania (Oslo), 1919.

7. It may be mentioned that this evidence has been doubted by other authorities; but as far as I can understand, the text quoted directly confirms Falk's identification. See also Leif J. Wilhelmsen, *English textile nomenclature,* Oslo, 1943.

8. Some authorities have lately advanced another origin of the word *fustan* from the Latin *fustaneum* ('of wood'), quoted from twelfth century sources. Cf. Meyer-Lubke, *Romanisches Etymologisches Worterbuch,* Heidelberg, 1935, and S. Gamilscheg, *Franzosisches Etymologisches Worterbuch,* Heidelberg, 1928. This derivation, however, does not exclude the possibility that the name of the important trading city of Fostat has very much favoured the use of trade mark *fustan.*

9. The discovery of the meaning of the word *seter* was for the first time presented by a Swedish scholar, Dr. Ingegered Henschen, in a work on printed fabrics in Swedish, Tygtrycki Sverige, Stockholm, 1942.

10. Schiller Lubben, *Mittelniderdeutsches Worterbuch,* Bremen, 1878.

11. Karl Lokotsch, *Etymologisches Worterbuch der europaischen Worter orientalischen Ursprungs,* Heidelberg, 1927.

12. The world *baldacchino* (Fr. *baudequin*) originally meant that the fabric was made in Baghdad (known in Italian as Baldacco). But in Scandinavia from the thirteenth century it was used for precious fabrics even of Italian make. *Pell* (Fr. *pail;* Latin, *pallium*) was another kind of precious silk.

13. Meaning literally, 'heathen piece' — a term often applied to precious materials of oriental origin.

14. Father Coeurdoux's account is quoted in full by G.P. Baker, *Calico painting and printing in the East Indies,* London, 1921.

A Type of Mughal Sash

Milton Sonday and Nobuko Kajitani

The Textile Museum has in its collection a Mughal "sash" which has presented the authors with an unusual challenge. It is related to six in the Los Angeles County Museum of Art[1] by common features including extremes of length and width,

---

Editor's Note: The detailed analysis of Mughal brocade is important for students of Indian textiles as a number of Indian textiles of very fine quality are often identified as Persian. There has been a tendency to look at all very fine silks as having originated in Iran. A detailed study of motif and structure of the fabric however has indicated often that their origin is Indian.

An extract of the article printed in the *Journal of the Textile Museum,* Washington D.C., 1970, reproduced here with the kind persmission of the authors and the Museum of Textiles.

woven structures, patterning techniques, finishing details, and probable use. The patterned areas are laid out according to a common plan. At each end of the very long fabrics with a narrow border along each side is a horizontal panel containing a row of either six or four plants bordered with a narrow band at top and bottom. A field with a continuous or all-over pattern fills the expanse between the two horizontal panels. Each fabric at a glance can be seen to have two contrasting surfaces: one for the horizontal panels and all borders, and another for the long narrow field.

One end of a Polish sash

Two flowering plants in a panel and floral vine borders in red, orange-pink and green outlined in black on a silver background. Two alternating horizontal floral bands in orange-pink, red (or blue) and green outlined in black on a silver background fill the entire field. Metal fringe attached. Evidence of four central lengthwise folds.

Previous Page

Detail of Textile Museum sash 6.29. Length, end to end: 375 cm. (12′ 4¼″. Width, selvedge to selvedge: 51.5 cm. (1′ 8¼″

Four plants in dark green, yellow-green, two reds, and ivory on a gold background within a horizontal panel at each end; floral vine borders; red field with alternating rows of pairs of small wavy bars; yellow warp stripe the entire width of each vertical side border.

The probability that these fabrics were used as sashes[2] is reinforced by the following. There is a difference in the weight of the fabric of the field and the fabric of the end panels by nature of the structures used and the amounts of metal in each. The lighter fabric of the field allows for increased flexibility in folding and tying, while the heavier fabric of the horizontal panels adds weight to the two hanging ends. The plant motifs which decorate the horizontal panels can be said to be in their natural growth position only when seen from each end — a position which would result from a tie with two hanging ends. Also, the fold, instead of cutting a motif, would have divided six into two groups of three; and the four into two groups of two. The fringe, of course, adds the appropriate finish plus added weight.

It has been said that fabrics of this type were used as sashes wrapped and tied around the waist. Indeed, all are long and narrow. The widths of the fabrics hardly vary, the average being about 19$^1/_2$". The lengths, on the other hand, vary greatly, the shortest being 7' 8$^7/_8$" and the longest 12' $^1/_2$". Observe that each fabric was folded in half along the length thereby reducing the average width as worn to about 9$^3/_4$" A sash of any length folded in half lengthwise, wrapped once around a waist of indeterminate size, and tied overhand (with or without a loop) leaving two ends hanging, seems to be a standard article of Mughal dress as seen in the miniatures. It is conceivable that sashes were woven to conform to a standard width but the length had no such standard except as set possibly by fashion, social position, or national origin.

Everything about these fabrics: the placement of pattern areas, the use of a structure in a specific area, the juxtaposition of a light and a heavier weight fabric, the contrast of surfaces, the patterns themselves, the skillful use of colours, contributes to their intended use — a sash to attest the significance and worth of the wearer. This affirms the artistry of the designer and the skill of the weaver.

For the moment, let us accept that these sashes were used and possibly manufactured in India sometimes in the Mughal period. Jehangir in his

Brocade, Andhra Pradesh

This stylized gold brocade with *meenakari* of silken colours woven into the motif is similar in style to enamel patterns in gold jewellery. (Collection: Crafts Museum).

One end of a Persian sash

Five flowering plants in green, yellow and light blue outlined in rose pink within a horizontal panel on an ivory background. Rose pink and ivory floral vine borders. Two alternating horizontal floral blands in rose pink and ivory, rose pink and blue, or ivory and green fill the entire field. Wide patterned heading and plied warp fringe. The sash was not woven with the pattern in mirror image. Evidence of a central lengthwise fold. T.M. 3.19.

Below

Fragment of one end of a sash

Six plants in blue green, yellow green and two reds on a gold background within a horizonal panel. Floral vine borders. Red orange field. Height: 17 cm; width, selvedge to selvedge: 47 cm. T.M. 6.31

memoirs[3] constantly mentions the robes and other items of dress he presented as gifts of honour to generals, statesmen and members of his family. In the 12th year of his reign (in about 1617) he claims to have invented a dress:

".... Having adopted for myself certain special cloths and cloth-stuffs, I gave an order that no one should wear the same but he on whom I might bestow them. One was a *nādirī* coat that they wear over the *qubā* (a kind of outer vest). Its length is from the waist down to below the thighs,

and it has no sleeves. It is fastened in front with buttons, and the people of Persia call it *kurdī* (from the country of the Kurds). I gave it the name of *nādirī*. Another garment is a *tus* shawl, which my revered father had adopted as a dress. The next was a coat (*qabā*) with a folded collar (*batū girībān*). The ends of the sleeves were embroidered. He had also appropriated this to himself. Another was a *qubā* with a border, from which the fringes of cloth were cut off and sewn round the skirt and collar and the ends of the sleeve. Another was a *qubā* of Gujarati satin, and another a *chīra* and waistbelt woven with silk, in which were interwoven gold and silver threads." In about 1621 (in the 16th year of his reign), he states: "... I presented my son Shahriyār with a jewelled *chārqab* (coat), with a turban and waistbelt (*kamarband*), and two horses, one an Iraqi, with a gold saddle, and the other a Turki, with an embroidered saddle."[4]

And, in about 1615 (in the 10th year of his reign), he says: "... On the 5th of the month ten turbans (*chīra*), ten coats (*qubā*), and ten waistbands were given to Karon...[5]"

These random quotes are meant to establish the sash as a status symbol and increase our curiosity about what fabrics were used by the court and manufactured in Mughal India and what the style of the sash was from decade to decade.

The common feature of all the sashes is the two free hanging ends with patterns concentrated at each end. In a brief survey of miniatures of the Mughal period, one cannot help but notice that the sashes worn during the period of Jehangir (who ruled from 1605 to 1627) seem to have been patterned with motifs in a geometric arrangement. Those patterned with growing flowering plants in naturalistic arrangement seem to appear during the reign of Shah Jahan (1627-1658) and most often during the reign of Aurangzeb (1658-1707). Though by no means conclusive, this suggestion seems to date this latter style to no earlier than the second half of the 17th century or to a style begun by Shah Jahan and popularised by Aurangzeb.

Obviously more work needs to be done on the styles and patterns of the Mughal Indian sash. All of them need to have been patterned by a complex loom mechanism. Were some printed, painted or embroidered? What influence did the Mughal sash have on those of other countries? What were the traditions of the Persian sash and what styles were contemporary with the Mughal

Detail of a sash in the Los Angeles
County Museum of Art, L.69.24.173

period? What were the traditions of the sash in the ancient Near East and how did they develop into the sashes we have been discussing?

We have often remarked that a structure or weaving technique is less subject to change than motifs and patterns. The former may survive wars and change of dynasty whereas the latter may change suddenly according to personal whim. The structure-combination of two structures with four sets of elements: 3/1 twill and plain weave, may be one of long duration. Are there fabrics having this structure earlier than these sashes for which, as we have explained, it is so well suited? On the basis of the colours and drawing of the motifs of one of the sashes in the Heeramaneck collection in the Los Angeles County Museum of Art (L.69.24.173) and the ends of what was probably a sari in the Metropolitan Museum of Art, we would extend the use of this structure into the 19th century.

The attribution of India as the country of manufacture at this moment seems quite possible. Statements to this effect have been made generally on the basis of pattern and vary from scholar to scholar. Persia as an alternative attribution raises the question as to who was weaving what and where and at what time. To date, not enough research has been done on the structures and patterns of woven fabrics (not necessarily sashes) attributed to either country to be able to confirm areas of manufacture. We have begun to note a variety of fabrics each with a twill face patterned by several colours including large amounts of metal — this group of sashes being but one of the types. it is our hope that this discussion will at least establish a group which in time might be contrasted with an analysis of the structures of another group. Only in this way will we arrive at a sensible conclusion. Concerning these sashes, we can say — be they short, extra long, plain or splendid, woven or painted, tied or untied — they seem to have been worn proudly by Shahs, herdsmen, civil servants, as well as by ladies of the harem.

FOOTNOTES

1. We wish to thank Mrs. Mary Kahlenberg, Curator of Costumes and Textiles, for providing us with an opportunity to study the following sashes in the Heeramaneck Collection in the Los Angeles County Museum of Art.

2. Fabrics of this type have also been called girdles, waistbands, *kamarbands* or *patkas*. We have chosen the word sash which today has a more general connection. For a discussion of the word sash, see: Irwin John, "A Note on the Indian Sashes of King Gustavus Adolphus", Journal of Indian Textile History, number IV, Ahmedabad, 1959, p. 69.

3. Jehangir, *The Memoirs of Jehangir*, translated by Rogers and Beveridge, Royal Asiatic Society, London, 1909, Vol. 1, p. 384.

4. Ibid., Vol. 1, p. 202-3

5. Ibid., Vol. 1, p. 290

Naksha Bandhas of Banaras

Pupul Jaykar

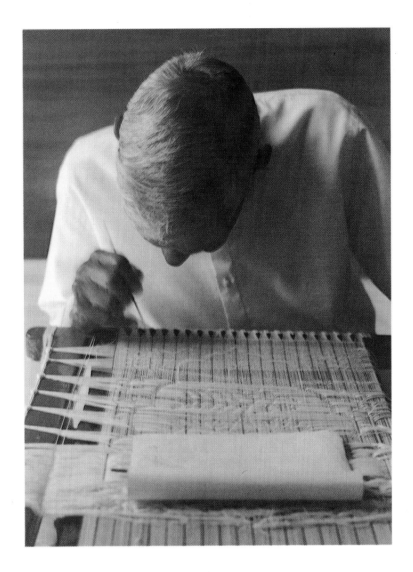

The history of textile design in India, though obscure, is of considerable interest, particularly in relation to the origin of the art of *naksha* making and the place it has occupied in the development of ornament.

The earliest records of the use of ornament in textiles is in the Satapata Brahmanas where enumerating the various deities who preside over sections of cloth worn at the time of the *yagna*, ritual, *alankar*, or ornament is mentioned and the

Originally published in the *Journal of India Textile History* of the Calico Museum of Textiles, Ahmedabad. Reprinted with the kind permission of the author and the Calico Museum.

nakshatras, the planets, are recorded as the presiding deities of this element of the cloth. Kautilya's *Arthashastra,* writing of the royal workshops for weaving set up in the court of Chandragupta Maurya, gives details of the various functions in existence for the manufacture of fine garments for the royal wordrobe. Fine spinners and weavers are mentioned and the great praise and encouragement given to those artisans by the gifts of oil, *anjan* for the eyes, scent, flower garlands and other adornments. There is, however, no mention of any designer or *naksha* maker, and it is obvious that the ornamental cloths which were woven at this time, introduced design into the cloth not by any mechanical contrivance but by a process similar to that practised in the *patola,* tie-dye or double *ikat* of Patan in Gujarat, or in the methods used to this day for weaving ornamental *butas* in the cotton *jamdanis* of Tanda as well as in the elaborate border designs of Paithan, the ancient Pratishthan.

An examination of the Paithan type of weaving of ornament reveals the same use as in the *jamdani* cottons, of tiny bobbins, one for each ornament along the weft. The process is akin to embroidery, and no mechanical contrivance or *naksha* is used to manipulate the warp threads in order to produce the design.

This raises the question as to the origin of the art of *naksha* making and the place it has occupied in the development of ornament. It is likely that *naksha bandhas* or designers familiar with the art of producing integrated patterns in various colours with the use of mechanical contrivances, were brought to this country in the time of Muhammed Tughlak. Tradition in Banaras, the main centre where the *naksha bandha* tradition prevails, indicates that the Muslim invaders from Central Asia brought in their wake Iranian *naksha bandhas* who were great masters of the art of tying designs on to the loom. The memoirs of a Damascus traveller — Shahab-ud-din Abdul Abbas-Ahmed who came from Egypt to this country in the reign of Muhammed Tughlak (A.D. 1325-1350) mention[1]: "The Sultan keeps in his service 500 manufacturers of golden tissues, who weave the gold brocades worn by the wives of the Sultan, and given away as presents to the Amirs and their wives."

The great interest taken by Zain-ul-Abidin, ruler of Kashmir (A.D. 1420-70) in the textile arts is mentioned in the Jain Rajtarangini. It records that in his time master craftsmen "adept in original designs regarding him as the Wishing Tree

Previous Page

Naksha tying for brocades, Varanasi

The art of creating the thread Jacquard, *jala,* in Varanasi, is an ancient technique. It has been used from the Pre-Mughal period and continues to be used even today for raising the warp threads so as to facilitate the weaving of brocades. The late Ali Hasan was one of the finest *jala* makers and the tradition is being continued by his son seen here working on a frame traditionally used for creating the *jala.*

came from long distances like swarming black bees." The local artisan weavers of Kashmir learnt the art of introducing new designs through the use of the *naksha* from these great craftsmen. There is a further record of the extraordinary quality of these elaborate designs — "the painters seeing the patterns (*chitra*) and creeper designs (*lattkritih*) obtained by intricate weaving process (*vichitravtyana*) are reduced to silence as the figures in a painting."[2]

Further light on the *naksha bandhas* is to be found in the *Ain-i-Akbari* of Abul Fazl. It is likely that a large number of foreign *naksha bandhas* came to teach new techniques to the local weavers in the Imperial workshops set up by the Emperor Akbar at Lucknow, Agra, Fatehpur and Ahmedabad. There is mention in the *Ain-i-Akbari* of a Ghias-i Naqshband. Ghias was born at Yazd and it is recorded that the world had not seen a weaver like him. Besides he was reputed to be a great poet. He was reputed to have brought a piece of "*mushajjar*" brocade to Shah Abbas (1585-1629) on which there was among other figures, that of a bear between some trees.

Today Banaras is one of the most important weaving centres where *naksha bandhas* function. So skilful are the craftsmen that their services are requisitioned from distant parts and it is they who tie the design for the silk and brocade weavers of Surat as well as for the intricate gold and enamel weavers of Chanderi.

Mr. Yusuf Ali in his monograph on the silk fabrics produced in the North-Western Provinces and Oudh mentions two noteworthy *naksha bandhas* of Banaras — Tajamul Hussain and Muhammed Hussain, both of whom had been to the Empire of India Exhibition of 1895-96.

A recent enquiry in Banaras from Shri Hafiz Ali Hasan who belongs to one of the most important hereditary *naksha bandha* families gave the following information on the history and legends associated with *naksha* making. He traced the introduction of silk weaving into Benares to a great fire which took place in Gujarat in A.D. 1300. He maintains that weavers, to escape the big fire, fled to various regions and settled in Delhi, Agra, Benares, Madras and Ajmer. It is strange how tradition links most silk weaving centres with an association with Gujarat. This is so with regard to the silk weavers of Murshidabad as well as the "Saurashtros" of South India. That migration of silk weavers took place from Gujarat from the earliest times is established by the inscriptions of the eighth century found at Mandasor, recording the building of a temple to the Sun by the silk weavers from Gujarat.

Hafeez Ali Hasan mentioning the tradition associated with the origin of *naksha* making says:

"The first human being to appear on the earth was Hazrat Adim Ali Salam who started the work in agriculture. After him his elder son Hazrat Shish Paigamber Ali Salam invented the art of weaving and this is why even today all those who start to learn this art first offer FATEHA in the name of Hazrat Shish Paigamber Ali Salam. During the year either 708 or 718 Hijari corresponding to the year A.D. 1288 or 1298, was born a big WALI named Hazrat Khwaja Bahauddin and he invented the art of making *naksha* and since then he has given the title of Hazrat Khwaja Bahauddin Naksha-Band Bokhari Rahamtulla Alia. The art of *naksha-bandi* so originated continued to be in existence since then and all those who wish to become disciples in the art of making *naksha-bandi* have necessarily to offer FATEHA in the name of Khwaja Bahauddin Saheba Nakshaband and then only adopt such a title. Khwaja Bahauddin Saheb Nakshaband died during the year 791 Hijari or A.D. 1371, and his Mausoleum (*Mazar Sharif*) is in Bokhara. It may be possible to trace out further history if someone goes and contacts the descendants and disciples of his *gaddi.*"

The specimens of traditional designs in the possession of Hasan Ali show that the designs were first made with steel pens on *abrak*, mica. These designs were of the actual size required on the fabric. They were permanent records kept by the master designers. The actual *naksha* which was tied on to the loom was an arrangement of threads built in such a fashion that by fixing it on the loom, the weaver was enabled to lift the required warp threads to form the desired design on the fabric. This was used on the Indian system of harness. The *naksha-bandha* first determined the construction of the fabric, i.e. the number of warp and weft threads per inch. From this he calculated the total number of warp ends and picks on which the design repeats. The design was then divided equally by drawing parallel lines vertically and horizontally. The number of sections were a measure of the number of ends and picks required in the repeat. Thus each section repeated a certain number of warp and weft threads. The design was now ready for preparing the *naksha*.

**Ganga-Jamuna brocade, Varanasi,
19th century**

A rich brocade from Varanasi woven
in thick silk as yardage to be used
for making garments. (Collection:
C.L. Bharany.)

The process of making naksha in Banaras*

Naksha may be defined as the indigenous equipment to weave complicated designs on handlooms. It takes the position of the Jacquard of modern weaving, but is reduced to simplicity since the whole equipment consists only of a group of threads and no complicated moving parts. The whole idea is to weave one complete design in a group of threads and duplicate it on the fabric wherever it is required by attaching these threads to the loom and to the threads of the fabric in a suitable way.

1. Winding the Naksha String on a Parita

The *naksha* string is a strong multistrand one usually made locally. It is available in hanks and is known as *pindi*. The hank is opened out and separated for winding. This is done by placing it on, what is called a swift (*natai*). From the swift it is transferred on to a swift of a different shape called *parita*.

2. Warping the Narba String

From the *parita* the strings are arranged side by side. The *parita* is placed on the floor and the *naksha* maker pulls out the string and winds it diagonally on two sticks driven in the ground at a distance of 40 to 42 inches (100 to 105 cms). If the design requires 400 threads, which is calculated depending upon the size of the design and the type of yarn used and the number of threads of yarn required per inch of the cloth, that is the number wound on these two sticks.

3. Putting a Lease Thread

It is important that these threads should not entangle. It should be possible for one to take out these threads in successive order i.e. first one, second, third one, etc. For doing this, a lease thread is attached.

4. Tying up the Naksha Threads in the Middle

The *naksha* threads are tied in the middle to prevent the threads from becoming loose and giving way during the succeeding processes.

5. The *naksha* is finally to be supported in a vertical form. Therefore, a bamboo stick is used to which all these *naksha* threads are tied individually or sometimes in groups of 4, 8, etc. The loops are taken so that the strings are fixed firmly. One person takes out each thread in succession and hands it over to the other man who ties the knot.

6. The Naksha-making Frame

The frame is made in dimensions to suit different sizes of *naksha*. Generally the *naksha* maker sits on the floor and does the work.

7. Fixing the Bamboo Stick

The bamboo stick, as mentioned in 5 above, has now all the *naksha* threads fixed with it. It is to be fixed to the *naksha*-making frame on to one side.

8. Arranging the Naksha Threads

One end of all the *Naksha* threads is fixed to the bamboo stick which in turn is fixed to the *naksha*-making frame. Now the other end remains. This is also fixed to the opposite side of the frame tightly by the *naksha* maker. Here the threads will be in small groups at irregular intervals. If they are at irregular intervals, it would be difficult for the *naksha* maker to pick up each thread to make the *naksha*. In order to arrange each thread at regular intervals a process called putting the "*shivren*" is adopted. This is simply twisting another thread round each of the *naksha* threads in such a way that all the *naksha* threads are laid side by side at regular intervals. This is done at both sides of the frame so that the spaces between each thread of the *naksha* are the same at both ends.

9. Tying up of Kheva Threads

The *kheva* threads are tied on to another thread by the side of the *naksha* threads in groups. These are tied in groups so that the *naksha* maker can pick each thread conveniently rather than taking one thread individually at every time. These threads, since they are in groups, are liable to get themselves entangled. So a lease is put for these threads as well.

10. For starting the design a tracing is placed in front. This traced design is divided into a definite number of parts longitudinally. The *naksha* threads are also divided into exactly the same number of divisions, this being marked by the colouring of *naksha* threads at intervals. For example, if the original design is divided into 20 parts, there should be 20 coloured threads in the *naksha* which divides the whole group of *naksha* threads into 20 equal divisions. The traced design will also be divided vertically into a definite number of parts. For each vertical division a definite number of *kheva* threads are also put. It is clear that in each division of the traced design there will be only a part of the design. This part of the design is transferred into the corresponding divisions of the *naksha* thread by the *naksha* maker by using his needle. By mere practice he knows that for a particular line or for a small square or for a dot how many threads are to be lifted or lowered in the *naksha* threads. Different weaves like twills and satins are also introduced by the *naksha* maker to bring out the design and to bind the threads to give a firm texture. This process continues till the whole design is completed.

11. Looping the Kheva

The loop is to be made in every *kheva* thread so that it may be supported by a string later on.

12. Introducing a Separate Thread (Nathia)

A separate thread is introduced through every *kheva* thread.

13. Setting up the Naksha on the Loom

The loom is first to be set up by tying the *paggia* thread or horizontal threads. There will be as many *paggia* threads as there are *naksha* threads. Each *naksha* thread and end is tied to a corresponding *paggia* thread. Two people are generally required for this work. When all the *naksha* threads are tied to the *paggia* thread the loom is ready for starting the work.

14. When there are a number of *nakshas* with a weaver he usually stores them by affixing a tag.

15. Duplicating the Nakshas

When a number of looms have to be worked on the same design it is not necessary that for each loom a sepaarate *naksha* is to be made. When one *naksha* is made it can be duplicated. The original one is tied in a vertical way and attached to horizontal threads of equal number. The interlacing arrangement of the vertical threads is transferred to the horizontal threads by lifting the vertical threads by taking out the *kheva*, Any number of *nakshas* can be duplicated from one original.

Indian Velvets

Jasleen Dhamija

Velvets woven with lustrous silk pile and gold thread were among the most sumptuous products of the loom. Their heavy texture, rich colours and the subtlety with which the colours changed in different lights made them the most suitable material for use as drapery in rich courtly surroundings.

The fact that velvet could effectively be combined with gold thread embroidery made it a favourite material for the use of royalty and also as robes of honour, *khilit.* Equally it was coveted by those

This monograph was prepared for the Calico Museum of Textiles, Ahmedabad, in 1971 and remains unpublished. It is published here with the kind permission of Calico Museum.

who could afford it for use as curtains, canopies, hangings and floor covers. Its softness made it specially suitable for cushions.

Examples of Indian velvets are very rare. Those which are available so far belong to the Mughal period. These velvets are of a very fine quality and distinctive style, and appear to be products of the culmination of a technique and style practised over an extended period. During the time of Akbar the Great, velvets of very fine quality were being woven in India and could be compared with the finest brocaded velvets of Kashan and Herat.[1] It is likely that velvets were being woven in India before the Mughals and might originally have been introduced into Western India by the Arabs, through the Tiraz factories which were a part of the Arab court organisation during the medieval period.[2]

The earliest mention of velvets in India is by an Arab geographer of the 9th century[3] when he talks of the kingdom of Rahma — identified by Eliot and Dawson[4] as a kingdom in Bengal, but most likely was a kingdom in Gujarat judging from the description of the bordering kingdoms with whom it was constantly embroiled in battles. He writes of the wealth of the kingdom and mentions, along with 500 elephants, fine velvet cloths, *al-kham-liyat*[5].

Later, in the early 10th century another Arab geographer even mentions places of velvet manufacture. These are given as Kalhin and Jalhandar,[6] identified as a town in Central India and Jullundur of Punjab, respectively. Here garments of velvets, *thiyab makhmal,* are specifically mentioned.

After this period, mentions of velvets being produced in India are rare. We know, however, that velvet was an important product for trade and a brisk demand existed for it. During the 14th century, in the court of Mohammed Tughlak at Delhi there was a court manufactory employing thousands of craftsmen.[7] The craftsmen wove, embroidered, made garments and robes of honour, as also articles to be presented to other courts. One of the materials being woven in Delhi was *khazz*. This has been identified as "plushy velvet material made of silk and wool."[8]

During this period Ma Huan, a Chinese traveller,[9] also visited India. In the detailed account of his travels, he lists a number of goods manufactured in India which include important textiles from Bengal, one of which has been identified as velvets made from cotton.[10] It is interesting that this type

53

of velvet made from cotton and coming from the Eastern region finds a place in the list of different types of velvets mentioned in the *Ain-i-Akbari* which were purchased for the royal household and is listed as the cheapest available velvet.[11]

In Dr. Moti Chandra's[12] study of textiles of the Sultanate period, references to velvets are common in the stock list of textiles compiled by Gujarati and Rajasthani writers of the 14th and 15th centuries. The words *kathivu* and *katipba* are obviously derived from the Arab word for velvets *al-katifa.* Two types of *kathivu* are described — one a *patani* and *phirangi.* The *phirangi* is the European velvet while *patani* possibly refers to the *ikat* velvet woven in Western India for use as hangings, cushion covers and spreads, and can be seen in the Calico Museum collection (accession No. 1364).

Western India had a tradition of velvet weaving, and Ahmedabad is mentioned as an important velvet producing centre.[13] Cambay is also referred to as a place for the weaving of a variety of textiles and coloured velvet of poor quality; *"myutos velads beix pintados"* which translated freely would mean "cheap painted velvets.[14] This refers to the plain velvets of a poor quality woven in Gujarat and stencilled or hand-painted with gold colour similar to the style of hanging of the Mughal period, carrying tree patterns or the portrait of Akbar which can be seen in the Calico Museum (accession No. 704) and in the Jaipur City Palace Museum's collections of tents and awnings.

The fact that very few textiles earlier than the Mughal period have survived in India is possibly due to several reasons. The contrasts of climate, from extreme dryness to the humid monsoon weather, would easily affect textiles. The uncertainty of the times, the wars with its attending pillage and arson and destruction must have led to a wide loss of textiles as well. Further, India had not previously attached much value to old textiles and the question of conservation and preservation did not arise. The only value seen was in the silver and gold threads used in the weaving. Until very recently many collections in old princely states have been lost by being burnt for the silver and gold content of the heavily worked gold thread *kalabatun,* which used originally to be pure silver wire covered with real gold. Today if textiles have been preserved in India, they could be perhaps found in some of the Jain *bhandars,* as book covers and wrappers. It is possible that a thorough study of the book-covers might reveal some early covers of the pre-Mughal period, substantiating

the literary evidence of the early origin of velvet found in local records, the *bahikhatas,* account books, of the states as well as in the descriptions of the travellers to India.

Technique

Without a full discussion of the technique of weaving velvets, no study can be complete. The technique of velvet weaving is complicated and since velvets, as they were woven upto the beginning of the century, are no longer being woven in India or Persia, it would be of interest to make a detailed study of the different techniques used in the weaving of velvets.

The most distinctive feature of velvet as a fabric is its pile. This is composed of tufts and cut threads which stand from the flat surface of the ground cloth, similar in appearance to the pile produced by carpet weavers. There is however a technical difference: the carpet weavers produced a pile by knotting separate threads to the warp, velvet weavers produced a pile as an integral part of the weave by placing extra warp threads below the main warp.

While preparing the loom for velvet weaving, an extra warp running parallel to the foundation warp was laid on a separate beam, placed below the beam of the foundation warp. While starting a new piece of velvet, a small section was woven in plain tabby or satin weave, whichever was being used for preparing the foundation cloth. After this, the extra warp thread was raised and a thin rod with a groove on the top, known as a pile wire, was introduced. The extra warp was then lowered and the weft was woven in closely and beaten down so as to tie the extra warp pile to the foundation cloth. Normally three lines of weft were woven in and another pile wire was introduced by raising the extra warp. This process was repeated until three or four pile wires had been introduced whereupon the loops of the earlier pile wires were cut with the help of a sharp knife, *trevette,* which fitted into the groove of the pile wire. This was the basic technique for weaving of single colour plain velvets.

Later, refinements were added to velvet weaving by varying the techniques. One variation was the weaving of figured velvets through introducing different colours in the extra warp. Here it was necessary to have a separate beam for each colour or a creel with — multiple extra warp threads on separate bobbins, each weighted down with metal pieces thus controlling the let-off. The figured velvet was mastered in Persia, where they developed a technique of introducing a variety of colours even while weaving the fabric, by twisting the extra warp threads with the basic warp thread of the ground material. A simple harness with the use of cords or a Jacquard device was used for producing the design in different colours of the velvet pile.

Voided velvet was another interesting variation. Here the pile was produced in selected sections of the material while the other areas were left void. The voided section generally carried extra weft gold thread twisted over silk or gilded paper, *lamé*. Voided velvets also had variations: in one variety, motifs were worked in different coloured silk pile while the background was of plain foundation cloth covered with gold thread laid down by being woven into the background material. This gave a rich gold effect. In some Indian velvets and especially in Chinese velvets, the voided area carried brocaded patterns worked in gold thread. This was a complicated process since brocades were normally woven from the reverse side whereas velvets were woven face upwards. The handling of brocaded patterns being worked with extra weft threads, along with velvet patterns, with the use of multiple extra warps, required total mastery over the weaving techniques. This style was developed very effectively in India during the Mughal period. In the second variety of voided velvets, the background was worked in one colour velvet pile with a larger motif worked in different coloured pile' only selected areas, such as the centres of flowers or other smaller details were kept voided and worked in gold thread. This style was commonly found in the Turkish velvets produced in Bursa.

Yet another variation was known as *terry*. Here, sections of woven loops were left uncut and others had a cut pile. This created a contrast of texture and a seeming variation in colour though only one colour was used for the weaving. The overall effect was monochromatic. Stamped velvets were another variety. Here, on a plain single colour velvet, the pattern was created by depressing areas with the use of pressure. Both of these styles created a variation in single coloured velvets and were mostly to be found in Italian or Japanese velvets.

Ikat velvets form an important variation. Here the extra warp thread was tied and dyed so that the pattern emerged in different colours as the extra warp thread was woven in loops and cut. The outline of the design was correspondingly hazy.

This technique was found in Persia, Central Asia and in India.

The technique employed in Indian velvets as seen in various collections as well as important museums in India and abroad was essentially single colour plain velvets woven with a cotton warp, cotton weft and silk pile or silk warp, silk weft and silk pile. The second kind is velvets with woven patterns on the surface, of which only a few pieces have been identified so far. Most of them carry only two to three coloured extra warp threads since the colour variations are few. The weaves in the case of plain velvet and the patterned velvets are generally satin.

The personage velvet to be seen in the National Museum, New Delhi, and the County Museum of Art, Los Angeles, are distinctive pieces and need to be discussed separately. The controversial velvet piece at the Royal Ontario Museum (No. 962.60.1) with embroidered additions which has been accepted so far as Persian, needs to be re-analysed since the treatment of figures, of the floral motif, the overall movement in the design of the pieces, as well as the quality of the *kala-batun*, gold thread, are indicators that it is from India rather than Persia.

The most important variety of velvets of the Mughal period are the voided velvets. From a detailed analysis of the velvets, it has been found that practically each piece varies in its technique. The common factor is that most of them have been woven with the use of the satin weave and by using two to three extra wefts of silk. The extra weft gold thread has often been laid with the twill weave since many of the pieces have the gold thread intact. Only a few of the earlier pieces, possibly belonging to the end of Akbar's reign and the beginning of Jehangir's, have gold thread laid on loosely with a satin weave, with the result that most of the gold thread has come apart from the foundation material.

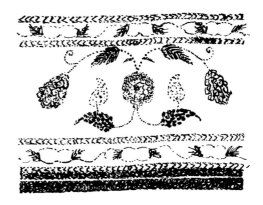

For weaving the motifs, the drop repeat pattern is used so that the multiple extra warp threads can be laid down in variations of three to four colours in stripes and make the weaving easier.

The ikat velvet pieces which have been located so far and can be identified as Indian are similar in style to the *mashru* being woven in Western India. Some of the ikat velvet pieces have cotton warp and cotton weft for the basic foundation and this may have been prepared specially for the conservative Muslim who did not use silk thread next to the skin.

There are a number of descriptions in the *bahi khatas,* the account books of the Rajasthan states, to another style similar to the voided velvets made in Turkey. Here the design is woven all over the surface with the introduction of coloured pile. Only a small section of the material was left voided. One velvet piece of this style carrying lotus flowers all over the surface was in a private collection in Bikaner and was made of four lengths of material stitched together with a woven border, a central band and smaller side bands running on all four sides of the velvet. This velvet accorded exactly with descriptions found in the *bahi khatas* of the Udaipur household.[15]

The earliest dated velvet is in the Jaipur City Palace Museum collection and has an all-over repeat pattern of a flowering shrub in two colours, woven on a yellow ground. The original label, still attached to the velvet, is dated 1605. The piece has been woven with a silk warp, a silk weft and three extra warp silks threads which produce the pattern. The velvet is a typical example of Jehangir's period when there was a preoccupation with detailed studies of flowers, birds and animals, and is very important in analysing the techniques and stylisations prevalent during the period.

Mughal Velvets

The organisation and development of court crafts was initiated in a grand manner during the reign of Akbar. Babar, though he conquered India, did not really belong here. He was an alien and things that were Indian irritated him:[16] the people were uncouth; their way of life was uncultured and even the melons were not sweet! He however accepted one aspect as a boon to his ambitions as builder of an empire — there were a number of craftsmen available in India who could adapt their skills to the needs of the patron.[17]

Humayun, a man of great sensitivity, with a love for beauty,[18] was never able to develop his court ateliers since he was unable to rule India undisturbed. His period of exile in the court of Shah Abbas in Persia made him aware of the large number of painters, textile designers and craftsmen who worked under the direct patronage of the great Shah of Persia. Humayun was responsible for bringing along with him some of the court painters of Shah Abbas and settling them in India. It is probably during his times that the Mughal style of miniatures which blended the Indian tradition with the Persian was developed.

It was during the reign of Akbar that the large workshops attached to the court were developed and he took personal interest in the organisation and development of the craft traditions. Akbar was fully conversant with the situation of crafts in other countries and knew of the status enjoyed by well-known master-weavers in Persia. The *Ain-i-Akbari* mentions that Akbar was acquainted with the world of Persia's master brocade-designer, Giyatyad-Din Ali Naqshband of Yazd, who was a man of considerable wealth, a poet, a collector of precious art objects, and a privileged member of Shah Abbas's court.[19] The *Ain-i-Akbari* also mentions that Akbar received textiles signed by Giyatyad-Din Ali Naqshband as a part of the presents received from the Persian court.[20]

During the time of Akbar, master-craftsmen were invited from important centres outside India to come and work in his royal *karkhanas* and settle in India. The conditions of service offered to them were an inducement to make India their home. It was because of this fact that some of the best weavers from Turkey and Iran settled in India and mingled with Indian craftsmen who had an excellent tradition of textiles. In a short period the products of the royal workshop could compete with the very best. This can be seen in the description of products from different centres given in the *Ain-in-Akbari:*

A. *Gold stuffs*
Brocaded velvet *(Makhmalai Zarbaft)* from Yazd per piece 15 to 150 *Mohurs.*
Brocaded velvet from Europe per piece 10 to 70 *Mohurs.*
Brocaded velvet from Gujarat per piece 10 to 50 *Mohurs.*
Brocaded velvet from Kashan per piece 10 to 40 *Mohurs.*
Brocaded velvet from Hirat per piece 10 to 40 *Mohurs.*
Brocaded velvet from Lahore per piece 10 to 40 *Mohurs.*

B. Silks, etc.

Plain velvet from Europe per yard 1 to 4 *Mohurs.*

Velvet from Kashan per piece 2 to 7 *Mohurs.*

Velvet from Yazd per piece 2 to 4 *Mohurs.*

Velvet from Mashhad per piece 2 to 4 *Mohurs.*

Velvet from Hirat per piece 1.1/2 to 3 *Mohurs.*

Velvet from Khafi per piece 2 to 4 *Mohurs.*

Velvet from Lahore per piece 2 to 4 *Mohurs.*

Velvet from Gujarat per yard 1 to 2 rupees.

Qatifa-yi-I Purabi per yard 1 to 1.1/2 rupees.

From this list it is clear that by Akbar's time velvets were being woven in India in Gujarat, Lahore, Eastern India and possibly Bengal. Good quality voided velvets, *Makhmalai Zarbaft,* were produced in Gujarat and Lahore and could compare favourably with those of Kashan which was then an important velvet producing centre. The royal workshop was located in Lahore and produced excellent quality brocaded velvets. It was only in the plain velvets that the quality of European and Persian velvets was superior to those being woven in India.

References to the specific uses of velvets also became more frequent. In the *Ain-in-Akbari,* while describing the encampments of journeys, *sayabans,* awnings, of gold embroidered brocade and velvet are mentioned. The inside of tents was ornamented with brocade and velvet. The demand in India, we learn was for "some velvets wrought with gold" and "good velvets, to wit, crimsons, purples, reds, greens and blacks."[21] In a description of the court in 1616, Sir Thomas Roe[22] described the scene: "..... before the throne the principal men had erected tents which encompassed the court and lined them with velvett, damask and tafety."

In another description given by Bernier,[231] he describes the King giving audience "under a spacious canopy of velvet." He also records visiting a fine house in Delhi where "each mattress has a large cushion of brocade to lean upon and there are other cushions placed around the room covered with brocade velvet of flowered satin."

During the reign of Jehangir (1605-1627), velvets as an item for trade and for use by royalty of the Mughal court as well as of the smaller states came into greater prominence. Hawkins[24] gives a graphic description of the *Nourouz* celebrations:

"The Emperor (Jehangir) keepeth many visits in the years, *Nourous* which is in honour of the new year's day. This visit continueth 18 days and the wealth and riches are wonderful. That are to be seen in the taking and setting forth of every man's room or place where he lodgeth. Whence it his turn to watch for every noble-man hath his place appointed him in the palace. In the midst of the spacious place, I bespoke of, there is rich tent pitched but so rich that I think the like cannot be found in the world. This tent is curiously wrought and hath many *semianas (shamiyanas* — canopies) joining round about it of most curiously wrought velvet, embroidered with gold and many of them are of cloth of gold and silver. This *shamnas* put shaddowes to keep the sun from the compasse of ..... At least two acres of ground so richly spread with silk and gold carpets and hangings in the velvets imbroydered with gold, perls and precious stones."

There is also an interesting reference to voided velvets with a gold background in the early travels of Edward Terry[25] (1616-19) in which he talks of a coach presented by the East India Company to Jehangir:

"The coach sent was lined within with crimson China velvet' which when the Mughal took notice of, he told the Ambassador that he wondered that the King of England would trouble himself so much as to send into China for velvet..... England's King had much better velvet near home..... And immediately after, the Mogol caused that coach to be taken to pieces and another made by it..... then pulling out all the China velvet..... put a very rich stuff the ground silver wrought all over in spaces with variety of flowers of silk, excellently well suited for their colours, cut short like a plush..... and with a richer stuff than the former the ground of gold mingled like the other with silken flowers......"

This is one of the finest descriptions of voided velvets being produced by the yard in India, having a silver or a gold background with the motifs worked in velvet pile.

The fact that the use of velvet was not only confined to the King's court is brought out in Jehangir's observation — "on the 28th I went to the house of Asaf Khan and this velvet was presented to me there. From the palace to his house was the distance of about a *kos.* For half the distance he had laid down underfoot velvet woven with gold and gold brocade and plain velvet, such that its value was represented to me as ten thousand rupees."[26]

During the reign of Jehangir, a new custom had been introduced in the Rajput states that during the *Raj Tilak* ceremony when the prince ascended his ancestral throne, the special cover for the throne for the ceremony was sent by the Emperor of Delhi. This is brought out in the records of the Rajasthan states of that period. The first reference is found in the *Bahi of Raj Tilak* of Sur Singhji of Bikaner 1671 Bikrami Samvat (A.D. 1614)"[27] The *bahi* mentions that Gadowaria Tej Singh brought a special throne cover of "*jari roh makhmali daree*", gold thread worked velvet woven carpet. For bringing this throne cover he was awarded 1100 rupees and a *bigha* of land by the Maharaja as a reward.

The examples of velvets of the Jehangir period available in the City Palace, Museum, Jaipur, the National Museum, New Delhi and in the collection of the Calico Museum of Textiles are some of the finest and fit in with the description of velvets in the writings of the period. It appears that during this period velvets were also exported out of the country, for we find that Sir Thomas Roe mentions that the Sultan of an Arab Kingdom at the mouth of the Red Sea "met us with all his pomp..... His clothes are of Surat stuff after the Arab manner a cassock of wrought velvet red and white and another of green gold.....[28]. During the reign of Shah Jehan (1628-1658), the royal workshop continued to produce fine quality textiles and from the records of the Rajasthan states besides Delhi, Agra, Lahore, Ahmedabad and Surat, Jaipur is referred to as a centre for the production of fine quality velvets.

The decorations of the Red Fort for its inauguration were more sumptuous and the court decorations richer during the reigns of Shah Jehan than even the descriptions given in the Jehangir period.[29] There is a description of the *Diwan-ai-Am* (the hall of public audience) decorated with the rarest textiles. "Its compartments and rooms were decorated with curtains of gold embroidery and velvets." A large *shamiana*, canopy, 70 yards in length and 45 yards in width was specially prepared at Ahmedabad at the cost of a lakh of rupees and was erected in the Red Fort with the help of 3,000 people. By the side of this tent were similar canopies of *makhmalai zarbaft* supported by silver and gold pillars. The royal throne was also decorated with *makhmalai zarbaft*.

After the period of Shah Jehan, references to velvets are to be found in the records of Rajput states and these convey the importance that was attached to them and the role that was played by the velvet decorations in the ceremonies and celebrations at the court.

During the marriage of Maharaja Anoop Singh of Bikaner with the princess of Udaipur held in A.D. 1643[30] a velvet carpet was spread for the bride which was green in colour and carried pink flowers and a golden border. This spread was then presented to the bride on her nuptial night. During the same occasion when a special religious ceremony was performed a red velvet curtain was presented to the local temple as an offering to propitiate the gods to bless the marriage.

There is an interesting description of an incident at a marriage, which gives an indication as to how valuable velvets were considered. For receiving the bridegroom a fine quality velvet was spread on the wooden *takht*, platform. The bridegroom while standing on the velvet spread was so enamoured by it that he tactfully asked the host, the Rana of Udaipur, if a similar one could be available for sale. The host called a conference of his ministers to discuss the matter and finally reluctantly decided to present the velvet spread to the bridegroom.[31]

In another description of the same period[32] the Queen Mother of Bikaner, Rani Shri Rajwatji, was approached by the family priest who had performed a special *puja*, worship, of Shri Ganesh, asking for a gold worked velvet carpet, *makhmal zari roh galicho*. The Queen Mother explained that she herself had no velvet carpet to sit on, leave alone one to give away in charity. Since however the brahmin had to be appeased, specially after his conducting a *puja* to Shri Ganesh, the Queen Mother presented him with 378 gold *Mohurs* and 27 gold brocade pieces, *kim khab than*.

Velvets thus were used as canopies, walls of tents, *kanat*, seat covers, floor spreads for receiving special visitors, door curtains, as well as palanquin covers. From the lavish manner in which the palaces of the kings and the nobles were decorated, it is obvious that a fairly large amount of velvet must have been produced in a number of centres in India as well as imported from outside.

With the weakening of the Mughal empire, the royal *karkhanas* lost their patronage. In fact during Aurangzeb's time (1658-1707) a number of special craftsmen in the royal *karkhanas* had been dispersed, but they found patrons amongst the *rajas* and *nawabs* of smaller states which were becoming more dominant and wealthy with the decline of power in the centre. Forster who visited India during the end of the 18th century gives a very clear picture of the situation.[33] The native princes and chiefs..... afforded constant employment to a vast number of indigenous manufactures, who supplied their masters with gold and silver stuffs, flowered and plain muslins, a diversity of beautiful silk and other articles of Asiatic luxury." He however goes to on to say that during this period, because of the courts' "constant strife and struggle for power many branches of rare manufacturers have evidently declined and some of the most precious are now no longer known. The distracted and impoverished conditions have lessened the great demand which was made by those States."

The techniques of producing velvets which required a high degree of skill deteriorated very fast, the finest quality was possibly from the reign of Akbar to the end of Shah Jehan's reign in 1658. Only a limited number of craftsmen continued to work on velvets and the deterioration of velvets by the 19th century can be seen in some of the dated 19th century album covers in the City Palace Museum, Jaipur. The Delhi Exhibition of Crafts conducted during the second half of the 19th century, which covered all the crafts practised in the country, does not include velvets nor is there any mention of this technique in the survey of arts and crafts carried out at the end of the 19th century. The weaving of velvets therefore ended with the fall of the Mughal empire.

FOOTNOTES

1. Abu-al-Fazl 'Ain a Akbari translated by H. Blochmann and Col. H.S. Jarret, 2nd edition, Calcutta, 1927-49.

2. (i) Sergeant R.B., Islamic Textiles "Ars Islamica, Vol. 16
   . (ii) For details see Masudi Murudj-al Dhanabhy, A.D. 943 (322 Hijri)

3. Ibn Khurdazabah (A.D. 826-912) as quoted by Elliot and Dawson. History of India as told by its own Historians, 8 vol., London, 1867-1877.

4. Ibid

5. Ibid

6. Hadud al Alam. Translated by M. Minorsky, Gibb Memorial Series XI, London, 1937

7. Ibn Batuta. Rehla. Misr (Egypt), 2nd edition, AH 1322.

8. Chandra, Moti. Costumes & Textiles of Sultanate Period, Journal of Indian Textile History No. VI, 1961.

9. Geo Phillips "Ma Huan's Account of the Kingdom of Bengal". Journal of Royal Asiatic Society, 1895.

10. Munshi. Cultural History of the People of India, Vol. III, Bharatiya Vidya Bhavan, Bombay

11. Abu-al-Fazl. A. Op. cit.

12. Chandra, Moti. Op. cit.

13. Hakalyt Series II, vol. XLIV

14. Barbosa Duarte. The Book of Duarte Barbosa — An Account of Countries Bordering on the Indian Ocean and their Inhabitants. Translated from Portuguese by M.L. Dames, 2 vol., London, 1919-22

15. Bahi Khatas of Udaipur. Uncatalogued. Rajasthan State, Archives, Bikaner

16. The Babar Nama: Autobiography of Emperor Babar. Translated from Turki by A.S. Beveridge, 2 vol. London, 1912-22

17. Ibid

18. (i) Ishwari Prasad. The Life and Times of Humayun, Calcutta, 1955
    . (ii) Gulbadan Begum. Humayun Nama. Translated by A. Beveridge from Turki, London

19. Pope A.V. History of Persian Art, vol. II

20. Abu-al-Fazl, Ain-i-Akbari. Op. cit.

21. Edwards M.A. Letter written on 8th August 1566 and 16th June 1567. Principal Navigations. Hakluyt series, Vol. III

22. Foster W. The Embassy of Sir Thomas Roe to the Court of the Great Moghul, Oxford University Press, London, 1826

23. Bernier, Francois, Travels in the Moghul Empire — Translated by Archibald Constable, London, 1891

24. Hawkins, William. Early Travels in India, 1608-13 Hakluyt Series.

25. Terry, Edward. Voyage to East India, London 1655.

26. The Tuzuk-i-Jahangiri. Translated by Alexander Rogers and edited by Henry Beveridge, London.

27. Bahi Raj Tilak Sur Singhji, Bikaner 1671 Bikrami Samvat. Uncatalogued record of Rajasthan State Archives, Bikaner.

28. Foster W. Op. cit.

29. Kahlenberg M.H. The Relationship between a Persian and an Indian Floral Velvet in the Los Angeles County Museum, LACM Art Bulletin

30. Bahi of Marriage of Maharajah Anup Singh of Bikaner. V.S. 1710, Rajasthan State Archives, Bikaner.

31. Ibid

32. Bahi of Raj Tilak of Raja Gaj Singh of Bikaner, A.D. 1729. Rajasthan State Archives, Bikaner

33. Forster. A Journey from Bengal to England, 1790

Kashmir Shawls

Moti Chandra

The history of shawl-weaving with which the history of wollen textiles in this country is closely associated, is rather obscure. No connected account of textile materials except a short notice in the *Arthasāstra* is available, and for the history of early Indian textiles we have to depend on casual references whose interpretations are not wholly certain. Even in later works such as the *Varnaratnākara* and the *Āin-i-akbari* which give long lists of textiles, the difficulty of interpretation is great as the articles are not properly described. Recently Mr. John Irwin[1] in the article on the

Extract from an article published in the Bulletin of the Prince of Wales Museum, and reprinted with the kind permission of the author and the museum.

Kashmir Shawl has discussed certain interesting facts about dating the shawls. He has utilised mainly the European sources some of which are inaccessible for research in India. Mr. Irwin, however, is not certain about the origin of the shawl industry in India and records the tradition current in Kashmir of Zain-ul-Ābidīn (A.D. 1420-70) who is said to have introduced Turkestan weavers in Kashmir for the purpose. Mr. Irwin examines the possibility that the original Kashmir shawl weavers might have been immigrants, as certain unique features of the industry distinguish it from the traditional weaving in India proper; the most significant is the technique which has a parallel in Persia and Central Asia but nowhere in the Indo-Pakistan continent. This is the twill-tapestry technique in which the wefts are inserted by means of floating wooden bobbins, *tojis,* on a simple loom without the use of a shuttle. The weft threads alone form the patterns and do not run the full width of the cloth, being woven back and forth round the warp threads only where each particular colour is needed in the pattern. It is possible that the technique of twill-tapestry weaving may be of foreign origin, but whether it was introduced in India in the 15th century is open to doubt as will be seen presently.

The earliest information about the woollen fabrics manufactured in India is available from Vedic literature. The references, however, being scanty, their interpretation at times is doubtful. It is however certain that sheep wool was used for spinning and therefore the sheep was called *ūrnavatī*[2] and the wool *āvika.*[3] The valley of Sindh has been called *suvāsā ūrnāvatī*[4] because sheep's wool and cloth were available there in plenty. The sheep of Gandhāra were famous,[5] and the regions through which the Rāvī flowed was noted for its washed or coloured woollen fabrics:[6] Pushan is mentioned as a weaver of woolen fabrics. *Kambala,* a generic term for blankets and shawls, appearing for the first time in the *Atharvaveda*[7] is according to Pryzluski an Austric loanword in Indo-Aryan.[8] *Dūrsha* from which probably *dhussā,* a rough woollen *chādar* from the Punjab and Kashmir derives its etymology, occurs for the first time in the *Atharvaveda*[9] but it is difficult to say anything about the form or material used in the manufacture of Vedic *dūśa.* Another fabric mentioned in the later *Samhitas*[10] and the *Brāhmanas*[11] is *pāndva* which the kings wore at the time of sacrifices. The *Brihadāranyaka Upanishad*[12] mentions *pīndvāvika* which was made from the sheep's wool and was possibly a woollen *chādar* or a shawl.

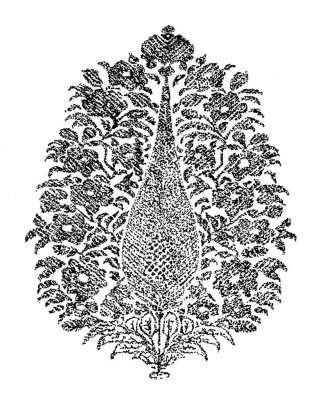

Opposite Page

Kashmir shawl, 19th century

This typical cross border intricately woven Kashmir shawl has the tree of life motif. At each end are broad flowing borders and smaller guard borders. The small green edging was woven by a separate set of weavers, as was the end border. The latter is similar to the narrow borders used on the *dhussa,* a self coloured woollen shawl traditionally worn by men. The finishing of the shawl is done with multi-coloured pieces joined together and richly embroidered.

It is not known whether the goats' wool from which the modern Kashmir shawls are woven was used in the Vedic period, though the sacred nature of the black antelope skin has been emphasised at many places in Vedic literature.[13]

Whether the woolen fabrics in the Vedic age were patterned is not known. However, there are references to show that brocades were known.[14] Perhaps *ārokāh*[15] also expresses some kind of fabric with decorated borders. *Pesas* seems to have been a general term for embroidery[16] and needlework profession.[17]

Some interesting information could be gathered about the woollen fabrics and shawls from Buddhist literature and the *Mahābhārata* and the *Rāmāyana*. It is interesting to note that needlework *(pesakākara-sippa)* was considered to be a low form of handicraft,[18] perhaps it was practised by low caste people. In Punjabi and Hindi even now *dhūssā* means a rough woollen *chādar*, but in Buddhist times it seems to have been a very costly shawl. Banāras also seems to have manufactured a kind of shawl of mixed fabric in which woollen and linen threads were used. Jivaka Kumārabhritya is said to have received such a shawl as gift from the ruler of *Kāsī*.[19] It is called *addha Kāsika-kambala*. Buddhaghosa explains the term *Kāsī* here as equivalent to a thousand *Kārshāpanas* and thus *addhakāsiya* was a shawl costing five hundred. It is possible that the shawl had a very light texture as even now very light muslin in Hindi is called *addhi*. Kodumbara.[20] also produced fine woollen fabrics. If Kodumbara and Odumbara are the same then in ancient times the region around Pathankot near Amritsar was a great centre of shawl weaving. While discussing the variant readings *Kochchhairabakahamsalakshanaih* in the *Saddharma Pundarīka*, p.82, verse 87, Pryzluski restitutes the correct text as *Kotamabakairhamsalakshanaih*, the Kotambaka cloth ornamented with figures of geese.[21] It shows that the geese pattern was a favourite motif of the ancient Audumbara weavers.

The *Arthasāstra* of Kautilya assigned to the Maurya period contains some interesting information about woollen textiles, blankets and shawls.[22] Woollen fabrics, *āvika*, were usually made of sheep's wool and were either plain white, deep red or light red. The shawls are divided into four categories — *khachita*, *vānchitra* and *khandasamghātya* and *tantuvichchhinna*. The commentary describes *Khachita* as *sūchīvānakarmanishpāditam* which may either mean "made by weaving and embroidering" or "made by twill-

tapestry process" — the *suchī* standing here for the *toji* of modern times. If the second explanation is correct then it indicates that even in those ancient days the *tīlīkār* process in Kashmir in which the patterns are woven on the loom and *amlīkar* process in which the patterns are embroidered existed. In *khachita* shawls apparently both processes were employed. The commentary describes *vānachitra* as *vānakarmanā kritavaichitryam*. Apparently in this process, as in the modern *tīlīkār* process, the designs were woven on the loom. The *khandasamghātya* in the commentary is described as *khachitānām utānām vā bahūnām khandānām samghātena nispāditam*, i.e. the shawl made by joining many *khachita* or woven pieces. It is apparently a form of Kashmir shawl in which patterns are woven on many strips measuring from twelve to eighteen inches; these are either joined to obtain a complete pattern or simply attached to a shawl. These strips are at times embroidered. The *tantuvichchhinna* is described by the commentator as *anutaviśrishtaih tantubhih madhya-kritavichchhedyam jālakopayagi cha*, i.e. obtaining patterns in the middle by unwoven yarn or a trellis pattern. It is possible that the netted border of a shawl made by tying the unwoven ends is meant here.

It is notable that *ranku* from whose hair costly shawls were made has simply been mentioned as an animal in the *Amarakośa*.[23] But there is little doubt that *ranku* is the same as *rang* or the shawl-goat mentioned several times by Jahangir in his memoirs and also noticed by Wood.[24] Thus *rānkava* is the equivalent of modern *pashmīna* or *aslī-tūs*. Elsewhere it is mentioned that when Hormuzd II (A.D. 302-310) married the daughter of the king of Kabul the bride's trousseau containing the wonderful products of the looms of Kashmir excited admiration.[25] But whether Kashmir is actually mentioned in the account could not be verified.

From the accounts of woollen fabrics and shawls in ancient India, it is clear that shawl weaving was not connected with Kashmir; the industry seems to have flourished in Swat, the North-Western Frontier Province, Punjab, etc. There is very little material to construct the history of shawl-weaving in Kashmir. Literary sources, however, reveal that the shawl industry of Kashmir was of greater antiquity than the 15th century. Kshemendra (c. A.D. 990-1065), a versatile writer of medieval Kashmir, seems to have been fairly well acquainted with the shawl-weaving industry of his country. In his *Desopadesa*, V.21,[261] he refers to *tūsta-prāvar-*

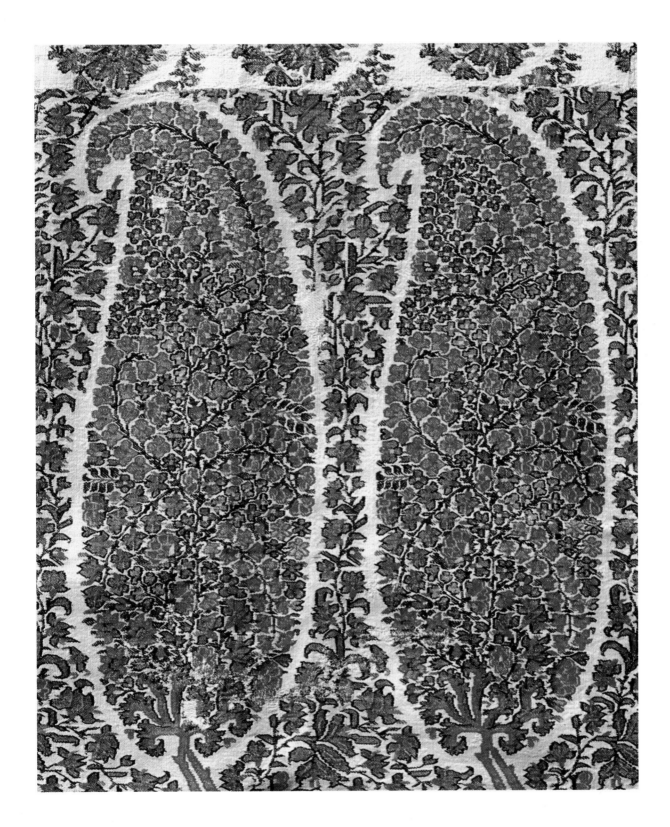

Kashmir shawl, 19th century

This long shawl, with an elongated paisley pattern, a highly stylized 'tree of life', was woven for the European market. Though the centres in France and England were already producing shawls with the use of the Jacquard, the Kashmir shawl was highly prized.

Following Page

Kashmir shawl, early 19th century

This shawl carries an elaborate *boteh* which conforms to the description found in Persian literature — the motif has a base, *piaeh,* a stomach, *shikam,* a fluting neck, *gardan,* and a *sir,* the head.

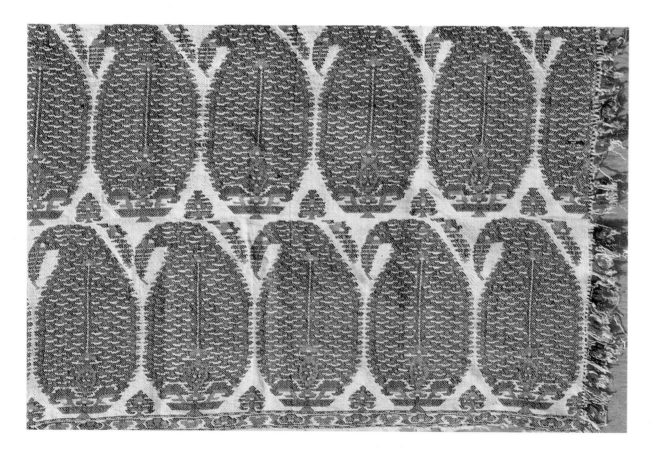

ana. In the *Narmamālā*,[27] *paryanta-tūstaka*, which seems to have been some inferior variety of shawl with borders, is mentioned.

There is little doubt that the *tūs* shawl of the *Aīn-i-Akbarī*[28] made from the wool of the animal of the same name is meant here. The *lohita-kambala* similar to the red shawls of *Gandhāra* and *Uddīyāna* mentioned in the *Jātakas* is mentioned.[29] Shawl-weaving seems to have been a cottage industry in 11th century Kashmir. At one place in the *Narmamālā*,[30] Kshemendra observes that the teacher employed in a *Kayastha's* house for teaching the children of the house instead of carrying out his duty whiled away his time in spinning *(kartana)*, drawing out the patterns *(likhanam)* and weaving the patterns on the strips with *tujis* or eyeless wooden needles *(sūchīpattikāvānam)* — the process analogous to the modern shawl-weaving in Kashmir. All these references to shawl manufacture in Kashmir prove its existence in Kashmir before the 15th century.

That in the 13th century shawls and other woollen goods from Kashmir reached Western India, is referred to by Udayaprabha Sūri in his *Dharmābhyudaya* (written c.1233). He says that along with other articles Kashmir shawls *(kāśmira-vasana)* were used for worshipping in the *samghas* and *chaityas*.[31]

The existence of the shawl-weaving industry in Kashmir in the 13th and 14th centuries is further supported by a reference in the *Sarūr-us-sudūr*, a work of Muhammad Bin Tughlaq's time, containing the sayings of Shaykh Farīd-ud-Dīn. It mentions that in Alāuddīn's time (1296-1316) Kashmir shawls were available in Delhi and that Shaykh Nizāmuddīn Auliyā had one such shawl.[32]

Zain-ul-Abidin's interest in textiles is shown in the *Jaina Rājatarangīnī* which says that hearing of the great reputation of Zain-ul-Ābidin many Indian rulers sent him presents. For instance Rana Kumbha (A.D. 1433-1468) of Chitor sent him a printed cloth known as *nārīkunjara*,[33] apparently decorated with the composite figures of women in the shape of an elephant, a favourite art motif of the 15th century. Sultān Mahmūd Beghrā A.D. (1458-1511) sent to him cloths such as *katepha, saglāta*, and *sopha*[34] which could be identified with *qatīf*, a silken stuff, *saqlāt*, scarlet broad cloth and *sūf* or woollen cloth mentioned in the *Aīn-i-Akbari*. Such was his reputation as a lover of art that in the words of the poet "a large number of artisans adept in original designs regarding him as the Wishing Tree came from long distances like swarming black bees".[35] "The Kashmiris mastering the intricacies of the shuttles *(turī)* and looms *(vema)* now weave beautiful and costly silks". "The special woollen textiles *(aurna, sopha)* of foreign origin, worthy of kings, are now woven by the Kashmiris".[36] "The painters seeing the patterns *(chitra)* and creeper designs *(latākritih)* obtained by intricate weaving processes *(vichitravayana)* are reduced to silence as the figures in a painting".[37] "The country and the costume of the king became famous on account of the silks made of endless yarns, and carefully dyed *(varnavichchhitti)*".[38]

From the above account it is clear that in Zain-ul-ābidin's time the art of textile weaving in Kashmir, specially the manufacture of silk, had received great impetus and that a large number of artisans, in order to show their art, came to Kashmir to seek the patronage of the ruler. It is also significant to note that certain woollen goods which came formerly from distant lands were, in the time of Zain-ul-ābidin, being manufactured in Kashmir. Herein possibly lies the origin of the tradition that Zain-ul-ābidin had invited Turkish weavers and thus laid the foundation of the shawl manufacturing industry in Kashmir. The tradition is further supported by Srivara's assertion that artisans came from distant lands to seek the patronage of the king. Turkestan is not specially mentioned, but the possibility that it was one of the countries from which artisans came to Kashmir could not be ruled out.

Considerable light on the shawl manufacture of Kashmir in the 16th century is thrown by the *Ain-in-Akbari* of Abul Fazl who has given exhaustive lists of all kinds of textiles. He points out the great interest which Akbar took in various stuffs — the reason why Iranian, European and Mongolian articles of wear were available in plenty in the country. Besides this, his interest in textiles had attracted a large number of foreign craftsmen and workers who taught the local people an improved style in textile manufacture. The imperial workshops at Lahore, Agra, Fatehpur and Ahmedabad were noted for their excellent products whose patterns, knots and varieties of fashion astonished the travellers. Akbar himself had acquired a practical knowledge of the whole trade, and the encouragement he gave to the indigenous workers brought all round improvement. All kinds of hair-weaving and silk-spinning improved so that the imperial workshops could manufacture all the stuff produced in other countries. There was a constant demand for fine materials and this gave an occasion for a grand display of draperies.

In keeping with his interest in textiles Akbar showed great interest in the shawl manufacture of Kashmir. We are informed in the *Ain* 31[39] that

to the generic term *shāl* Akbar gave his own Hindi designation *paramnaram,* very soft. The *Ain* 32[40] gives a fairly good account of Kashmir shawls. At that time the trade names given by the *Ain* are obscure, but some light could be thrown on them with the help of a mid-seventeenth centtury manuscript of the *Āin-i-Akbarī* in the Prince of Wales Museum, Bombay. It bears marginal notes which either give the correct spellings of the words or offer short explanations. The translation of the text on shawls differs at places from Jarrett's translation in the light of the new manuscript. "His Majesty improved the department (shawl department) in four ways. The improvement is visible first in *tūus* shawls, which are made of the wool of an animal of that name whose natural colours are black, white and red but chiefly black. Sometimes the colour is pure white. This kind of shawl is unrivalled for its lightness, warmth and softness. People generally wear it without altering its natural colour: His Majesty has had it dyed. It is curious that it will not take a red dye. Secondly, in the *safīd ālchas* (any kind of coloured stuff) or *tarahadārs* in their natural colours, the wool is either white, black or mixed. The first white kind was formerly dyed in three or four ways: His Majesty has given order to dye it in various ways." ..... "Fourthly, he improved the smaller size of the shawls and enlarged them as to make complete suit out of them."

"His Majesty encourages in every possible way the manufacture of shawls in Kashmir. In Lahore alone there are more than a thousand workshops. A kind of shawl named *mayan* is chiefly woven there; it consists of silk and wool mixed. These are of standard size. Both are used for *chīrahs* (turbans) and *fautahs* (loin-bands)".

From the above account of shawls, many points are clear. Firstly, the *tūs* shawl was made from the hair of the *tūs* goat. In the 19th century when Moorcroft visited Kashmir there were two kinds of goat-wool: *pashm shāl* obtained from the wool of domestic goats and *aslī tūs* obtained from the hair of wild goats and sheep. It was chiefly black, white or reddish. Secondly, the corded and patterned shawls *(tarah* shawls) were made of either white, black or mixed wool. The white kind was formerly dyed in three or four colours but in Akbar's time the number of colours increased. Thirdly, attention was paid to the manufacture of the following varieties of shawls: (1) *Zardozi* — Apparently this shawl was embroidered with gold wire and sequins. (2) *Kālabatūn* — The design seems to have been brocaded with gold wire. (3) *Qashidah* — In this variety the pattern was em-

Tree of Life motif Kashmir shawl,
19th century
detail

(Collection: C.L. Bharany)

broidered and not woven. (4) *Qalghai* — this type was made either of silk or gold wire and bore pine cone patterns *(qalghi)*. (5) *Bāndhnūn* shawls had tie-dyed pattern. (6) *Chhint* shawls were apparently painted or decorated with floral patterns in the manner of calico prints. According to Moorcroft[41] even in the early 19th century some shawls with green flowers tied in small hard knots to protect them from the action of the dye, were made. When united, each flower was surrounded by a small white field to which small eyes or spots of yellow and red were added by the embroiderers. (7) *Ālchah* was a white banded stuff. (8) *Purzdār* is described by Jarrett as a different kind of stuff of which the outside is plush-like. But according to the Prince of Wales Museum manuscript, it was known in Turkish as *Karh* and in Hindi and *rūsā*. The note further explains that the *purzdār* was either a big piece made of various strips joined together or had a marbled *(abrī)* design, or was given its name due to its good quality. There is little doubt that the *purzdār* is the kind of shawl in which the size is obtained by joining together several strips — the *khandasamghātya* of ancient times. Further, it seems that the shawls before Akbar's period were narrow. By Akbar's order, however, shawls of a suit's length were being made. Finally, Lahore, with more than a thousand workshops became a centre of shawl weaving and produced a stuff called *māyān* used for turbans and waist-bands.

There are several references to the shawl industry of Kashmir in the 17th century. Jāhāngîr, in his memoirs,[42] makes the following remarks: "The shawls of Kashmir to which my father gave the name of *parmnarm* are very famous: there is no need to praise them. Another kind is *taharma (naharma* is printed versions); it is thicker than a shawl and soft. Another is *darn*. It is like a *jul-i-khirasak* and is put on a carpet. With the exception of shawls they make other woollen material better in Tibet. Though they bring the wool for the shawls from Tibet, they do not make them there. The wool for the shawls come from a goat which is peculiar to Tibet. In Kashmir they weave the *pattu* shawl from wool, and sewing two shawls together they smooth them into a kind of *saqarlāt* (broadcloth) which is not bad for a rain coat."

Besides the stuffs mentioned above, we are told that Jahangir once presented to Mirza Raja Bhao Singh a special Kashmir *phup* shawl.[43] *Phup* here is certainly coming from the Hindi *puhupa* derived from the Sanskrit *pushpa,* flower. Apparently it was a flowered shawl. At another place[44] it is said that the *tūs* shawl was a special prerogative of the king. It could only be worn when ordered by the king.[45]

Bernier, on his visit to Kashmir in 1665, has left the following account of shawls manufactured there:

"Large quantities of shawls were manufactured which gave employment even to children. These shawls measured 1 1/2 ell* long and an ell broad, ornamented at both ends with a sort of embroidery, made in the loom, a foot in width. The Mughal and Indian men and women wore them in winter round their heads, passing them over the shoulders as a mantle. One sort was manufactured with the wool of the country and the other with the wool of the shawl goat of Tibet. The price of the *tus* shawl ranged from 50 to 150 Rupees. Great pains were taken to manufacture similar shawls at Patna, Agra and Lahore but they lacked the delicate texture of Kashmir shawls.[46]

By the end of the 17th century the shawls of Kashmir were being exported to other countries. The shawls imported by the East India Company in 1685 and 1704,[47] according to Mr. Irwin,[48] were almost certainly intended for use as tablecloths or counterpanes. How the demand for Kashmir shawls in Europe grew and how it dictated the contemporary fashion has been ably dealt by Mr. Irwin and need not be recapitulated here.

Forster in his travel to Kashmir in 1783 has made certain interesting observations on the shawl industry of Kashmir. As a matter of fact he travelled in the guise of a Turkish shawl merchant proceeding to purchase shawls in Kashmir.[49] At Bilaspur he met a *tumboo (tambū)* shawl caravan on its way to Delhi and Lucknow. It was through the help of their agents that he could clear himself from the Bilaspur customs.[50] According to Forster, shawls exported from Kashmir were packed in oblong bales, whose outward coverings were made of buffalo's or ox's hide, strongly sewn with leather thongs. They were opened only in the destined markets.[51] The shawl wool was brought from Tibet. Originally of a dark colour, it was bleached with rice flour. The yarn was dyed as desired; the shawls were also washed after fabrication. Richly patterned borders were attached to the shawls so neatly as to allow no joints. The price of an ordinary shawl varied from 8 to 40 rupees, but the value of a flowered shawl was considerably greater. A portion of the revenue of Kashmir was returned to the Afghan capital in shawl goods. The shawls were in three sizes: the long and the square ones were in common use in India; the other long and very narrow ones with black preponderating in their colour scheme were worn as girdles by the Northern Asiatics.[52]

The best account of shawl manufacture in the early nineteenth century has been given by Moorcroft.[53] During the course of his journey he found that Amritsar had become an important centre of shawl manufacture owing to the migration of a large number of Kashmir craftsmen from their country to escape the Afghan tyranny. Before Moorcroft's time, shawl yarn sent to Amritsar came from Kashmir, but its export was banned to discourage the foreign manufacture of shawls. However, when he visited Amritsar the wool came from Tibet and Bokhara. The Amritsar shawls with double warp and weft were fairly thick and soft. The meagre wages of two annas daily left the weavers miserably poor.[54]

Moorcroft has left an interesting account of shawl manufacture in Kashmir[55] which has been supplemented by Mr. Irwin from the original papers in the India Office. According to Moorcroft the *pashm* wool employed for shawl manufacture was obtained from domestic and wild goats and was brought from Tibet, Ladakh, Yarkand and Khotan by the Mongols who exchanged it for shawls.[56] In its first disposal the importer *(baqāl)*, the retailer *(pashm-farosh)*, and the broker *(muqīm)* were concerned, the payment made in each or two months' credit.[57]

Women purchased the wool from the retailer for spinning. It was first packed and cleaned with the solution of rice flour and then torn to pieces. Then after separating the fine quality from the second quality, extracted for strong shawl *(Pattu)* cloth, it was arranged into square elastic pads. Then the pads were rolled and carefully stored. The fine wool was spun in the lengths of seven hundred yards which were again cut into two hundred lengths to suit the length of the warp. The retailers purchased the yarn from the spinners and sold it to weavers who, having ascertained the patterns in demand, handed over the skeins to the dyer. For shawls with a plain field a second yarn was used to weave patterns to get an enhanced effect. The dyer professed to give sixty-four shades such as crimson *(gulenar)* obtained from cochineal, kermes, logwood for other reds and blue and green from indigo. Carthamus and saffron yielded various tints of orange, yellow, etc.

The *nakatu* adjusted the yarn for the warp and the weft; the warp yarns, measuring 3.1/2 yards and consisting of two to three thousand threads were double-ply while the weft yarns were single. Then the warp was dressed with thickly boiled rice water. Silk was used for border warp for strength, and as a colour contrast. Narrow borders were woven with the shawl, but the broader ones were woven on a different loom and then sewn to the shawl by the darner in such a manner that the joints could scarcely be detected. The warp was then drawn through the needles and then taken to the loom. After the warp had been fixed upon the looms and the pattern drawn, the *naqqāsh,* the *tarahdār guru* and the *tālīm guru* determined the proportion of the yarn of different colours. The *naqqāsh* prepared the drawing of the pattern, the *tarahdār guru,* after considering the disposition of the colours, called out the colours beginning from the foot of the pattern, the number of threads to which it extended and the colour by which it was followed till the whole pattern had been described. From his directions, the *tālīm guru* took down the particulars in a short-hand and delivered a copy to the weaver.

The workmen prepared *tujis* or needles containing about four grains of dyed yarn. These eyeless needles had sharp ends. Following the instructions of the *tarahguru,* the right side of the cloth was placed next to the ground, the work being carried on the reverse on which the needles hung in a row numbering 400 to 1500. As soon as the work on one line was completed the count was brought down with force.

The shawl-cloth was generally of two kinds: one, plain with two threads, and the second, twilled or with four threads. The twilled cloth, which was frequently of irregular texture, was usually twenty-four *girah* broad. To ensure a good field the borders were woven separately and joined to the field by the *rafugar.*

When finished, the shawl was handed over to the *purusgar* who removed discoloured hair with tweezers or by shaving. Then the shawls were sent to the collector for stamp duties which amounted to 26%. After that they were handed over to the sellers and brokers. They were than washed and calendered, packed separately in coloured papers, pressed and then the bale was sewn up in strong cloth over which a cover of *tūs* or birch bark was laid. Finally, the whole was sewn smoothly and tightly in a raw hide.

Besides the shawls manufactured and described above, *doshālī umilī* shawls were embroidered with needles using woollen thread. Tracing paper with holes through which charcoal and coloured powder mixed with gum arabic was pounced, was used. Sometimes wooden blocks were also used.

Among the plain shawls Moorcroft mentions *pattū, pashminā* made of *asal tūs* or coarse shawl wool (4 gaz × 1^1/2 gaz); *shāl phiri* made of seconds; turban-cloth and *johar shāl-sādū* with a narrow edging of coloured yarn 3 to 3¾ gaz × 1^1/2 gaz).

The following shawls measured 3^1/2 gaz × 1^1/2 gaz: *Shāl-hāshiyādār, shāl do-hāshiyādār* and *shāl chahār hāshiyādār* had one, two and four borders respectively; *hāshiyādār khosar* of *khalīkhāni* had two borders and two *tanga* with or without flowers in the corners. *Hāshiādār kiiungrīdār* had the border of the usual form with another inside, or nearer the middle resembling the crest of the wall of an Asiatic fort furnished with narrow niches or embrasures for wall pieces; *dhūrdār* in which an ornament ran round the field between the border and the field; *matandār* had flower or decoration in the middle of the field; *chādār* and a circular ornament in the field; *chautahīdār* had four half-moons; *kunj būte-dār* had a group of flowers at each corner; *alfīdār* had green sprigs without any colour on a white field; *Kaddār* had a large group of flowers in the form of the cone of a pine with the ends of point straight or curved downwards; *do-kaddār* had two such motifs; *sehkaddār* had three rows and so on to five and upwards; in the latter case, the cones were somewhat small.

Moorcroft has also given the definitions of some technical terms about patterns. Thus *hāshiyā* is the border; the *zanzirī* or chain runs above and below the *patta* and confines it; the *dhūr* or running ornament situated inside the *hāshiyā* and *zanzir* enveloped the whole field; *kunjbūtā* is a corner ornament; *metan* is the decorated part of the field and *būtā* is a cone in one or several rows; after five rows it is *tūkaddār*. The constituent part of a *būtā* is *pāi* or foot or pediment of leaves, the *shikam* or belly and *sir*, the head, which is straight, curved or inclined. The sloping *būtā* is *būtā-kaj*; the *thal* or net separates the different *būtās*, sometimes the interspace being plain. *Jāmewār* meaning literally a gown piece in many varieties such as *khirkhabūtā*, large compound flowers consisting of groups of smaller ones, etc. It was used by the Persians and Afghans.

The *rezābūta* (small flowers thickly set), *thāldār* (network), *mehramat, khaterast, marpech, kalamkar, zakheangūr, chaporast, dogul* (two flowers), *sehgul* (three flowers), *chahargul* (four flowers), *barghe-beed, gule-sant, duzdehkhat, dazdeh rang, gule parwāne, kaddār, kayhamu, sabzkār* and *safed* were exported to India proper where they were dyed, the small flowers being tied previously in hard knots.

The square *rumāls* for women were known as *khatdār, mehramat* and *islimi* with other patterns of *jāmewār, chahārbāgh, hāshiya, chānd, chautahi, shāhmantohi, firangi* (exported to Russia), *tarah Armeni* (exported to Armenia and Persia), *tarah Rūmi* (exported to Turkey) and *sādā* for domestic use.

Besides the articles mentioned above there were also *shamlas* for the waist (8 × 1½ gaz — exported to Tibet), *gospech* or *patkā* (turban, 10 × 1 gaz), *mandila* with or without *zanzir* (8 to 10 gaz × 12 girah), *kālin* (*pashmina* shawl carpet made of any size), *naqsh* (trousers with or without seams, the former in two pieces sewn by a darner and the latter by a *jurrab saz* or a stocking maker), *chārkhānā* or netted cloth (1 to 1½ gaz), *gul-*

badan (breadth 14 girah to 1 girah), *lugi* (3½ × 1½ gaz), *tākhīn* (caps), *jurrab* (short stockings) flowered or striped *(mehramat), moze pashmina* (long stockings), *sakkahposh* (canopies) *darparda* (curtain), *kajjarī asp* (saddle cloth), *kajjarī fil* (elephant's cover), *bālaposh* (quilt or coverlet), *galāband* (cravat), *pistānī-band* (neckerchief), *langot* (waist-belt), *postīn* (lining for a pelisse), *paipech*, legging, *izārband, takiā* (pillow case), *khalitā* (bags or purse), *kabarposh* (shrouds), *tākposh* (hanging for cupboards or recesses) and *khwān-posh* (dish cover or napkins).

It is peculiar that in the above list the *shikārgāh* or hunting pattern of the Kashmir shawl has not been mentioned by Moorcroft, though shawls with such patterns are available. It is possible that this pattern had already fallen into disuse in the beginning of the 19th century. It is however clear that when Vigne visited Kashmir, figured shawls were being manufactured. According to him, Maharaja Ranjit Singh had ordered, at a cost of Rs.5,000, a pair of shawls to be made, which represented his victories.[58]

The dispersal of Kashmir shawl weavers and embroiderers in the late 18th century to Amritsar and possibly to the Hill States of Kangra was due to the tyranny of the Afghans and the rigorous exactions of the Sikh rulers. Vigne notes that after

1830 he found that at Srinagar only six hundred shawl frames had remained, and most of the weavers had migrated or had taken to some other profession.

As mentioned by Moorcroft in one of his letters dated 1882, quoted by John Irwin, at Srinagar he met merchants from the cities of Chinese Turkestan, Uzbek, Tartary, Kabul, Persia and Turkey and from the provinces of British India getting the shawls manufactured after the patterns and quality for which there was demand in their respective countries. But as Moorcroft has observed elsewhere, political events in the 19th century had reduced Kashmir's trade with Persia, Turkey and Punjab while the demand from British India had decreased. One encouraging feature, however, was the increase in demand from Russia and Turkestan which probably helped the industry to tide over its difficulties for some time.

The increased demand for Kashmir shawls in Europe led to their imitation in England, and in the closing years of the 18th century, from 1814 onwards, Paisley became the main centre of shawl manufacture in Britain. By 1818 Paisley shawls were being exported to India though they could never compete with the quality of Kashmir shawls. French design also exerted great influence on Kashmir design. France produced new varieties of the cone palmette design, the pattern being known in the English trade as the "fill over" design because the patterns covered the whole field of the shawls instead of the borders only. They became so popular by 1830 that Paisley weavers ceased to copy the originals and followed the French patterns. The effect of the new French patterns which had great demand in Europe and America also led to the copying of French patterns by the weavers of Kashmir.

The shawl industry in Kashmir survived till 1870, when the change in fashion in the West killed the export market with consequent suffering to the weaver. The internal demand persisted for some time but it was too inadequate to support the industry.

FOOTNOTES

1. Irwin, John: *The Kashmir Shawls*, Marg, VI, I (1952) pp.43-50
2. *Rigveda*, VIII, 67.3
3. *Brihadāranyaka Upanishada*, II, 3, 6
4. *Rigveda*, x, 75, 8
5. *Rigveda*, I, 126, 7
6. *Rigveda*, IV, 22 2; V, 52, 9
7. *Atharvaveda*, DIV, 2, 66-67
8. Bagchi, *Pre-Aryan and Pre-Dravidian*, pp.6-8
9. *Atharvaveda*, IV, 7, 6; VIII, 6, 11
10. *Maitrāyani Samhitā*, IV, 4, 3
11. *Sat. Brā.* V, 3, 5, 5, 21
12. *Brihadaranyaka Upanishad*, I, 3, 6
13. Moti Chandra, *Prāchina Bhāratiya Vesha-Bhūshā*, pp.11-12
14. *Hiranvān prati atkān, Rigveda*, V, 55, 6
15. *Satpatha Brahmanas*, III, 1, 2, 13
16. *Rigveda*, IV, 36, 7
17. *Väja. Sam.* XXX, 9
18. *Jātaka*, IV, p.251: *Suttavibhanga Pāchittiya*, II, 2, 1
19. *Mahavagga*, VIII, 1, 4; VIII, 2
20. *Jātakas*, VI, 500, gāthas 1786, 1801
21. *J.A.*, 1926, p.23
22. *Arthasāstra*, ed. by J. Ganapati Sastri, Vol.1, p.193; Ib. ed. by Samasastry, pp.89-90
23. *Amarkosa*, II, 6, 111
24. Wood, A., *Journey to the Sources of Oxus;* Introduction, p.57, London, 1872
25. B. Laufer, *Sino-Iranica*, p.161
26. *Desopadesa and Narmamāla*, ed. by M. Kaul, Poona 1923
27. *Narmamāla*, I, 72
28. *Ain Akbari* 32
29. *Narmamāla*, I, 111
30. *Narmamāla*, II, 45
31. *Dharmābhyudaya*, I, 71, Bombay, 1949
32. *Indian History Congress Proceedings of the 18th Session*, Nagpur, p.168
33. *Jaina Rājatarangini*, VI, 137, Bombay, 1892
34. Ibid VI, 25
35. Ibid VI, 27
36. Ibid VI, 29
37. Ibid VI, 30
38. Ibid VI, 31
39. *Ain-i-Akbari*, I, 89
40. Ibid I, 90-91
41. Travels, II, 191-192
42. *Tuzuk*, II, 147-178
43. Ibid I, 297
44. Ibid I, 384
45. Ibid I, 384
46. Bernier's *Travels*, pp.402-403, London, 1891
47. Birdwood, *Report on Old Records*, p.27
48. Loc. cit. p.47, fn.8
49. G. Forster, *A Journey from Bengal to England*, I, p.191, London, 1798
50. Ibid I, p.211
51. Ibid I, pp.247-248
52. Ibid I, pp.18-19
53. *Travels in the Himalayan Provinces.....* by Moorcroft and Trebnech from 1819-25, London, 1841
54. Ibid I, pp.110-113
55. Ibid II, chapter III
56. Ibid II, pp.164-166
57. Ibid p.167
58. G.G. Vigne, *Travels in Kashmir, Ladak and Iskardo*, Vol.II, p.124, London, 1842.

Kashmir Shawls and Iranian Termeh

Jasleen Dhamija

The finest textiles ever woven in wool are the shawls of Kashmir during the Moghul period, and the *shale termeh* of Kerman and Mashhad, woven in the Safavid period. Scholars hold different opinions on the origin of this technique. Some are of the opinion that the technique was developed in Persia and was introduced from Persia into Kashmir. Others, however, consider that the technique was introduced into Persia from India. The local tradition in Kashmir is that the art of patterned shawl-weaving was introduced with the help

An extract from the catalogue of the exhibition of Royal Iranian Termeh and Kashmir Shawls from the collection of Rahim & George Anavian.

of Turkish weavers by the enlightened ruler Zain-ul-'Abidin (A.D. 1470). This tradition is confirmed by references found in the history of Kashmir (in *Jaina Rajatarangini*), where, in a discussion on the skill of the weavers in the reign of Zain-ul-'Abidin, mention is made of the special woollen textiles "of foreign origin, worthy of kings, which are now being woven by the Kashmiris."

Kashmir, however, had an ancient tradition of weaving fine woollen *tus* shawls which were woven from the wool of the undercoats of goats that lived at very high altitudes: these were perhaps the finest shawls woven in Asia. Reference to such shawls is found as early as the 10th century A.D. It is likely that the expert spinners and weavers who were known for their fine shawls, had mastered the art of twill-tapestry weaving in wool with great speed, and had rapidly surpassed the products of the original centre of production. The availability of wool of the finest quality, in combination with the skill of the weaver in Kashmir, contributed to the extremely fine quality of Kashmir shawls. Moghul records state that although the weaving of shawls was practised in the royal workshops in Agra, Lahore and Delhi, none were so fine as those woven in Kashmir.

Technique

Detailed accounts of the organisation of the shawl industry in Kashmir are given by Moorcraft, an Englishman who travelled in the Himalayas between 1819 and 1825. He notes the great systematization and describes it at length:

Separate groups of workers — invariably women — sorted and spun the wool. The raw wool given to them was very dirty and had to be immediately sorted and separated according to its different grades. Different colours of wool had also to be matched. The finest quality was wool from the undercoat of goats living in high mountain areas, who often rubbed against brambles and thorns, leaving tufts of wool to be collected. This was priced as first quality wool.

Wool of the second quality was that taken from domesticated goats, and even in this, there were variations. As always, the wool from the undercoat was finer in quality than wool from other parts of the same Pashmina goats.

After spinning, the next workers concerned were the dyers who prepared the colours and dyed the wools according to samples provided to them. The art of dyeing was very well developed, with a

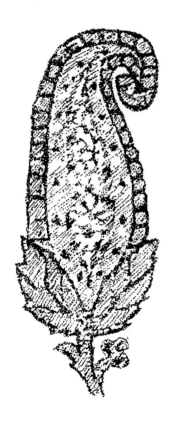

Previous Page

Mehramat, striped Kashmir shawl, late 19th century

This striped shawl is based on the striped *termeh* made for garment edgings.

Opposite Page

Kashmir shawl, 19th century

The all-over pattern is of a *boteh*, tree of life, and is typical of the shawls made for the Indian market.

range of three hundred shades available, according to tradition.

At least six specialists were involved with the coloured wools before weaving could actually begin. These were: the warp-makers, the warp-dresser, the warp-threader, the pattern-drawer, the colourist and the *tālim*-writer. The master-weaver controlled the loom by calling out the colours to be used in the *tālim*, the coded pattern-guide, which would be followed by the weavers.

Warp-makers had the job of twisting the threads into the required thickness for the two to three thousand threads required for the preparation of the warp. The warp-dresser had to stretch the warps so that they could sustain the strain of the weaving process and the constant pressure and movement of the heddle. The warp-threader had to pass the yarn through the heddles of the loom.

Once the warp was ready the pattern was required, and the pattern-drawer who worked out the complete design, had the most important role. The pattern,, once drawn, was then passed to the expert colourist who coloured the design. Sometimes the pattern-maker and the colourist would be the same person but often this job would have

been done by two specialists. The importance of the pattern-maker and the colourist, or *naqqash,* can be seen from the fact that the highest wages in the whole operation were paid to this person or persons. The total number of pattern-drawers in Kashmir were very few, and during the period when the shawl-weaving industry was expanding, the work was still confined to five or six families.

Often the colourist did not actually colour the drawing itself but matched the different shades by means of a colour-card — a *range-tikat* — on the basis of which he annotated the drawing. From such annotated drawings the *tālim*-writer produced a written shorthand indicating the number of warp threads to be covered with different colours so that by following the written instructions the weaver could reproduce the pattern. This technique of annotating the designs, so that each stitch was written down, was possibly responsible for the development of the most intricate of patterns woven in an extraordinarily wide range of colours.

It was only then that the master weaver would start to weave the shawl, with the help of two or three apprentices who worked with him on the loom. For the patterned portions, he would call

Kashmir shawl loom, Kanihama

The village of Kanihama still has a
few weavers who weave traditional
shawls using the *talim* and the
tradition of multiple weft threads for
weaving the designs. The *tojis*,
small pools seen here with multi-
coloured threads, are woven in by
the deft fingers of the young
weavers, as the master weaver calls
out the colours and number of
threads from the written code of the
talim.

Opposite Page

Kashmir shawl border, detail

This *kani* shawl border is woven in
twill weave with non-continuous
weft threads.

out the design and they would be woven in with
the use of fine needle-like spools, *tojis*, employed
by the weavers in place of shuttles. They were
made of fine light wood with sharp edges on both
sides, charred to prevent their becoming rough or
jagged when they were actually in use. The design
part was always on the underside and the weaver
inserted his spools from above. After each line of
multiple-wefts had been completed, the comb was
vigorously pulled down so that the weaving would
be very close. Because of the great variety of patterns and the complicated designs, which took
such a long time to produce, the actual weaving of
one shawl would be divided among ten looms,
each loom working on a particular section of the
shawl.

These sections were finally handed over to a
group of specialists whose task it was to repair any
defects in the shawl and to join the pieces in such
a manner that the join would not be visible.

Today, should one wish to determine whether a
shawl being offered for sale is a true Kashmiri
shawl or a copy made in Europe, the easiest test is
to see whether it has been joined from many
pieces or whether it was woven as a single piece.

It is clear, thus, that Kashmir shawls are woven in
a twill-tapestry technique, having multiple weft-

threads and woven in a number of pieces later joined together.

As regards the manner in which shawls were woven in Iran, we have no such detailed accounts. But from a study of the silk-textile traditions of the Safavid period, it is not hard to deduce that the same kind of organisation found in Kashmir must have existed in the centres of weaving in Iran. The only difference was that the technique of using the *tālim*, the written annotation, was not employed in Persia. Instead the graph method was utilised for evolving the pattern. The result was that Persian shawls rarely display large patterns: instead they have smaller designs with many repeats. More complicated designs, with medallions in the body and multiple borders, are also very uncommon and do not appear to have been used after the 17th century. Woven *termeh* was really meant to be used as lengths, cut up and either stitched into garments or as ceremonial bath mats, *souzani,* as wraps, *boghcheh* or as quilt-covers with additional borders that were traditionally made from striped *termeh.*

Kerman shawls are distinguished by their isolated design motifs and are loosely woven with floating threads on the back of the textile. The wool used is also coarser in texture, but the colouring is very subtle, all of which differentiates them from the shawls of not only Kashmir but also of Mashhad

and of Yazd. Mashhad shawls generally display an all over pattern of *botehs* interconnected with staghorn motifs, *shakhe gavazn* or linked *botehs* of different sizes and shapes. Yazd shawls are of two qualities, the more common being thinly striped with an extra weft pattern. The stripes may be narrow and in two colours, used for borders and edgings of garments, or woven in many colours, *haft-rangi,* and used as girdles. Textiles with wider *haft-rangi* stripes are specifically made for the loose pants, *shalvar,* worn by Zoroastrian women. Another type is still woven with narrow stripes of many colours with the same patterns, then stitched together to make a *shalvar,* traditionally meant to be stitched from strips of different coloured materials. Until the beginning of the twentieth century, the dyes used for these textiles were derived from organic substances well described by R and G. Anavian in *Royal Persian and Kashmir Brocades.*

Designs and Styles of Shawls

Existing examples of both Persian and Indian shawls can be found from the 18th century in some quantity. Very few pieces survive from the 17th century and both Indian and Persian examples are rare, the Persian ones especially. The few that do survive are quite restrained, both in their colours and in their design motifs. From a study of those pieces that have come down to us or which are known from travellers' descriptions, three distinct types of shawls woven in Kashmir can be identified as belonging to this period, and from the fragment of a shawl in the Anavian collection, we may perhaps conclude that the same may have been true for Persian shawls.

One distinct type would be the *chahar ghadi*, a square shawl which carries floral motifs distributed over the surface with a narrow but finely detailed four-sided border. Sometimes, they have a circular medallion in the centre with quartered medallions at each of the four corners. The second type woven in Kashmir, and possibly also in Persia, consists of sashes or girdles, known as *kamarband* in Persia and *patka* in India. These were long and narrow, with a four-sided border and a cross-border at the end. The third variety was the long shawl woven for the Indian market, wide and long with a narrow border and a cross-border of stylized *boteh* or tree-of-life designs. This was draped over the shoulder and was a part of the formal Indian dress for both men and women.

The more elaborate patterns were developed later, as can be seen in pieces dated in the latter half of the 18th century. It is possible that the all over patterns known commercially as *jamevar*, to be used for making cut and stitched garments, might have been developed in Kerman and later influenced the development of Kashmir textiles. The French jeweller Chardin mentions that in India elaborate allover patterns were especially woven for the Persian market. The oldest surviving Kerman pieces display allover patterns but do not carry cross-borders — typical of the shawls woven in Kashmir and other parts of India. The later, more elaborate shawls with allover patterns are probably a development of this particular style.

Kashmir shawls are well documented not only in travel literature but also in the official documents of the Moghul Empire. In the *Ain-i-Akbari*, the biography of the Emperor Akbar (1556-1605), the different types of shawls woven in India are enumerated: "In former times shawls came from Kashmir; from time to time, people folded them in four-fold and wore them for a long time. Nowadays they are generally worn without folds and are merely thrown over the shoulders. His Majesty has commenced to wear it double which looks very well."

The fact that these shawls are very precious is brought home by the mention in the *Tuzuk-i-Jahangiri*, Jahangir's memoirs, that the use of woven shawls was the prerogative of the emperor and could only be worn by others when allowed by the emperor or when gifted by him.

The later study of shawls by Moorcroft in 1819-25 gives a very detailed description of the designs woven in the shawls. From the terms used we see that most of the terminology used is Persian and the words are similar to those used in Kerman, Yazd and Khorasan and exactly the same as those used by the Persian trade until the beginning of this century, when *termeh* continued to be woven in Persia and imported from India.

Hashieh or *Hashia* is the border; *zanziri* or the chain was the pattern that ran above and below the cross border and enclosed it. *Boteh* is either used for shrub or a cone. This is divided into three sections: the *piaeh (payeh)*, the foot or pediment of leaves, the *shikam* or belly and lastly the *sir*, head, which is either straight, inclined or curved. The sloping *boteh* is *boteh kaj*. The all over pattern without a border is known as *jamevar* for it was meant to be cut into pieces for making the upper coat known in India as the *jama*. The motifs were called *reezboteh*, small flowers; *thal dar*, a network of oval enclosures; *meharamat*, the striped pattern known in Persia as *moharamat*; *mar peech*, snakes curve or twisted branch; *kalamkar*, where designs were derived from the printing traditions; *dou-gul*, double flowers; *sehgul*, triple flowers; *chahar-gul*, quadruple flowers; and *barge beed*, the curving and drooping long leaves of the willow tree.

The names of different overall patterns were indicative of the markets for which they were meant. *Tareh Armeni* was exported to Persia. *Tareh Rumi* was for Turkey and *Tareh Farangi* for Europe.

The designers in Kashmir and Persia used a variety of techniques not only to evolve complicated patterns but also tried to overcome the limitations of the flat surface by giving a dimensional effect with the use of secondary patterns and subtle variation of colours.

The pieced shawls of Kashmir which were woven on at least ten separate looms and were then joined together by the *rafoogars* are a later development of the Kashmir shawl industry. The curving *boteh* is extended to nearly half the length of the shawl and is transposed on one side and the overall pattern flows over the entire surface, creating a rhythmic flow of colour and design, over the entire surface. These products of the 19th century are possibly some of the most complicated styles of weaving during any period.

The combination of the woven and embroidered shawl is a technique developed at the end of the 19th century when labour was becoming more expensive and the number of weavers had decreased because of the local economic situation, the method of taxation and the lack of patronage. Here the larger areas of colour were woven in the twill tapestry technique and the smaller areas were embroidered by the *rafoogars* who were experts in imitating the woven surface and in working out the outlines of the patterns. They however extended their skill to contribute another dimension to the shawl industry by working out the embroidery in such a fashion that the shawl could be used on either side. In certain cases they even went a step further to evolve a technique of embroidery where the warp threads could be split in half by passing the needle through them so that the embroidery would not be visible on the other side. The shawl thus became not only reversible but also had different colours on each side, *dou ruh* and *dou rukh* and were known as *akshi*, meaning reflection.

Embroidered Shawls

The *pateh doozi* of Kerman has been known for a long time. Marco Polo mentions that women in Kerman did very fine embroidery, indicating that embroidery was important economically and known even outside its place of manufacture. The basic background material known as *shal* was woven in twill weave and dyed in one colour, most commonly red. After that the cloth was given to the women to embroider. Mostly items for the household were made: curtains; *sofreh*, table spread; quilt covers and sometimes shawls; *chador* and *kamarband*, waist cloth.

The designs were pounced over the surface by using coal dust over perforated parchment and later thick paper. After this the outline was worked with a pen. The women then embroidered the piece with the use of woollen threads dyed in different colours. The outline was worked in stem stitches. Covering of the surface was worked in fillin stiches and sometimes with satin stitches. Very few old patterns have survived, and most extant pieces are of the late 19th or early 20th century. Each one shows the use of bold designs and colours but not a very fine type of craftsmanship.

According to the tradition in Kashmir, embroidery was only developed in the 19th century when the expert repairers, who could strip and recreate the defective sections of shawls and join pieces together invisibly, were used to recreate the woven shawls by embroidering the entire surface. An Armenian merchant, Khwaja Yusuf was responsible for this development. Khwaja Yusuf had been sent to Kashmir by a trading firm in Constantinople in 1803 to purchase shawls. On seeing the large number of merchants with their orders still unfulfilled, Khwaja Yusuf got the idea of utilizing the expert *rafoogars* to produce copies of the woven shawls by imitating the fine quality shawls, through embroidery. They even copied the texture of the twill weave used in weaving and the shawls were so well copied that they could be mistaken for the woven ones. The cost of production was much less and these *amli* shawls also escaped the payment of 25% tax on the value of the woven shawls which was being levied by the local government.

With the fall in the demand of the woven shawls, the cheaper hand embroidered shawls began to appear in the market. These were now being prepared for the local Indian market and by the middle of the present century, the embroidered shawls eclipsed the woven shawls and the number of the embroidered ones multiplied. Shawls were made specially for different clientele. The finest *shahtoosh* shawls with intricate embroidery were made as well as overall *jamevar* shawls on *pashmina*. Craftsmen kept in tune with the changing fashions and demands, making the reversible shawls which had different colours on each side and were known as *doranga*. They also embroidered the very fine shawl called *aksi* which means reflection — where the pattern was embroidered only on one side by splitting the warp thread into half.

The embroiderers in Kerman and Kashmir still continue to embroider and with the right patronage could embroider pieces as fine as those made earlier. There are even today a few weavers left at the outskirts of Kerman in the village of Hudk who can weave fine pieces of "*termeh*" as do the weavers of Kanihama in Kashmir.

Kantha Textiles

Stella Kramrisch

The *kanthā*, patched cloth, was made mainly in eastern Bengal (Bangladesh) and also in Bihar, of worn-out and disused saris and *dhotis*. After becoming threadbare, their thin, white cotton cloth

---

Editorial Note: *In India handloom weaving and certain processes of embellishing them have traditionally gone hand in hand. Handlooms therefore often include handworked and handcrafted textiles. The kanthā is one such process which is a combination of quilting and embroidery on handwoven textile. This particular research is a landmark in the study of symbolism in textiles.*

First published in *JISOA* Calcutta, 1939. Reprinted here from *Exploring India's Secret Art: Selected Writings of Stella Kramrisch,* edited by Barbara Stoller Miller, Philadelphia,, 1983, with the kind permission of the author and the Philadelphia University Press.

with its coloured borders were cut, patched, quilted, and embroidered. According to the thickness of the quilt and its size, it was used as a cover to be spread, as a wrap to be worn, or folded as a bag. The white ground of the quilt was embroidered and reinforced with coloured threads drawn from the coloured borders. The colours of the *kanthās* of the early part of the nineteenth century are mainly red and blue; in the later half of the century, yellows and greens, particularly linden green are also included. The materials of *kanthās* are rags and their threads. Joined afresh, these tatters are given a new wholeness. Their embroidered designs spring from this meaning. The *kanthā* is a work that gives wholeness to things that were of no use any more, to fragments without any significance. This rite of the restitution of wholeness is a domestic one, performed by women, though rarely by Brahman women. The more ornate *kanthās* are the work of *Kāyastha*, or middle-class, women from the homes of clerks and scribes. However, women of all castes and classes of the rural population, including Muslim women, owned or had embroidered *kanthās*. They were given as presents within the family or to friends.

Textile symbolism in India is hallowed by tradition. In the *Rg Veda* and the *Upanisads*, the universe is envisioned as a fabric woven by the gods. The cosmos, the ordered universe, is one continuous fabric with its warp and woof making a grid pattern.[1] Hence the importance of wholeness, not only of the uncut garment, like the sari or the *dhoti*, but also of the cloth woven all in one piece, on which a sacred picture is to painted.[2] Whether as cover for the body or as ground for a painting, the uncut fabric is a symbol of totality and integrity. It symbolises the whole of manifestation. Inversely, rags are offered to the gods. *Cindiyadeo,* the Lord of Tatters, gives a new whole cloth if a rag is offered to him. There are rag shrines all over the country. Their goddess is *Cithariya Bhavani,* Our Lady of Tatters.[3] The Buddha wore a patchwork robe (*sanghati*). Some of the reliefs of the Mathura School of the second century A.D. show him thus clad. Lord Caitanya (1485-1533), the apostle and visionary draped in a *kanthā,* the ecstasies which overwhelmed his body.[4] The colourful patchwork of the robes of saints forms part of miniature paintings of the Mughal period. The patched robe of the Buddha or of a saint belongs to him in his nature of Saviour. The rags are given a new wholeness. They clothe holiness.

Clothes being worn near the body are part of its ambience and are personal. Should an enemy get

A square *kantha*, end 19th century

The central lotus form dominates with intensely worked patterns built one on top of the other. The petal is like a ripple which vibrates outwards and is echoed by four lotuses created in each corner. The border carries cameos from *Krishna Lilas,* and scenes from nature.

hold of any bit of the cloth, he might practise black magic against the former wearer.[5] The patch-work quilt, a collection of tatters, guarantees immunity from black magic, protection and security, as do even the rags themselves when offered to the gods.

The symbolism inherent in the patchwork of the *kanthā* is the ground, which is embroidered with nearly equal perfection on both sides.[6] The act of making whole demands perfection throughout. The design is drawn by the embroiderer herself or by another woman. It is neither the work of a professional artist nor is it copied from anywhere. No two *kanthās* are ever alike; each is an original creation although *kanthās* from the same district follow certain types and these have more in common than those from villages at a greater distance.

The design of the square of rectangular field of the *kanthā,* in principle, relies on a central circle occupied by a lotus flower. Four trees mark the four corners. The central, wide-open, many-petalled lotus is an ancient Indian symbol of universal manifestation and of this world in particular. The four trees are symbols of the four directions; their meaning stems from Mesopotamia. The disc of the many-petalled lotus, when drawn as *alpona*, on the floor, would support a vessel filled with water. The deity is invoked and known to be present in a vessel filled with water. In the design of *kanthā*, the central lotus is inscribed in a square. The entire ground of the quilted cloth between the lotus and the directional trees is filled with figures, objects, symbolic devices, and scenes whose shapes and combinations are dictated by the imagination of the artist. Themes from ancient myths and legends are laid out next to scenes and figures commenting on contemporary life, and both are permeated with purely symbolic devices. The design of the *kanthās* provides wide margins for showing the contents of a woman's mind. Their figures and symbols are freely associated and rhythmically assembled. In some *kanthās*, the figures are those of animals only. A Muslim *kanthā*, faithful to the precepts of a noniconic art, shows nothing but scroll work. On the underlying central and directional composition of the *kanthā*, as its framework, is displayed the personality of the embroiderer. It shows not only in the planar composition but also in the selection of themes from the common reservoir of the tradition as it is lived by her at the moment of her needlework, especially in the selection and spacing of the stitches and the resulting texture and form of the embroidery.

The stitches are of the simplest kind, the running stitch being not only the main but also the most ingeniously employed. According to the length and spacing of the single stitches, they circumscribe, and this is their truly creative function, they organise a surface in a multitude of small squares and triangles so that its speckled texture of ground and embroidery is light or dense with colours. Closely parallel running stitches give a more gliding quality to the ground cover which they produce. Both of these modes and their combinations filling a given surface, are bounded by a continuous line, which the backstitch yields. Within its firm contour, be it red or blue, the running stitches, according to their density, not only produce different colour values, but together with a particular texture of the surface, they give a totality of its own to each *kanthā*. Moreover, they are conducted so as to produce an effect of modelling of its own kind on the textured surface. Modelling by means of running stitches appears to be an invention of the embroiderers of the *kanthās*. It is a purely textile equivalent of modelling with brush and colours. In this the "classical" tradition of Indian painting, as in Ajanta, excelled. Visualisation in terms of the modelled form, an

***Kantha* wrap, a detail, end 19th century**

A typical square *kantha* with an auspicious lotus in the centre, a flowing border of lotus flowers and religious themes. It depicts the story of the *vastra haran* from the life of Krishna, where Krishna hides the clothes of the *gopis,* the milkmaids. Instead of creating the tree in the corner, the form of Krishna represents the tree. The end border created with a running stitch imitates a woven pattern, similar to the *kanthas* made by the women of the weaver community.

irrepressible sense of a plasticity, are essentially Indian. This age-old and "classical" Indian quality was given form by textile means in the art of the *kantha* of East Bengal in the 19th century. The effect of modelling is produced by the closely spaced rows of stitches running parallel with the outline of a figure. This brings about an area of uniform texture and tone. Towards the interior of the outlined surface, the density and direction of the stitches change, producing other areas set off from their neighbour zones. This, together with the speckled textural effect of the stitches, which leads the eyes in more than one direction, also yields effects akin to op art but having representational intentions. The op art effect is bounded by the outline of the respective figure of the elephant or the horse.

The figure of the *kantha*, "modelled" by these colourful stitches, which allow the white ground to shine through, are also foreshortened, and their limbs may overlap without, however, their giving the effect of any spatial context. The figures are scattered rhythmically over the white ground, and if limbs or figures overlap, their area is part of the embroidered ground, for though the figure may be modelled in terms of stitching, the modelling has no substance to it.

It suggests volume by directional movement. Far from creating an illusion of the body, its embroidered form is dematerialised. Often the figures are shown in a contraction of front and profile. At other times, an x-ray view allows one to see across them. As an outcome of this, some *kanthas* create their own figures, having the shape of a man, with or without a body, the number of limbs also being at the discretion of the artist. This, though, does not refer to their multiplicity which iconography may postulate in the case of the figures of deities but to their reduction, to stumps instead of limbs, contraction of two limbs into one, or omission of one limb or the other according to the needs of identification, rhythm, and compositional clarity.

By the middle of the century, the embroidery stitch is more frequently resorted to than it was earlier. It adds more compact areas and stronger hues to the *kantha*. But these stronger accents too sink into the ground of the *kantha*. The ground between figures, as often as not, is reinforced all over with stitches running in closely set parallels around each figure. For this, white thread is used and, less frequently, blue or red thread. These colours give a pointillistically muted tonality to the vibrant texture of the ground of *kanthas* and make them assignable to the turn of the century.

Thematically, the art of *kantha* is an enriched textile version of the art of the *aripana* or *alpona*, the painting on the floor, its magic purpose being enhanced by the textile symbolism of its material and the way this is used. Stylistically, its form is entirely its own, adjusting an ancient propensity of India's classical art to its own textile and planar sensibilities.

The art of the *kantha* is a rural art. While it is imbued with Hindu myths, it is also perceptive of the life of India in the nineteenth century with some of its manners and fashions derived from those of the West, an imaginative blend of the actuality of living where every day contributes some novelty to be absorbed by the stream of the tradition and integrated into its style. It is an art of leisure.

Sophisticatedly primitive, the quilt of the *kantha* integrates many layers of the fabric of Indian life, tribal as well as urban, in its conception. The magic that underlies its purpose is that of love — not of coercion, as that of the diagrammatic floor drawings whose purpose is wish fulfilment. A *kantha* is given as a present, it is conceived with an outgoing mind and brings the entire personality of the

maker to the person for whom it is made. Its composition is a ritual being laid out around the centre of the lotus of manifestation. Its symbols have universal validity in the four directions. To their whirls and waves, to the lotus and the life trees are assigned the innumerable figured scenes of the mythic, ever-present past together with episodes of the passing scene.

All of them are firmly stitched into a reconstituted, vibrant wholeness. The *kantha* is the form, by textile means, of a creative process of integration within each woman who makes a *kantha*.

Succumbing to what were, in India, the belated effects of the Industrial Revolution, the art of the *kantha* died after the first quarter of the twentieth century. It is not known when this art began. Its upsurge in a narrowly circumscribed area has not its like elsewhere. *Kanthas* from Bihar are without the wealth of associated content and textile imagination. Although made by the same technique, their widely spaced design is an adaptation, in terms of embroidery, of the staid, placid lines of a certain type of painting of Bihar. The Bengali *kanthas* resemble a form of painting in Bengal only insofar as their overall character stems from the magic art of the *alpona*. As much as the South Indian sanctuaries, teeming with their hundreds of clay horses, clay cattle, and clay human figures offered in sacred groves express in their form the mystery of autochthony, the *kanthas* of East Bengal are saturated with and express a numinous power, the *sakti* of this region, working through its women and given form by innumerable disciplined stitches. Both these forms of art, that of the South Indian half-Brahman priest-potter and that of the Bengali Hindu matron — it was the older women, as a rule, who made the *kanthas* — represent traditional village art in fulfilment of rites of offering.

FOOTNOTES

1. RV 6.9:3: 10.130.1, also Br Up 3.8.3-8 and MUp 2.2.5

2. M. Lalou, Iconographic des etoffes peintes (pata* dans le Manjusrimulakalpa (Paris, 1930) p.27.

3. Crooke, *Popular Religion*, p.161

4. Sarkar, *Folk Element*, p.33

5. Cf. K.K. Ganguli, "*Kantha, The Enchanted Wrap*", Indian Folklore 1, No. 2:3-10

6. *Kanthas*, however, made by women of the weaver caste, imitate the effect of weaving and are meant to be seen on one side only. G.S. Dutt, "The Art of *Kantha*", Modern Review (Calcutta, October 1939)

Indian Resist-Dyed Fabrics

Alfred Bühler

There is a large group of Indian textiles, which are patterned by means of resist techniques. These dyeing methods serve to decorate textiles in colour by partially reserving or resisting the fabric before dyeing and removing these resists afterwards. What distinguishes these patterning methods from others is that the ornamented motifs are produced neither by weaving nor by applying them onto the fabric as in painting, applique work or embroidery, but rather that they are left undyed on coloured ground. The process can be repeated for producing multi-coloured designs.

Reprinted from *Treasures of Indian Textiles: Calico Museum, Ahmedabad,* Marg Publications, Bombay, 1980, with the kind permission of Marg Publications.

All types of resist-dyeing techniques are based on two elementary forms: folding and screening. In the first case, parts of the fabric form the resists; in the second, additional materials are used for covering certain portions of the textile. These two basic forms were combined with each other in many ways and developed into the following main types:

1. Fold-resist-dyeing

   The fabric is crumpled, knotted or pleated into folds. Thus, when dipped into the liquid dye, the solution cannot penetrate into the folds. As a result one gets a strongly blurred pattern corresponding vaguely to the folding.

2. Stitch-resist-dyeing

   Either folds or pleats are fixed by stitching through them or leading threads through the material in simple running stitches. Then the fabric is pushed or drawn together as close as possible on the threads which are knotted on the ends. Folds and perforation points, rarely the running thread itself, form the pattern. For this technique, the Indonesian term *tritik* is now generally used.

3. Wrap-resist-dyeing

   Rolled or folded material is partially wrapped in such a way that no dye can penetrate the reserved places. Simple wrappings yield striped patterns. If the material is folded in a second direction after the first dyeings, one gets a chequered design. In Rajasthan and Gujarat fabrics patterned in this way are called *laheria*, literally meaning waves.

4. Tie-resist-dyeing

   Individual parts of the outspread fabric are lifted and completely or partially tied in such a way that one gets spherical or mould-like forms. Once again the coverings act as resists. They decide the pattern by their actual forms and sizes as well as by the way the thread is wound around the part and tied. Variations are also possible by different ways of folding the material. Generally the Indonesian term *plangi* is used for this technique. In India and especially in Gujarat, it is known as *bandhani* and in Rajasthan as *chundari*.

5. Stencil-resist-dyeing

   Stencils that prevent dyes from penetrating into the fabric are fixed on it before the colouring is applied. This method, however, is more suitable for painting or for spraying the dye on the fabric than for dyeing textiles.

Opposite Page

Padmatola panch kothari bandha, five-square lotus pattern. Single-ikat saree from Baragarh, Orissa, contemporary

Detail of the *palau* which is typical of the *bandha* sarees of this area with rows of extra weft patterns.

Double ikat *patola*, Patan, early 20th century

This double ikat *patola* with ikat patterns on the border and cross border and a simple striped body was made by the Salvis for a Maharashtrian client. (Collection: Crafts Museum).

Opposite Page

***Telia rumal*, Poochampalli**

The tie-and-dye ikat square *rumals* were traditionally woven in Andhra Pradesh for local users and for export.

6. Paste or wax-resist-dyeing

Parts of the fabric are sprayed, painted or coated with paste, like mud, lime, gum, or with molten substances like wax, which when drying or cooling, become hard. They then serve as reserves which can be removed after dyeing by immersing in hot water, and by washing, dissolving or rubbing off. *Batik*, again an Indonesian term, is generally used for this technique.

7. Mordant-resist-dyeing

As against covering the fabric partially to protect it against the dye, one prepares parts of the textiles for dyeing with mordants whilst the unprepared parts do not take on the dye, i.e. act as resists. In the most popular process of this kind, used on cotton, mordants containing alum or iron are applied, as in the famous *kalamkari* technique.

8. Resist-dyeing of yarn to be woven after patterning.

Certain parts of the yarn for warp, weft or both are made to resist the dye by wrapping. This dyeing is carried out on yarn bundles from which the wrapping is removed after the dyeing. The process may be repeated if one wants to produce multi-coloured patterns. If the de-

sign should show clear and definite, not diffuse or blurred, patterning the yarn has to be arranged before tying and dyeing in the same way as it will be used in the loom. Only then the motifs will come out clearly. For the same reason one must be very careful not to disturb the arrangement of the yarn and to avoid displacing it during the dyeing process and later in the loom.

The technique of resisting yarn for fabrics is best known as ikat, also an Indonesian term. If it is applied on the warp above, then one speaks of warp-ikat. Weft-ikat is patterned in the weft, compound-ikat in both yarn systems, independent patterns, double-ikat in both systems as well, but in such a way that the patterns of warp and weft correspond to each other. This is the most complicated, incredibly intricate technique of all the tie-dye techniques. The famous *patola* of Gujarat belongs to this group.

Of the techniques listed in our classification, only those which use ties or wrappings as resists are dealt with here. Thus the following remarks concern themselves exclusively with wrap-resist-dyeing, tie-resist-dyeing and resist-dyeing of yarn. These three techniques are very well known in India. Unfortunately up to now it has not been possible to survey all the places where they were used or where they are still in use. The most important centres, however, are well documented, amongst other publications by two important books of the Calico Museum of Textiles, one on *Ikat Fabrics of Orissa* and the other one on *Tie-Dyed Fabrics*.

Laheria, wrap-resist-dyed fabrics from Rajasthan.

For patterning, the fabric is rolled from one corner diagonally to the selvedge and tied very tightly at intervals with strong thread or string. Thus, after dyeing the reserved portions appear as white diagonal stripes. Only very thin, loose and not too wide cotton fabrics are suitable for this process. In thick material the dye would not penetrate properly. For every new colour old ties must be opened and new ones applied. Over-dyeing is also possible. Sometimes only individual parts between two ties are dipped into the dye or the latter may be applied by hand.

If the fabric is rolled from one corner for the first stages of tying and dyeing and then, for the last stages, from the other one, instead of stripes a chequered effect is achieved. Even greater variety is possible if, at the end of the process, parts of

the colouring are discharged, thereby breaking up the stripes obtained in the first stages.

Laheria fabrics are mostly used as turban cloths and saris. Single-coloured turban cloths are known as Rajasthani *laheria,* multi-coloured ones as *panyla.* The variety of technical possibilities leads to a surprising number of different patterns.

The *laheria* technique is probably quite old, but nothing definite is known about its origin. Present centres of fabrication are Udaipur and Jaipur a well as neighbouring villages and towns such as Nathdwara near Udaipur.

Above

This double ikat fragment is from a saree woven in Gujarat. The dyes used for creating the ikat pattern have the soft tones of indigo blue and *majith* red.

Below

Popat kunjar patola, Gujarat, late 19th century

The parrot and elephant double ikat is enclosed into a trellis which has, at each corner, a jewel-like lozenge enclosing the cross of a *mandala.* Rows of flowering shrubs stand in between and alternate between red and green parrots and white elephants. This design is greatly valued amongst traditional Gujaratis and is considered auspicious.

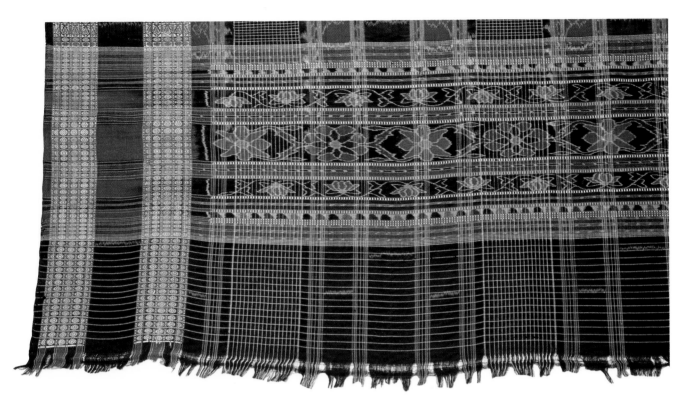

The fabrics are mostly tied and sometimes dyed in the houses, sometimes in small workshops. The dyeing is done mostly by professionals.

Bandhani, tie-dyed fabrics from Gujarat and Rajasthan.

Almost any kind of fabric may be used for this technique: cotton, silk, wool and even synthetic textiles. Today one uses mostly industrial products, such as *malmal,* a thin cotton tissue, and georgette, a loosely woven silk, but artificial silks are also quite common.

The process of tying and dyeing the fabric is very simple on principle but actually it demands much experience and skill. It is also very lengthy as the following example from Bhuj, Kutch, may illustrate.

The fabric obtained from the dealer is bleached, if necessary, then folded into several layers, mostly four, which are carefully placed one above the other and then fixed by stitches at the borders. The *rangari,* colourer, now marks the layout of the design on the top layer. He is a specialist who does only this work, but for various workshops. With the help of burnt sienna mixed with water and put on a cord, he draws lines for the various fields of the design. Into these fields he stamps the individual patterns with wooden blocks by using the same red-brown pigment as for the lining. Now follows the tying of the motif-parts which

Vachitrapuri saree, Sambalpur, contemporary

Vachitrapuri sarees were traditionally worn for weddings. They carry a combination of *bandha* and woven patterns. The warp ikat patterns are on the body, combined with checks worked in natural silk, as well as extra warp patterns on the border in two coloured silk. The woven patterns are of stylized fish and *rudraksh,* typical of most Orissa sarees. The *pallu* is of weft ikat.

Chanderkhani sado, simple moon
pattern. ***Bandhani odhani*** from
Kutch, Gujarat, beginning of 20th
century

The centre of the *bandhani* is the
white background colour and the five
moon forms are in black, with the
red outline dominating. The centre
is framed by multiple tie and dye
borders with the patterns emerging
in red. The technique of dyeing
requires great mastery, so as not to
get any surplus dye on the white
background. The cloth is dyed in
sections by tying the edges before
dipping it in red, section by section.
The tie and dye work is then
executed of the fine motifs which will
emerge in red. The portions
surrounding the roundels which are
to remain red are also tied. After this,
sections of the cloth are dyed in
black. The black borders and the
roundels are edged with red,
producing a dramatic effect by this
juxtaposition of contrasting colours.

Mashru, Patan, contemporary

The mixed cotton and silk cloth known as *mashru,* literally, "allowed" was possibly developed in the Tiraz factories in Syria for the orthodox Muslims who were not permitted to wear silk next to their body. The silk warp was woven with a satin weave which brought the silk yarn on the face of the fabric, while the cotton weft touched the skin. The designs for the *mashru* were created by combining extra warp patterns and warp ikat in the stripes. Though an ancient tradition, the look of *mashru* has a contemporaneous quality.

have to remain in the original colour of the fabric. It is mostly carried out by women and girls, rarely by men. The layers of the folded cloth are pushed from below with the pointed nail of the small finger while the left-hand thumb presses the material together. Thus results an arching-out of the material, which can now easily be wrapped. This process is continued from one dot to the other.

The first dyeing, which follows now, is done in the lightest colour, mostly yellow. The fabric is soaked in cold water, wrapped in a cloth to make sure that the ties will not open and then dyed in a hot solution of a synthetic dye, rinsed, squeezed and dried.

Probably with the use of modern fast dyes, which can be applied cold, it has become popular to dye individual parts of the white pattern on the yellow ground by hand, with pink and orange. All these dots, along with the ones left uncoloured are now tied again.

It follows the dyeing with the next darker colour, mostly red or green.

If the border, the *pallav,* the end pieces, and perhaps a few spots in the main field of the textile should remain bright red or green while the borders are meant to become dark red or even black, then all the lighter shaded and white parts of the textile have to be covered again. If big spots or broad parts of the fabric have to be reserved they are nowadays protected by plastic foils.

After the dyeing, the fabric is washed, and, if necessary, starched.

The ties of the *bandhani* fabrics, especially of the folded ones with small dots remain on the textile until they are sold or, at the most, they are opened in a corner to show the colour scheme. As long as the ties remain, the customer can be sure that he is not buying a printed imitation. For removing all reserves, the fabric is forcibly pulled crosswise so that all the ties open at once and fall.

Of course this method, although it is principally the same in all centres of fabrication, varies in details from place to place. The same goes for designs and sizes of the fabrics.

Bandhani-work is used for saris, *odhanis*, *duppattas* as well as for turbans, shirts, skirts and trousers. There are comparatively simple and cheap fabrics and magnificent pieces with gold brocade work added, used by well-to-do town communities at their wedding ceremonies. The so-called *ghar-cholu* form part of this group. The main field of these cotton fabrics is divided in squares by brocade work in gold thread while the squares are filled in with *bandhani* designs. Fabrics of this kind serve as *odhanis* for the brides of many communities in Gujarat.

Another striking group is characterized by the incredibly fine dots of the geometrical or floral patterns on dark red, reddish blue or black ground. These fabrics are known as wedding clothes used by Hindu and Muslim Khatri communities in Kutch. They are worn as *odhanis* but can also be made up into garments like trousers, *kurtas* and shirts.

It would lead too far to describe all known groups of *bandhani* fabrics produced in different parts of India. Only the main centres can be mentioned here. The most important ones are situated in Gujarat and Rajasthan. In the first state the largest and best-known workshops are found in Saurashtra, especially in Jamnagar and other equally famous centres in Kutch. There are also a number of *bandhani* production centres in Rajasthan. It is said that the best tie-dye work, with the finest single motifs, is done in Bikaner and Sikar to the north of Jaipur. Other centres are Jaipur itself, Jodhpur, Barmer, Pali, Udaipur and Nathdwara. Many of the fabrics are produced for local people

and show traditional designs. But here, as in Gujarat, owing to the production for town people and their modern taste, the designs have become more and more uniform.

In Madhya Pradesh extremely fascinating *bandhani* textiles are manufactured in Shivpuri, dark blue cotton fabrics with white figurative patterns, made for local farmer communities. Apart from that, modern production is made from different places e.g. Indore.

In South India, especially in the region around Madurai, Saurashtri speaking groups, emigrants from Gujarat, produce *bandhani* fabrics with large and coarse design on cotton fabrics.

Lastly it should be mentioned that Sindh and the parts of Punjab, now in Pakistan, have been and are still, important centres of *bandhani* production.

Bandhani-work is undoubtedly a very old technique in India. It is mentioned in the *Harshacharita* of the seventh century and around the same time illustrated on the wall paintings in a cave of Ajanta. In the later periods, if not genuine *bandhani* work, then at least printed imitations of such fabrics were found in Egypt. They were imported from Gujarat and dated from the fifteenth century onwards.

Mashru, semi-silk fabrics with ikat-stripes in the warp.

In these textiles silk is used as warp and cotton as weft. The weave is satin which causes a smooth right side of the fabric with nearly invisible cotton parts. The designs consist of length-stripes in different colours, sometimes enriched by small stripes with very simple woven patterns or with equally simple ikat patterns in block or arrowhead form. Sometimes these *ikat* patterns may cover the whole surface of the fabric.

Mashru means permitted. Originally it denoted textiles used by orthodox Muslim men who are forbidden to wear garments of pure silk. However, the fabrics were and still are quite popular among non-Islamic communities, especially used for petticoats, skirts and vests. In earlier times they were also in general use as lining material, for coats and jackets, for pillow covers, umbrellas, borders of embroideries, etc.

Today one of the main centres for *mashru* fabrication is Patan, where about 250 families are occupied in this field of activity.

Ikat in Orissa

The ikat technique of Orissa has been dealt with in an excellent publication of the Calico Museum of Textiles: *Ikat-Fabrics from Orissa and Andhra Pradesh,* by Prof. B.C. Mohanty. The patterns of these textiles are partly resist-dyed, partly woven. The ikat-technique is used for the warp as well as for the weft of the same cloth. Apart from very simple motifs like squares, however, the designs for the two threads systems do not cover each other. Thus we are dealing here chiefly with warp ikat, weft ikat and combined ikat.

The ikat products of Orissa are characterized by an exceedingly fine structure of the motifs and well-matched and soft colours as well as by their manifoldness. Quite a number of them are traditional. But during the last decades more and more new forms were introduced, many of them being original inventions, others copied from various Indian textiles.

According to Mohanty there are two main regions in Orissa, producing ikat fabrics. One of them comprises the Bargarh and Sonepur areas where Meher communities have developed the technique to an extremely high standard. It seems that originally cotton ikats were produced and these still prevail in spite of the silk and *tassar* fabrics being produced as well. The other centre, Naupatna, Tigria, in the Cuttack District is much older and traditionally produced only silk fabrics. Only in the twentieth century, cotton and tassar ikat were taken over as well.

Orissa ikats are very popular all over India. They are used as saris, bed covers, bolsters and cushion covers, table cloths and mats, napkins, scarves, stoles, door and window screens, skirt materials, *rumals,* etc. In all these cases, the weavers have found ingenious possibilities to adapt the design to the use of the fabric.

Ikat in Andhra Pradesh

The oldest ikat centre in this state is Chirala. During the last quarter of the nineteenth century and at the beginning of our century strinkingly beautiful cotton cloths, saris and *rumals,* were produced here for local use and for the wealthy sections of Muslim communities, amongst others in Hyderabad.

Typical of these older fabrics are sombre and extremely fine linear designs in weft ikat, combined ikat and simple double ikat. Sometimes these patterns are enriched by fine embroidered motifs or silver applications. Fabrics of this kind belong to the outstanding products of Indian handicrafts.

During the second quarter of the twentieth century rather crude red and black designs — figures, animals and even aeroplanes — were applied on turban cloths and *lungis.* They were known as *telia rumal* and, apart from local use, mostly exported to the Near East, Arabia and East Africa. According to two Swiss anthropologists, Nabholz-Kartaschoff and Fischer, who are preparing a comprehensive treatise on ikat in Andhra Pradesh, this production which was concentrated in Chirala, has almost entirely stopped.

Today the Nalgonda District near Hyderabad, with Pochampally, Puttapaka and other localities, is the centre of ikat production in Andhra Pradesh. The technique was introduced there by dealers and Chirala-weavers during the first quarter of this century, at first without much success. Between 1950 and 1960 however a tremendous extension started, and today one estimates that ikat fabrics are produced on about 10,000 looms in the district.

In these new centres the traditional work, formerly typical of Chirala, was given up entirely. Besides cotton, mercerised cotton and silk are used now, and double ikat was introduced as a technique for complicated patterns. A new style, adapted to the wishes of the customers, became fashionable; the weavers, belonging to the Padmasali community, proved to be most ingenious in inventing new designs as well as in copying traditional patterns from other ikat regions. Thus, Puttapaka specialized especially in imitating the famous *patola,* double ikat, from Patan in Gujarat.

At present ikat fabrics from the Nalgonda District are nearly as popular in India as the textiles from Orissa. They are mostly used as saris, but *lungis* and cloth for various purposes are made as well.

Nalgonda ikats are easily discernible by their comparatively crude patterning, usually with big motifs, and by very bright and often quite hard colours. In these aspects they are very different from Orissa products.

Patola, silk double ikats from Gujarat

Undoubtedly the most beautiful fabrics among the Indian resist-dyed textiles are the world-famous *patola* from Gujarat. They are outstanding examples of creative craftsmanship based on the experiences of countless generations and typical for a family craft in which the children begin to take part in the work and learn it from early childhood

Already ikat on the warp or on the weft are very complicated techniques which could hardly be described fully in a short article. Even less so is this possible for double ikat. Many different operations are necessary to match warp and weft both in size and patterning, to simplify the resisting by putting together appropriate parts of the threads and to prevent the tangling or dislocation of the thread throughout the whole working process until they are ready to be woven. The weaving as well, done on a simple horizontal loom without treadles, is very laborious.

There are at least forty different traditional types of patola, and with the exception of one form, used for cholis, they are all saris or odhanis. The arrangement of the patterns is the same in all these pieces. There is a main body with geometrical, floral and figural designs enclosed by length-borders with ikat patterns and simple stripes and pallav, panels, with cross sections in ikat as well as in plain red and, at one end, with gilt-thread parts.

In modern times new motifs have been invented and, apart from saris and odhanis, patola fabrics are used also as kerchiefs, rumals and curtains.

There are many divergent views on the age and origin of the patola technique. There is no archaeological evidence from the Middle Ages or older periods; only warp ikat, but not double ikat, has been established by the Ajanta frescoes. The earliest evidence comes from Kerala and Tamil Nadu in the South where patola-like patterns have been found on frescoes and paintings in temples and palaces of the sixteenth-eighteenth centuries.

Patolu (sing.), Patola (pl.) is a Gujarati word which may be connected with an expression for silk, but may also go back to the sense of colourful. In its present form it first appears in Indian literature in the tenth century and from then on with increasing frequency especially in Gujarati literature. But only from the eighteenth century can the fabrics clearly be established to be made of silk, and even in these sources nothing is said about the patterning technique. Nonetheless it may be assumed that the fabrics were done in double ikat.

From contemporary reports one may conclude that cloth termed patola began to be exported to Southeast Asia and especially to the Malay Archipelago at least in the thirteenth century. Here they acquired immense significance in various places.

Indian, Portuguese, Dutch and other merchants used them to barter for precious spices.

For the local Indonesian population patola were and still are one of the most valuable possessions, often being carefully guarded heirlooms. Their uses have a ceremonial, and a sacred character throughout and even healing powers are ascribed to them.

In India traditional use and fabrication of patola were almost entirely restricted to Gujarat. The patola weavers belong to the Salvi community. Outside of Gujarat they are also found in Jalna, north Maharashtra, and in Burhanpur, Madhya Pradesh, where, upto recent times, patola were woven. In Gujarat there were workshops in Surat as well as perhaps in Cambay and Ahmedabad. In earlier times the production must be very considerable. The craft declined, however, already at the beginning of our century. Before the Second World War there were only two Salvi families in Patan, who produced patola and the same is the case at present. It is to be hoped that the craft and with it these outstanding textiles will not disappear entirely.

Nowadays patola are worn on festive occasions by wealthy ladies in many parts of India. But their traditional use is far less widespread. They were and still are most popular in Gujarat, where they are traditionally used by Hindus, Anavil and Nagar Brahmins, Vaishnava, Gandhi, etc., Jains and Bohra Muslims. Further on there used to be a smaller dispersal area in Maharashtra-Madhya Pradesh, in Jalna-Burhanpur region, and in South India in Kerala. Both in Gujarat and Central India patola used to play an important role in wedding ceremonies, being worn, however, more often by the mothers of the bridal couple and other female relations rather than by the bride herself. Men, too, used them during certain parts of the wedding ceremony as shoulder cloths, Hindus and Jains used them for ritual acts, for instance — as is also the case for the Bohra Muslims — during a pregnancy ceremony. In South India their main use was as temple hangings, clothing for idols, elephant blankets for festive occasions and gifts by princes.

All these traditional functions express clearly that patolas used to be not only symbols of wealth but they were — just as in Indonesia — considered indispensable for certian ceremonial occasions. Special powers were evidently attributed to them, and even today they are thought to signify more than just wealth and luck. They possess a sacred or even a magical character.

Cotton Jamdanis of Tanda and Banaras

Pupul Jayakar

The cotton *jāmdānī* is the rarest and most sophisticated product of the Indian handloom. The extraordinary comprehension and knowledge of colour that is the genius of the Indian craftsman is manifested in these fabrics, the finest of which are woven in two or more tones of white, yarn of varying thicknesses being used for effects of light and shade, transparency and opaqueness.It is the projection of a highly developed perception rooted in an aesthetic where white is acknowledged as a colour with nuances and tones. The *Vishnudharmottara* differentiates five tones

First published in *Lalit Kala* (Ancient), No.6, 1959. Reprinted with the kind permission of the author and the Lalit Kala Academy, New Delhi.

of white — bright gold or "light" white, tooth white, pure sandal white, autumn cloud white (clouds in which rain is spent), autumn moon (*shard*) white. In another place, in writing of the *rasachitras*, white has been referred to as the colour of *hāsya* (laughter). The *jāmdāni* cloth is a response to the challenge of the terrific summer heat of the Gangetic plains. The fierce scorching sun demands a cloth that is bereft of colour and yet has its tones and nuances. A cloth that is light to the body, that moves to the gentlest breeze, a cloth that is of great beauty recalling flowers and running water and moonlight.

The word *jāmdāni* has come to mean loom embroidered or figured, and is applied both to the woollen weaves of Kashmir as well as to the cotton flowered weaves of the Gangetic plain. The technique of weaving and the nature of the textile is ancient, but the word *jāmdāni* does not appear till very late and is likely to have been derived from the word *jāmā* or coat. The *jāmdāni thān* is woven in coat or *angarakhā* lengths of 3¾ yds. (3.43 metres).

Jāmdāni are very fine textured muslins in which floral, animal or bird ornaments are woven on the loom. The warp is, as a rule, unbleached grey yarn, the motifs being woven in bleached white

A *jamdani* weaver, Bengal

A *jamdani* weaver bends over a loom working in the tiny spools of threads to create the intricate patterns which are absorbed into the fabric of the woven cloth.

Opposite Page

Jamdani saree, early 20th century, detail

Pallu of a saree woven with a silk warp and a cotton weft. The extra weft inlaid pattern is worked with a single cotton thread; after weaving the motif, the thread is not cut but is carried on to the next motif.

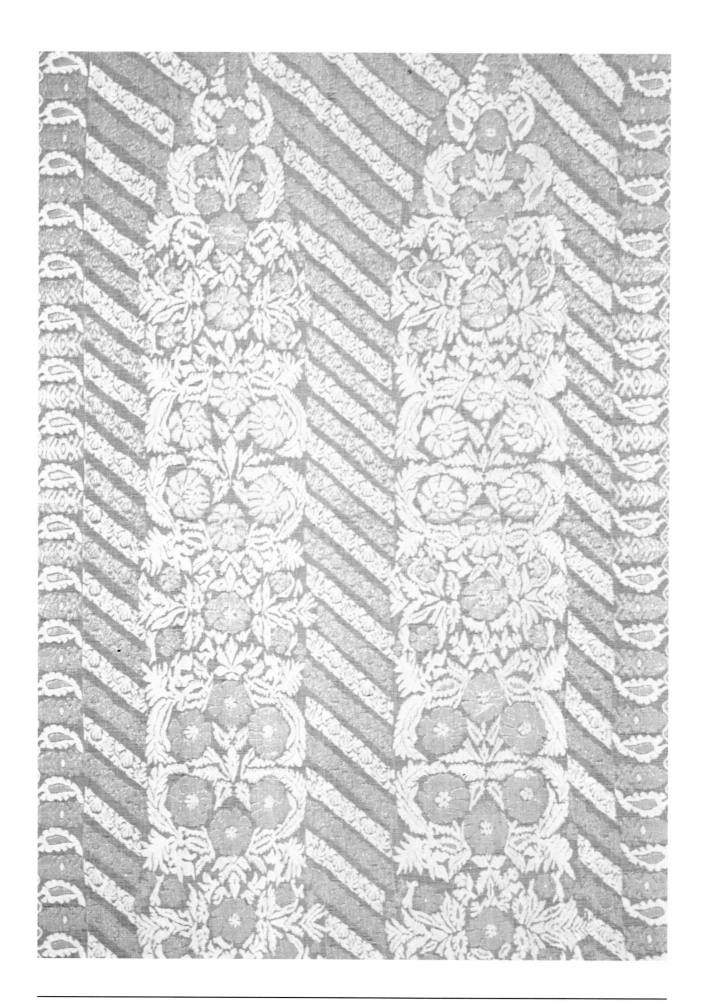

yarn. The most important centres of *jāmdānī* weaving in the Gangetic plain are Dacca, Tanda (Fyzabad district, Uttar Pradesh) and Banaras. In Banaras, gold thread is used along with bleached and unbleached white to weave the design. In Dacca, coloured cotton thread is used along with gold and white, but the Tanda cloths are of the finest quality, only white yarn being used in the ornament.

From the earliest times, the Gangetic plain was famous for its fine muslins. The *Periplus* speaks of the rarest of Indian muslins in Rome being known by the name of "Gangetic". Banaras was famous for its muslins and the finest of them are known as *kasivastra*. The *Majjhima Nikāya* mentions the fact that the great development of fine cotton production in Banaras was due to the growing of fine grade cotton, the presence of proficient spinners and the softness of the water for washing and bleaching. Moti Chandra in *Prāchīna Bhāratīya Vesha Bhūshā* has identified the *chitra viralīs* or picture muslins and the *pushpapattas* or flower-cloth mentioned in the ancient texts as *jāmdānī* fabrics. Megasthenes, describing the dress of the nobles at the court of Pātaliputra, writes of them as weaving flowered muslins — *pushpapattas*. Bānabhatta's *Harshacharita* is one of the richest sources of our knowledge of ancient

Jamdani weave, early 20th century

The traditional *jamdani* saree has an elaborate corner *kalga*, mango pattern. On an unbleached cotton background, the pattern is woven with the deep blue-black cotton of the *nilambari* colour. (Collection: Crafts Museum).

Opposite Page

Jamdani pallu, Bengal

A 'tree of life' motif worked for a *pallu* of a *jamdani* saree at Weavers Service Centre, Calcutta.

textiles. Describing the costume worn by the Goddess Lakshmi, Bāna speaks of a garment white as foam, of the finest muslin, waving in the breeze, ornamented with various flowers and birds. In another place he describes these fine transparent cloths as having the appearance of a cast-off slough of a serpent.

The Mughals with their sensitivity to beauty and elegance, their sophistication and the patronage extended by them to textile crafts, must have given a further impetus to the production of these figured muslins or *chitra viralis*. In the *Ain-i-Akbari*, there is no mention of the word *jāmdāni* in the list of cotton cloths acquired for the royal wardrobe. The name *tanjeb* however appears, and is used as an alternative word for a coat. This is likely to have indicated a coat made from the finer types of *jāmdāni* cloth, the words *tanjeb* and *pench* being used even today to denote the most expensive type of figured muslins. Earlier writers on Indian textile history have used words such as *ābrawān*, running water, and *shabnam*, morning dew, as referring to the fine plain cotton muslins. The words however seem more descriptive of a figured cloth, the all-over fine diaper in the *jāmdāni* muslin, with its alternating transparent and opaque cotton suggesting the movement of water and the fine dotted muslins suggesting dew.

Although no direct information exists, it is likely that royal *kārkhānās* were set up under the Mughals for the manufacture of *jāmdāni* cottons. Forbes Watson mentions special *jāmdānis* woven at Dacca for Aurangzeb costing £31 a piece.[1]

Two fundamental changes are however noticeable. The form of the ornament undergoes a change. In the court textiles produced by the royal *kārkhānās* of the Mughals, living forms of birds and animals disappear, and only floral ornaments are introduced into the cloth, this taboo being rigidly enforced in all textiles to be worn on the body. The same prohibition exists even today among the weavers of Chanderi. They consider it *harām* or unlawful to weave cloth in which living beings, human, animal or bird, are to be portrayed. The concept of colour also undergoes a change. In the list of colours mentioned in the *Ain-i-Akbari* as comprising the royal wardrobe, there is no longer mention of the various tones of white. The *korā* unbleached cloth which has ritual significance to the Hindu gives place to the bleached *jāmdāni* worn at the Mughal courts.

With the establishment of royal *kārkhānās* for the manufacture of fabrics for the royal courts, the centres of production of *jāmdāni* cloth developed and crystallised. Tanda in Fyzabad district of Uttar Pradesh and Dacca became the two main centres of *jāmdāni* production. Flowered cottons still continued to be produced in Banaras but strangely there is no mention under the Mughal Emperor of the estblishment of royal *kārkhānās* in Banaras.

This article does not deal with the *jāmdāni* muslins of Dacca. They have already been dealt with at some length by Forbes Watson in his *Textile Manufacturers and Costumes of India,* and by Ajit Ghosh in his article on Dacca muslins.[2]

It will be worthwhile, however, to mention some of the main points of difference between the *jāmdāni* of Tanda and Dacca. In the Dacca weaves, gold and coloured threads were used in weaving. In the finer *jāmdāni* only coarse bleached white yarn was used to weave the ornament on a fine unbleached background. This use of coarse and fine yarns led to the ornament appearing distinct against the fine background material.

In Tanda, a fine court bleached yarn was used for the ornament. Coloured or gold thread was never used. The distinction between the ornament and the background cloth was never accentuated. In the method of weaving too, the Tanda variety was different; the thread which formed the ornament was not cut at both edges, but was left dangling on the spool and was introduced into the next figured pick. Thus figures were introduced which did not fray at the edges nor did they work loose during wear. In the Dacca weaves, the thread was cut at both the beginning and end of the ornament.

The jāmdāni of Tanda

Tanda is a small town in the district of Fyzabad, in Uttar Pradesh. Its origin is associated with the Emperor Akbar who is said to have named it Khaspur Tanda, Tanda being the name for the local gangs of Banjaras who encamped there. It appears to have been held as *jāgir* by the royal washerman of Akbar's court, Malik Khas Zahīdī of Baghdad, who is said to have settled in Tanda, and his family came to be known as the Malika of Khaspur. No information is available on the origin of the *jāmdāni* industry there. But it is probable that Katwās and Julāhās from Banaras were taken and settled at Tanda in the early 16th century. The name of Sa'adat Ali Khān, Mughal governor of Oudh, is clearly associated with the development of the textile manufacture at Tanda, as well as Mahummad Hyat Khan of Rasulpur. The patronage of the court of Oudh gave a great impetus to the manufacture of *jāmdānī* cloth, and flowered muslin *angarkhīs* became the court dress of the Oudh rulers. It is likely that like the *jāmdānī* cottons of Dacca, the flowered muslins of Tanda ,were retained as a monopoly in the hands of the Government. In Dacca, *jāmdānī* weavers were forbidden under threat of corporal punishment to sell to any person a piece exceeding the value of £3/-. The Indian and European merchants were obliged to purchase muslin through brokers specially appointed by the Government. A detailed account of the later history of the *jāmdānī* industry in Tanda, has been left by H.R. Neville in *The District Gazetteer of the U.P. of Agra and Oudh.*[3]

In the 18th century, agents of the East India Company established a trading centre at Tanda which appears to have been famous for its cotton printing as well as weaving. Neville mentions the name of a Mr. John Scott who is said to have had an immense establishment in Tanda, where all the cloth made in the town was brought for bleaching and washing. All the washerman seem to have been in his pay. For the security they enjoyed, a tax of three annas in a score was paid by the weavers to Mr. Scott for the use of his place. Mr. Scott was followed by a James Orr who is said to have been paymaster in the British service. He introduced a number of changes in the manufacture of cotton fabrics and it appears likely that various other textiles such as tablecloths, towels, etc., on European demand, were woven at Tanda at this time.

By 1874, however, the number of *jāmdānī* weavers had decreased to 875. At the present moment there are about five weaver families with knowledge of the manufacture of the fabulous *jāmdānī* cotton fabrics. Mention has been made by Neville in the Gazetteer of the great skill of the Katwās who were Hindus and who were capable of producing and spinning yarn in counts ranging from 150s to 200s.[4] The Jūlāhas or weavers were Muslims. Till about fifty years ago very fine, handspun yarn was being used to weave the *jāmdānī* cloth. The flowered muslin cloth contained per inch 90 to 120 ends in the warp and 80 to 110 in the weft. The loom used by the *jāmdānī* weaver has remained to this day the old traditional type of pit-loom. No special attachments are needed. The spindle is known as *rach* and is made out of small bamboos or maize stalks. This spindle is about two inches long. As many bamboos splits are required as there are floral ornaments across the width of the cloth. The ornamental figures are woven by two threads of yarn of the same count as in the background, being introduced into the cloth by means of extra spools, the threads of which are passed under and over the ornament as many times as are required to form the design. The threads selected for this purpose are lifted up by the weaver with his fingers. No mechanical contrivances like the Jacquard or dobby are required to lift up the threads. There is no draw boy sitting near the looms pulling the cords to manipulate the harness. The weaver sits at the loom usually with one or two assistants.

This twill-tapestry type of weaving is very akin to embroidery — the bamboo spindle taking the place of the needle. The weaver works directly on the loom. The knowledge of the designs is carried in his head. No *naqshās* are used, nor is the design tied on the loom.

Apart from *than* intended for the production of *angarkhīs* the *jāmdānī* cloth is woven for caps and for *sārīs*. Borders, *pallavs* or end pieces of *sārīs* and the *būtā* (small motis) are woven. The forms of the ornament are floral. The flowers which ornament parts of the body of the cloth are woven either vertically or horizontally. The *chamelī, mogrā, juhī, khas pomera, gendā, khas kamana, ishqapench, harsingār, phūlbanjarī* are some of the common flowers used for the design. The following names of designs have been given by one of the best known *jāmdānī* weavers of Tanda.

Aribel (bel, meaning creeper or climber) — running figures arranged diagonally.
Lahariā (lahar, meaning a wave) — figured like the wave of the sea.
Harava — straight or wave-like vertical lines intersperesed with little flower-like motifs.
Kharībel — running figures arranged horizontally.
Kangūrā — border about 3" wide for *sārīs, dupattas,* blouses, etc.
Ārībel bhanjvara — big flowers, 2" apart.
Saro — vertically pillars or stylized trees; repeats spaced about 2½" apart.
Katār — crossed sword with shield motif, arranged in ½" wide stripes.
Lahar — waves arranged horizontally, about twelve waves in a 36;; piece.
Haravva — as in *ārībel,* running vertically across.
Patri — running horizontally figures.
Jāldār — ornamental figures arranged in the form of a network (*jāl* meaning net).

Purmatan — small intricate hexagonal figures with flowers all over the cloth.

Jāl guldastā — roses and leaves alternating within the ornamental network.

Phūldār — flowerlike ornament in the body of the *sāri.*

Pankala — ornate cones about 3" square with an ornamental motif within the cone.

Būtā — ornamental single motifs within the body of the cloth.

Fardī būtā — small dots arranged close together; a *sāri* takes four months to weave, there being one lakh figures required for a piece of 1 × 3 yds.

Masūr būtā — ornamental motifs of the size of a *masūr dāl;* it takes twelve hours to weave one inch.

Makkhī būtā — small dots of the size of a fly.

Shāhī būtā — design made by the use of one *killi* or *shirkī,* i.e. one small spindle.

Phūl annānās — pineapple motif.

Jāmewār — intricate all-over design in cotton.

Ishqapench — a pattern of fine leaves arranged in a creeper form.

The most important features that distinguish the flowered muslin of Tanda from other ornamental weaves are the use of the twill-tapestry technique of weaving and the absence of the *naqshā* and of the function of the *naqshband.* John Irwin in his monograph on shawls has traced the origin of the twill-tapestry technique to the time of Zain-ul-ābidīn (A.D. 1420-1470). He is of the opinion that weavers from Turkestan introduced the twill-tapestry technique into India. He supports this view on the basis that the twill-tapestry technique of weaving, apart from the *tilikar* weaving of shawls in Kashmir, does not exist in any other part of the Indian sub-continent and the technique used in the weaving of these Kashmir shawls can be traced to the introduction of artisans into Kashmir at the time of Zain-ul-Abidin.[5]

From a study, however, of the weaving processes to be found in cotton *jāmdānī* weaving, Irwin's views need further examination.

In the cotton *jāmdānī* weaving of Tanda and of Dacca, the weft threads alone form the pattern. They do not extend over the full width of the cloth, but are used on the warp threads to delineate the ornament. Unlike figured weaving in other parts of the world, the ornament is woven directly on the cloth without the aid of any form of technical devices as *naqshā.* This introduced an entirely new element into the twill-tapestry technique which in my opinion must have been indigenous to this country. Irwin does not seem to have given sufficient importance to the place of the *naqshband* in the twill-tapestry process of weaving as practised in Kashmir and in parts of Central Asia. It appears very likely that the function of the *naqshband* was of foreign origin and is likely to have been introduced into India into the indigenous twill-tapestry process of weaving as early as the beginning of the 15th century. That the *tilikār* or twill-tapestry process of weaving was known in ancient India is corroborated by Moti Chandra[6] in his article on Kashmir shawls.

It is also likely that *naqshbands* of great skill came to Kashmir in the reign of Zain-ul-ābidīn. Moti Chandra in the same article gives a description from the *Jaina Rājatarangini.*

There is apparently no word in Sanskrit equivalent to *naqshband* or *naqsh*-making, nor is there any description of this important function in the early texts, although all the other intricate processes of weaving have been explained in some detail. This would lead us to believe that the twill-tapestry type of technique practised in the *jāmdānī* weaving was the earliest form of indigenous weaving in this country and the later use of *naqshabands* in the *tilikār* shawls of Kashmir and the cotton and gold *jāmdānī* of Banaras was the impact of the introduction of *naqshbands* brought in by Muslim conquerors from Persia and Central Asia.

With the introduction of this new function of *naqshband* and the practice of tying the *naqshā* or pattern on to the loom, designs became more complicated and a large number of coloured threads began to be introduced into the cloth.

FOOTNOTES

1. Forbes Watson, *Textile Manufacturers and Costumes of India.* "The jamdanee or loom figured muslins, from the exquisite delicacy of manipulation which many of them display, may be considered the *chef-d'oeuvre* of the Indian weaver. From their complicated designs they have always constituted the expensive productions of the Dacca loom. Those manufactured for the Emperor Aurangzeb are stated to have cost 31, while some manufactured in 1776 reached the extravagant price of 56 per piece."

2. Ajit Ghosh, "Figured Fabrics of Old Bengal", Marg, Vol.3, No.I, p.38.
3. H.R. Neville, *The District Gazetteer of the U.P. of Agra and Oudh,* p.41.
4. Ibid., p.42.
5. John Irwin, *Shawls: A Study in Indo-European Influences,* London, 1955, p.2.
6. Moti Chandra, "Kashmir Shawls", Bulletin of the Prince of Wales Museum of Western India, No.3, p.4.

Light and Shade, Blue and Red: The Azrak of Sind

Françoise Cousin

Editorial Note: *One of the oldest techniques of printing in India is that of azrak; today however the finest azrak is printed in Sind, now in Pakistan. In India the tradition is maintained in Dhamadka in Kutch where Mr. Mohamedbahi Khatri has revived the tradition of using vegetable dyes. The detailed study of the printing technique and the use of the colours, as well as the evolution of the geometric patterns of azrak, common to Sind and Gujarat, has been carried out in great detail by Francoise Cousin. This article has been translated by Achille Forler.*

Printed originally in French as "Lumiere et ombre, blue et rouge: les azrak du Sind" in Objects et Mondes Volume 16, Fasc 2 - ETF 1976, Musee de l'Homme, Paris. Translated by Achille Forler. Reprinted with the kind permission of Objects et Mondes and the author.

The use of azrak[1] is widespread throughout the province of Sind, Pakistan. The azrak is a large, rectangular cloth put together from two strips of narrow cotton cloth. The patterns are printed in blue and red. It is used by the Muslim men of the region as a turban or as a shoulder cloth with which they cover themselves when it is chilly, or as a bedspread. It is given as a gift on numerous occasions. In short, it is associated with their everyday life. Women have also begun to use it: here the motifs are generally different but the technique remains the same. Today's fashion among the Sindhis, as well as their newfound awareness of their regional character, has transformed the azrak into a kind of symbol of self-identification and has opened up a new market for it among the upper class of Karachi. Nevertheless, it is with the men in the provincial towns and villages that its popularity is the greatest.

The technique of handblock-printing is used in Sind for the decoration of diverse fabrics: bedspreads, blankets, turbans for men, veils or skirts for women. The motifs are varied: some exclusively Sindhi, others as used in the neighbouring state of Rajasthan, India. They are traditional designs indicative of the religious or the geographical association of the wearer, sometimes suggesting even his social and professional group.

Though the basic technique of handblock-printing is the same for all different types of azrak, the process and the different technical stages may differ with the pattern. The printing of the cloth is done with a mordant, a resist, or both. When a mordant is printed, the dye reacts with it and only the mordant covered areas accept the colour. On the contrary, when a resist is printed it is those areas without resist which accept the dye. In the case of azrak the process is particularly complex and is the work of highly skilled craftsmen.

The villages where the azrak is printed — side by side with other fabrics — are situated in the Lower Valley of the Indus. Water is indispensable at all stages of the process and the presence of the river, with its numerous ramifications and canals, was an important factor for the establishment and development of the printing industry and the

Previous Page

Ajrakh print reversible bed cover
block printed from Kutch

Author's Note

Mr. Marc Gabroieau has kindly checked the translation of the Sindhi terms: it is J. Platts' A Dictionary of Urdū, classical Hindī and English, *Oxford University Press (1st ed. 1884, 1259 p.)* which has been used for the words that could be identified. I have also been advised, in the analysis of the lines of construction, by Mr. Piotr Perelys. I wish to thank them here as well as Mrs. Shireen Firoz Nana for the interest she took in my work.

growth of communities of printers.

Today, for economic reasons, printing is abandoned or considerably reduced in some villages. The two major problems which confront the craftsmen are the marketing of their product and the availability of imported raw materials. The latter problem is of recent origin. The Government of Pakistan has restricted the import of non-essential commodities, among which are included indigo and alizarine (madder) dyes which are essential to the printing industry. Traditionally, the printer purchases the raw materials and sells the finished product in the bazaar. This has made him financially dependent on the wholesale dealers. However, one witnesses today attempts to regroup. Some factories employing craftsmen grow by centralizing the demands of the wholesale dealers, but at the expense of less prosperous factories. Or, the craftsmen try to organize themselves by setting up a purchase cooperative which enables them to obtain an important licence for the essential raw materials.

The printers belong to a Muslim community called Khatri. They sometimes engage workers from other communities for subsidiary jobs, such as washing the cloth. For instance, in 1973, Tando Mohammed Khan employed among his workforce of thirty-five: three Sumro, four Mohana and three Shidi.[2]

As a general rule, printing and dyeing is done by men. However, in some factories, one can see women engaged in the subordinate tasks of preparation of the dyes and the resists, such as grinding of the seeds, etc... Whereas the work, which is eventually done by the women, is done in the living quarters themselves, most of the operations take place in workshops which are separate from but near to their living quarters. The workplace has both covered and open air spaces. For the washing, the cloth is carried to the river or the canal.

Among the printers one can distinguish between the master-craftsman and owner, the craftsmen and, sometimes, the apprentices. Strictly speaking, there is no specialization at the level of printing. Each one carries out all the operations of the process from beginning to end, with the apprentices themselves attending to the craftsmen in all the operations. However, in large factories, there are printers who specialize in the preparation of a particular design. But even in this case, where he is confined to the production of a particular cloth, the craftsman is in charge of all the stages of the printing process. The owner usually reserves for himself the task of preparing the dyestuffs and the dyeing baths.

The wages of the craftsmen vary according to whether or not they belong to the owner's family. Family members are not paid as they live together according to the joint-family system. In the case of hired labour, they are paid on a piece-rate. It is difficult however to give a precise figure; the wages vary according to the financial position of the firm or, in the workshops where specialization exists, according to the type of cloth prepared by them.

Technological Data

The preparation of the *azrak* is divided into numerous stages spread over several days.

The white cotton cloth, bought in bulk from the bazaar, is cut to the required dimensions.[3] The pieces are immersed into a copper container filled with cold water and soda ash. They are then hung on rods placed across a cauldron filled with boiling water. The steam goes through the cloth which is thus softened and bleached. After being washed in the river or canal and dried, it is spread over a copper pot filled to the three-fourths with water. Soap is applied on it and rubbed with the hands while the cloth absorbs the water. It is then plunged in a mixture of two oils and immediately taken out, twisted together and kept overnight. The next day it is again washed in the river and dried. Thereafter, it is soaked in a mixture of powdered *sakun* seeds[4] and oil, and dried again. At this stage the cloth has a beige colour.

These operations are for degumming the cloth so as to soften and prepare it for absorbing the dyes. The process is not always as complex but, even when simpler, it needs always to be done. As a matter of fact, this practice is imperative for, the better the cloth is prepared, the better the end result will be.

Thereafter, the first print *asul* (or *asil*) is done with a block called *asule-jo pur*. The printing is done with a mixture of gum from the tree *mimosa arabica*, *babur khunr*, lime, *cūnā*, and water. A little alizarine is added to give it a colour to make the work easier. The motif thus printed will be white or pale red on red after dyeing it with alizarine. The few spots which must remain shining white are printed with a mixture without alizarine. Printing is done from left to right. First the borders are printed, across the border first. The ground is printed last.

The second print, *kot,* is done with a block called *kot-jo pur.* A solution of ferrous sulphate, *hira kas,* thickened with earth, gum or grounded seeds, *ambika* of the *amli* tree, is used. This print will turn black after being dyed in alizarine.

The third print, *khor,* is that of a resist made of a mixture of earth, *metti,* flour, *āto,* khunr, aluminium sulphate, *phitkar* or *phitki),* and water, sometimes adding molasses, *ghur.* After printing, the cloth is sprinkled with rice bran, *kitti,* or powdered cowdung, *bhan,* with the help of a sieve to fix the compound. This resist covers all the parts destined to receive a colour other than blue.

Then comes the indigo dyeing. This process is carried out with the dye kept cold in a deep tank in the ground. The length of the cloth is folded fourfold, then pleated widthwise. They are dipped into the tank, pressed and made to dry. Finally, the cloth is vigorously washed in running water. This operation removes the resist but not the two prints, nor the aluminium sulphate which permeates the cloth and will produce the red colour in the alizarine dye.

The cloth is now dyed in alizarine. Water is boiled in drums in which a solution of alizarine and *sakun* seeds is thrown, after which the cloth is immersed. The operation lasts over two hours and the water is kept near boiling point all the time. The cloth is stirred to ensure a uniform dye while alizarine and *sakun* seeds continue to be added. The cloth, after being taken out, is left to cool until it can be picked up by hand. It is then put in water containing fresh camel dung, *ut-ji gissi,* and left to soak for twelve hours. The next morning, the cloth is taken to the canal and washed in water containing soda ash and caustic soda. This process is called *tapai.* It is followed by an operation called *cat* which consists in drying the cloth on a sandy bank, sprinkling it when it is half dry, five or six times. The term *tapai* is sometimes used for this last operation too. In the evening, the cloth is again washed and left to dry.

A new resist, *khor,* is then printed and the cloth is again dyed in the indigo tank. This operation is called *mina* and produces a second shade of blue.

The finishing consists in successive washing: first in water containing soda ash, then in water containing a detergent and, finally, in running water. Once the cloth is dry, it is beaten. In fact, just as a meticulous preparation of the work gives a high quality print and dye, it is through the finishing that the colours take their full luminosity and the whites their full eclat. Therefore, the more careful the finishing, the greater the value of the cloth.

In some *azrak,* and for some parts only, the woodblocks *asul* and *kot* are inversed: the block *asul* is used for printing the *kot* and vice versa. The expression *kataji cura* is used for such an operation which causes an inversion of the colours. This seems to be of recent origin.

One could conceive of a simpler procedure but at the expense of the delicacy of the lines and the precision of the superimpositions. In the same way, the recent introduction of chemicals containing naphthol results in a loss of quality in the colours.

Most of the raw materials have been mentioned in the sequence in which they are used. The use of natural products, vegetable or mineral, has almost completely disappeared. For example, the ferrous sulphate used as mordant, *hira khas,* is no more produced from iron scrap made to ferment with molasses in water. The same is true of aluminium sulphate for which potash alum was used, and for the dyes themselves, alizarine and indigo. Today, imported synthetic products are used. The only natural products still in use are the gums (gum from *mimosa arabica,* almond gum), oils (vegetable oil, castor oil), clay, molasses, lime, *sakun* seeds and, of course, water.

The cloth used is cotton, of diverse quality and manufactured in Pakistan. The craftsmen buy it in bulk from the bazaar.

For printing, the craftsmen uses woodblocks, *pur,* made by specialized craftsmen called *purgār.* The block-makers of village Radhan, in the district of Dadu, have a particular reputation for the quality of their work. The blocks, from ten to fifteen centimetres in thickness, are always made from a hard wood to keep the contours of the carvings sharp for a prolonged use. Yet, blocks that are used regularly have to be changed every year.

Several blocks are needed to complete the design of a cloth and each block has a particular name, depending on the operation for which it is destined.[5] Thus, one distinguishes *asul, kot, khor, phuli, minā* from the names of the different impressions. *Phuli* designates the small motif, generally star-shaped or circular, which remains spotlessly white. Sometimes it is obtained not with the help of a block but solely by plugging at the right time, with cloth or clay, the desired portion of the block. To this set of blocks one should add the

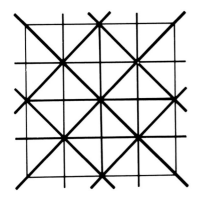 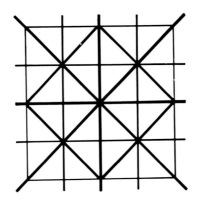 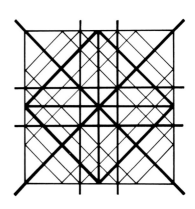

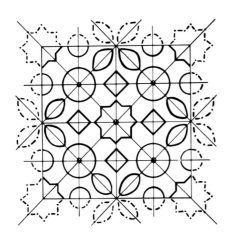 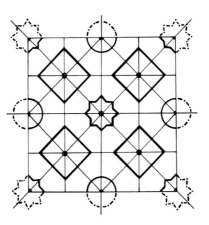 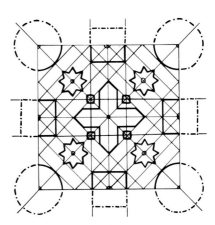

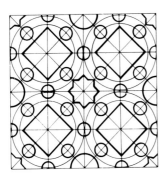 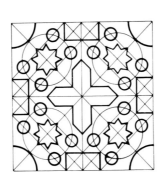

Square motifs whose pattern is based on diagonals and medians
a) *khorak*, date. This is the only motif which is done solely in red against a blue background.
b) *moru*, peacock.
c) *jileb*, a kind of sweetmeat. The presence of a central cross and squares is exceptional.

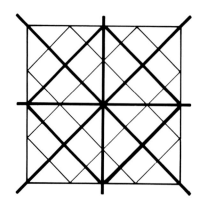 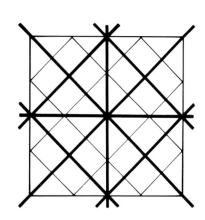

Square motifs whose pattern is based on the reduction of the diagonals

a) *dabuli,* round jewel-box, or *cakki,* millstone; this motif is organised around a central circular element.

b) *chap,* literally meaning print; this is the only instance when the name refers to the artisan's work and not to an exterior object.

c) *badam,* almond.

d) *ishq pech,* meaning a love affair; often symbolized by plants from the family of Convolvulaceae, such as the morning glory and the bindweed.

e) *chalo sarkari,* government seal; this refers probably to a ring with a seal and seams to go back to the time of British rule.

 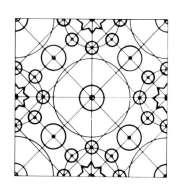

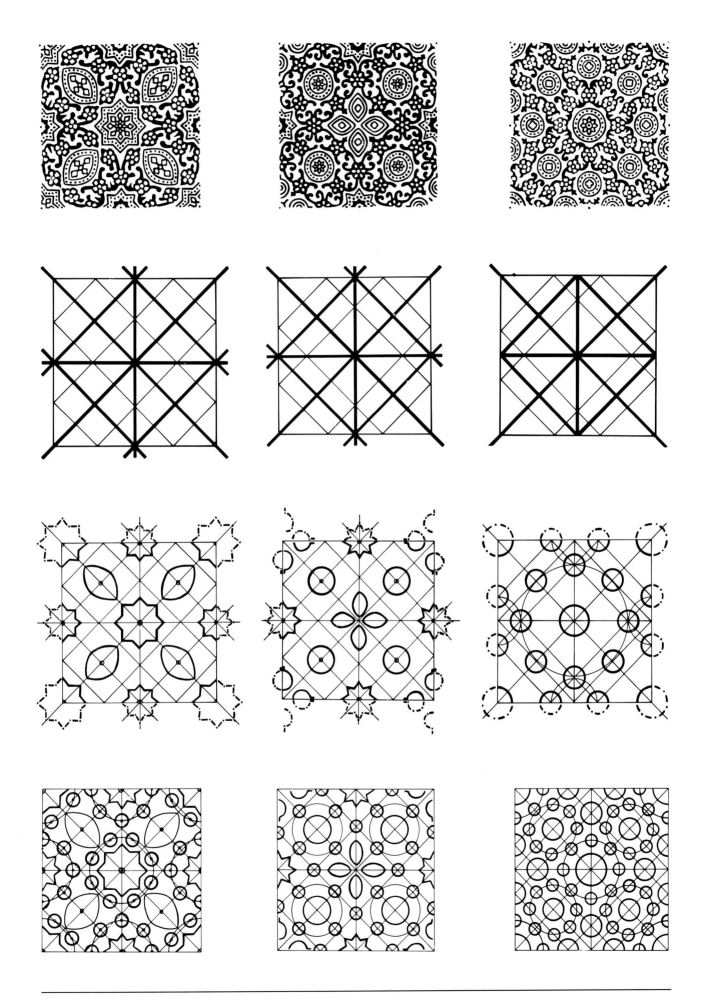

a) *coman*, garden; traditionally used only for bedspreads, this motif is borrowed today for some types of *azrak*.
b) *ghalica*, carpet; another motif borrowed from the printed bedspread decors.

rough blocks made by the craftsmen themselves which are used to cover the borders lengthwise with resist.

After use, the blocks are carefully cleansed with a pig-bristle brush and, eventually, an engraver's point is used to clean the holes in some blocks. They are oiled before being stored away.

The craftsman's working-table, *pathia*, is low and made by the local carpenter. On it are laid layers of cloth, *ghar*. The cloth on the top, *acharo*, is thickest. This layer makes the surface on which the cloth to be printed is placed, soft. A simple pad makes for a seat. To his right, either on the floor, or on a small support, he keeps the pot with the printing mixture. It consists of an earthen receptacle, rectangular in shape, called *chāti*. A screen made of reed, *chipri*, is placed inside; on it, a thick piece of cloth, jute or wool, with a layer of cotton cloth atop. The dye is poured slowly into the pot through the sides and is absorbed by the layers of cloth resting on the reed screen. The block, when pressed on this pad of cloth, receives a uniform layer of the dye or mordant. The resist is generally put in a broken earthen pot, *tibri*.

These are the main tools use for the printing process itself. Moreover, the craftsman uses a straw, *tili*, as a measuring instrument to measure the different parts of the pattern and the distance between the joints of the motifs and a piece of cloth or paper, *camri*, to "cut" the pattern.

For the grinding work a millstone similar to the one used for the grains at home is used. The preparation of the mordants is done in big copper pots, *degri*, while that of the resists is done in earthen pots.

Since the alizarine dye requires boiling, it is prepared in a huge copper pot, *charu* (or *charun*), placed over a fire, *bhati*. The cloth is continually stirred with the help of two sticks, *dhandio*. For measuring the quantity of alizarine, a vessel, *vati*, is used and two handfuls, *bhuk*, for the *sakum*. The indigo dye is made in an earthen tank, *kuni (or gundi)*, built by the potters. For stirring, they use a long wooden pole, *lāth*. Copper pots are also used for the washing at the river or canal. The cloth is beaten on a stone, *paro*, with a wooden mallet.

Study of the Patterns

There are two kinds of *azrak* those printed on one side only, *ek puri*, and those printed on both sides,

bi puri. The latter, of course, take more skill and time and are therefore costlier. The most famous ateliers produce only *bi puri azrak*, or so their owners claim. On the other hand, ateliers facing financial difficulties are compelled to produce *ek puri azrak*.

The *azrak* differ also by the organization of their pattern and by the motifs included. The buyer, according to his taste and his purse, has the choice between different types of patterns and, among each type, between different motifs[6] though some motifs appear only in particular types of *azrak*.

Almost all the *azrak* are printed against either a blue or a red background. If one describes them when mounted, the disposition of the pattern is as follows: at both ends is the cross border, *palad*. Restricted by these two cross borders are two borders that run lengthwise. Finally, we have the central rectangle, the ground, surrounded by one or more "frames". Lines of separation are printed between all these parts; they are the "frames" which help, it seems, to distinguish the different types of *azrak*.

Thus, there is a great variety of patterns. Some of them are very old while others are of recent origin. The novelty lies in changing the layout of the motifs by using sometimes a motif traditionally associated with another type of cloth. Such innovations show the vitality of the craft and the strength of the demand. It is true that the adoption of a handicraft by a clientele different from the traditional customers can be a sign of the decadence of the technique and the first step towards a decline of the quality; for the present, this phenomenon is marginal and the rapport between the two demands is far from being upset. The development of a new section of users does not correspond to a disaffection among the traditional clientele.

The simplest type of *azrak* is called *naro vari azrak*. At both extremities one finds a cross border with two registers, separated and aligned at the inside by a line consisting of a triple white stroke and called *naro*. The borders consist of a plain red stripe enhanced on the inside by a triple white line. The central rectangle is decorated with one of the *azrak* motifs.

The most elaborate type of *azrak* is called *thi hashe-ji azrak* (*azrak* with three borders). The cross borders, always with two registers, are emphasized by a line of separation named after its pattern, *sādi vat*, and which is found again on the inner side of a plain stripe to mark the longitudinal borders. Thus a rectangle is formed surrounded by three "frames", each one separated by the same line, *sādi vat,* and printed inwards with the following motifs: *parai hasho, seleimi hasho, parai hasho.* The angles are carefully executed so that there may be no overlapping or blank space but a perfect joining of the motifs. The ground is decorated with the *seleimi hasho* motif or some other *azrak* motif such as the *badām.*

In the disposition of the *pase-jo hasho azrak* one meets again the same cross borders as in the preceding cloths, terminated by a *sādi vat* line. The line also runs along the internal edge of the plain stripe placed on the longitudinal border. The central rectangle is framed with the *hasho* motif doubled width, without separation, and bordered on the inside by a *sādi vat* line. The ground itself is decorated with an *azrak* motif, here the *cakkī* (or *dabuli).*

The *sajo hashe yari azrak* presents the same across and longitudinal borders. The frame is made with the *parai hasho* motif printed in double width and bordered on the inside by a *sādi vat* line. The ground is decorated width the *seleimi hasho* motif.

Ghalica vari azrak has only recently been introduced. In this case, it is the motif that is new. On the transversal border one finds the same decor as in the other *azrak* but inversely printed: the block for *asul* is used for the printing of *kot* and vice-versa. We have already seen that this technique of inversion is called *kataji cura,* an expression which designates the operation itself and, by extension, its result. The longitudinal borders are the same as in the "classical" *azrak* already mentioned. The frame is made by printing the *ghalica* motif in double width and without the separation line. A line of separation surrounds the central rectangle decorated with the *val* motif, using the regular blocks.

In these four *azrak,* the difference lies in the preferential use of one or the other element. A separating line here or the exclusive presence of a particular motif there are enough to justify the distinction though the overall design be the same.

Finally, the last new type is called *tedi azrak.* The cross borders are limited by a line which is called after its pattern: *cher vari vat.* The longitudinal borders are composite: a stripe ornamented with the *azrak* motif *badām,* surrounded by the same

line of separation. The central ground is limited at both ends by a cross border which touches the longitudinal borders and is filled with the same *badām* motif. The newly made rectangle is then framed, the motif of the frame differing with the direction: *hasho* across and *badām* lengthwise. The inner separation lines cross each other at the angles, forming a square decorated with a flower motif, *phul.* For the decoration of the ground another *azrak* motif, different from the previous ones, is used: *cakkī* for example. The novelty lies in the presence of a composite frame, not found elsewhere, in the square corner motif and in the use of several motifs — which is a break from the sobriety of the "classical" *azrak.* Nevertheless, such a pattern is frequent in bedspreads.

The cross border, *palad,* has in all cases two registers. The external register consists of an arched line decorated with stylized floral motifs. Separated from this by a triple white line, *naro,* the second register is decorated with motifs so that the width of one of these motifs comprises two arches with perfectly synchronized joints. One can distinguish two different motifs for this register: one that is closed and one that is open. In the first, two multifoiled, symmetrically opposed arches rest on two columns; inset in the space thus circumscribed is a medallion with festooned borders decorated with a bouquet. The second is of a similar style: a multifoiled arch resting on two columns delimits an open space in which is a basin with flowers spread out.

The longitudinal border is simpler. It consists of a plain stripe of red if the background is blue and blue if the background is red.

The actual *azrak* motifs decorate the central part. The same motif is repeated all over the rectangular surface; this juxtaposition gives a pattern of intercrossing diagonal lines. The frame or the frames generally use a motif different from the central one.

Finally, the different parts of the pattern are separated by dividing lines, *vat,* which could also be called transition lines as they are not used without a purpose.

The simplest line is the *naro,* the triple white line already mentioned, appearing on all the transversal borders as well as on the fringe in the *naro azrak.* Of a more complex pattern, the *cher vari vat* and *sādi vat,* are used with a preference in some types of *azrak; cher vari vat,* which takes its name from the ankle bells, *cher,* presents a succession of tiny flowers separated by long stylised leaves giving the effect of undulating lines. A row of small triangles on either side completes the decor. Blooming flowers on a straight line decorated with small leaves make the *sadi vat.* Two thick, black, dotted lines make up the edge.

If by their name they evoke nature or the objects of daily life, the *azrak* motifs themselves show such a stylization that they are distinguished rather by the peculiar combination of often similar elements than by any realistic or figurative representation. The decor of the ceramic tiles of the tombs and mosques of Thatta are often used as a reference and, effectively, one finds an affinity of inspiration due to, or enhanced by, a decorative method. But it is perhaps hazardous to claim affiliation or a direct dependence and more prudent to speak of a convergence, after all quite natural. However, the reputation of the Thatta motifs is such, that it seems certain that, at one point, the printers must have transposed them on cloth. Such is the case for the *hasho* motifs *(pargi hasho* and *seleimi hasho).*

The inventory is probably not exhaustive but, of all the names actually cited to designate the motifs, only the *real* motif, an Arabian coin, is missing. The name of *taviz,* amulet, has also been given to me in the village of Khebar but it seems to designate the motif called *hasho* elsewhere. The names given to the motifs are certainly less stable than the motifs themselves.

As we have seen, the motifs are red on a blue background or inversely and, as the case may be, are called for example *lāl cakkī* or *garho kakar,* red wheel or red cloud, or *mīna badām,* blue almond.[7]

The *azrak* motifs are inscribed in the square or rectangular surface of the printing block. The first to be used are the blocks for the *asul* printing and it is these which determine the pattern; it is therefore on these that the following analysis is based.

Besides the square motifs, which are the most numerous, there are some inscribed in rectangles: *hasho, kakar* and *val.* These motifs are foreign, one could say, to the art of the *azrak,* either because they are borrowed from a different art (this is the case, as we have seen, of the *hasho* motifs inspired from the ceramic design), or because they were destined — originally or in priority — for a group different from today's traditional users: men, both Sindhi and Moslem. Thus, the *kakar* motif was reserved for the black slaves while the *val* motif is used primarily by women.

The *parai hasho* and the *seleimi hasho* are two variants of an identical theme. The same block is used in both cases for the first print, *asul,* and it is only with the *knot* block that the difference will begin. The pattern is therefore the same: two median axes divide the surface into four parts, each part again divided by two secondary median axes. A foliated scroll is used as setting for the *val* motif. As for the *kakar* motif, it is characterized by a geometrical pattern that is not coherent at the level of one motif alone. Repetition brings to light obliques between which lines undulate and twist without any immediately recognizable apparent order.

With the square motifs we come to the actual *azrak* motifs. If one tries to find the general lines besides the primary, diagonal and median lines, two major types stand out: the first, where diagonals, verticals and horizontals are associated, intercrossing at regular intervals; the second, which relies on the scaling of the diagonal only. On these two trellises are disposed the motifs inscribed in the geometrical figures thus composed or in the circles inscribed within these figures. These figures are never obvious, but only suggested by the very place of the different elements of the pattern.

The purpose is not at all to make an arbitrary, a *posteriori,* reconstitution of these geometrical constructions but, on the contrary, to find at the beginning of the chain of operations the first task which the craftsman who carves the blocks sets out to do; in other words, the plan according to which he will carve out or leave as it is such and such a portion.

The construction of the motifs follows two opposite but complementary tendencies. On one hand, the printing block, used as the basic unit, is a closed surface having a clear, coherent and balanced order: the centre is always clearly defined and the diverse elements of the pattern are solidly structured around it according to the pattern of the diagonals and medians. But on the other hand, and at the same time, this well-delimited construction opens outwards and by this very opening a new order is created, ruled by different laws. It is this balance between the centrifugal and the centripetal tendencies within one unit, translated by the surfaces (and of course by the alternating of the colours, not dealt with here) which will generate the harmony at the time of repetition; that is, at the moment when the part will merge into the whole. The balance is perfect when only a minute examination of the joints on the cloth reveal the size of the wooden block. In this sense, the *ghalīca* and *caman* motifs which are taken from printed bedspread decors, are cases apart. They can be integrated within the framework of the geometrical construction defined above as long as the play of the diagonal and the medians is respected. But, in another way, these geometrical lines build up a decor where the central element takes prime importance in regard to the whole; the polarization thus closes the decor and, ultimately, repetition is not a decorative necessity imposed by the motif itself.

The analysis reveals a unity and a coherence in the inspiration which is broken only in the case of motifs foreign to the art of *azrak*. These characteristics are part of a decorative tradition which covers a fairly large geographical area and a variety of applied techniques and it is within this stream that the original creation of the *azrak* must be seen.

FOOTNOTES

1. The term *azrak* is probably derived from the arabic *ajraq* which designates the cerulean blue.

2. On the Khatri and their activities, see esp. C.G.H. Fawcett: *A monograph on dyes and dyeing in the Bombay Presidency*, 1986, 43 p. The Mohana are a traditional fisher community. The Shidi (or Sidi) are the descendants of slaves from Africa. The Sumro, originating from Sind itself, are engaged today in different activities such as carpentary, dyeing, laundry. See Richard R. Burton *Sindh and the races that inhabit the valley of the Indus*, Karachi (1975), reprint of a book published in 1851. On the Mohana, pp. 251-253; on the slaves pp. 253-257. T Postans *Personal Observations on Sindh; and its manners and customs of its inhabitants; and its productive capabilities*. Karachi 1973, reprint of a book published in 1843. On the Mohana, pp. 58-60; on the slaves, pp. 73-74. H.T. Sorley *The Gazetteer of West Pakistan*. The former province of Sind (including Khairpur State) 1968. On the Mohana, p. 252; on the Sumro, pp. 239-240.

3. The cloth is cut into pieces of adequate length for the realization of the two *azrak*. As each *azrak* is made of two parts (joined by the user), each of these parts is therefore four times the length of an *azrak* and its width half of the *azrak's* width. Usually, *a than* (that is 40 yards, about 36.50 m.) is printed in succession, the length of seven such pieces being a *takia*.

4. This is the *sakur* referred to by T. Rostans, *op. cit.* pp. 96 and 100: "red dye, produced from the knot of the tamarisk shrub" and "The knots or berries found upon this shrub are used as a dye ..." These are the dried berries which I saw being used.

   According to the Gazetteer of H.T. Sorley, five different kinds of tamarisk grow in Sind (see *op. cit.* App.III, list of plants of former Sind and Khairpur. p.xiv).

5. The blocks used for the *azrak bi puri* must compulsorily have a small metallic point at each corner. In this way, a small scale hole is made each time the craftsman presses the block and when he turns the cloth for the reverse printing he can use these holes as guiding-marks. Moreover, lines are carved on the block's handle to distinguish left from right.

6. Besides these differences due to the printer's skill, there are differences in the quality of the cloth itself which will, of course, affect the final price.

7. The term *mina* designates the enamel as well as the particular shade of blue most used in enamel. Here it means blue. In other period cloths it will designate any colour that "gives shine", especially the vivid pink in which the cloth is soaked to give it eclat, but which disappears soon with washing.

Regional Weaves of India

Jasleen Dhamija

India has the largest variations in textiles — variations in techniques, in the use of materials, in the art of dyeing and in the form of design expression which is part of its cultural heritage. The most intimate element in a person's external being is the cloth with which he wraps himself or his loved ones. It is also closely associated with his inner life and with the stages through which a person passes. Though the rituals are similar, the enactment of rituals and the fabrics used in them are quite distinctive. The very lines of the lullabye sung by the mother are indicative of the magical ritual associated with the fabrics:

Jamadara lal gudhar baletah kuchar lita ena miha tai dayea

Nata tai dhota lal pat baletah kuchar lita mapou jaiah

When my jewel was born he was wrapped in a patched quilt, *gudri,* and the midwife carried him. When my jewel was bathed he was wrapped in silk and placed in the arms of his mother and father.

The *gudari,* the *kantha,* the *ralli* or *dharki,* made out of pieces of fabric and threadbare cloth is not only an expression of the ability to utilise and recycle all fabrics, but it is closely associated with the concept of the magical quality of joining different pieces of cloth together. This has always had important connotations for the Indian psyche. The concept of the *Kesa* cloth, a garment of pieced fabrics worn by Buddhist priests of Japan, is possibly a culmination of this belief, which is also very much a part of the Indian living tradition.

It is in this context that we have to look at the regional development of handwoven and worked textiles. The textile traditions were not only greatly influenced by the geo-climatic conditions but also by the socio-cultural traditions of the areas and absorption of the range of influence of migrations of many ethnic groups into India, by land and sea. As it is said about language that every 10 km, dialects change, in the same way every village or centre has a distinct style for weaving which a connoisseur can distinguish. In fact within the same village different communities produce fabrics which are quite distinct. The weaver in any case weaves a range of designs which are meant for different communities; in fact in some cases he will even refuse to sell it to others. This adherence to traditional use of fabrics has been responsible for retaining the distinctive regional styles. Variations were introduced yet the basic sense of design, the use of colour, the balance between the technique and the desired effect were retained.

Today with the far-reaching impact of the audio-visual media which carries across a rather bizarre image of an affluent Indian, the changing mores and the flooding of the market with synthetic fabrics which are longer lasting and easier to maintain, the traditional market for the fabrics is changing. The large-scale export market has also affected the design traditions. The subtle nuances which used to distinguish one product from another are now being lost. The imitation Baluchar of Varanasi is better than that woven in Murshidabad. The Surat *tanchoi* has become extinct because Varanasi has produced better quality and cheaper *tanchoi.* The Patan *patola* is facing competition from the silk Poochampalli and only the discerning will recognise the difference between the two.

Despite all these factors textile tradition has shown a remarkable ability to develop and grow. Today many of the techniques and design traditions which were extinct, before India gained its independence, have been revived. Some of the finest textiles which are mentioned in our ancient records have been woven once again.

North-Western India - Gujarat and Rajasthan

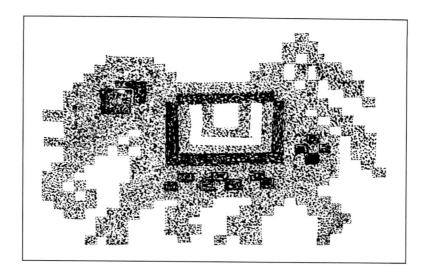

Gujarat, with its long coastline and easy land routes over which people could migrate, has had contacts with most parts of the world from ancient times. Excavations at the Harappan settlements at Lothal and at a number of ports point to the fact that Gujarat had a number of seafearing communities trading with the ancient world.

The presence of large numbers of spindles for spinning and twisting yarn, of needles for stitching, of hooks and awls found at excavations, as well as impressions of woven textiles, point out the weaving was extensively practised. The discovery of a fragment of mordant-dyed cotton found adhering to a silver jar not only indicates that cotton originated in India but also that the art of dyeing with the use of mordants was known 4000 years ago.[1]

Finds at Kalibangan in Rajasthan also indicate a knowledge of spinning and weaving. It is certain that contact existed between the different Harappan settlements, and that commodities and possibly techniques were exchanged.

The earliest known archaeological textiles of Gujarat are cotton fabrics dyed and printed with the use of mordants found at Fostat and at other recently excavated Red Sea ports. These have been identified as Indian cottons, having originated in Gujarat. It is possible that block printing and *Kalamkari* were practised in Gujarat from early times, even though the examples available are from the eighth to the 17th century.

Literary references to Indian dyed fabrics occur at a much earlier date. The *Periplus* and the writings of Pliny talk frequently of painted and dyed fabrics. Many of the patterns found in the excavated fragments are still being block printed by the *chhipas* of Ahmedabad, Anjar, Dhamadka and Khavda. Some of these have designs similar to the patterns found in prehistoric textiles and the more elaborate geometric patterns are based on the *yantras* used by the Jains and Buddhists in their rituals.

Gujarat has a wide range of techniques developed with the use of cotton, silk and wool. Some of these evolved through contacts with the outside world, which brought in a number of techniques that were absorbed and became a part of the repertoire of the weavers of Gujarat and later the whole of India.

Cotton was exported from the earliest times and it is possible that it was exported to Egypt and was even used to wrap mummies. It was certainly exported to the ancient world and later to the Roman Empire, for the Roman term for cotton, *carbasina*, is derived from the Sanskrit *karpasa*.[2] Woven cotton was also exported to the outside world and fine quality cotton was woven in many parts of Rajasthan and Gujarat.

Today fine weaving is confined only to a few towns — Dholka, Khambhat and Porbandar in Gujarat and the small village of Kaithon in Kota district, Rajasthan. Dholka, until 20 years ago, wove sarees with a subtle range of colours and a heavy *zari* border, shot with silver wire of *badla*. Porbandar used to weave checked sarees with gold *ashrafi buti* or a swan in the squares, using the *jamdani*

technique. These sarees were than tied for the *gharchola* pattern at Kutch and dyed a brilliant red in Jamnagar. The Masooria sarees, commonly known as Kota sarees, created a net-like effect by varying the count of the yarn as well as picks in the weaving. Handspun woven *khaddar* in thicker counts used to be woven all over the countryside and is even today an important product.

Gujarat has a number of centres in the rural areas where traditional fabrics for the different tribes continue to be produced. In Saurashtra and north Gujarat, a variety of *pachedis*, long white *lungis*, are woven. They have a simple red border and rich extra weft pattern on the cross borders at both ends. For the Bharwad community, the *pachedis* are woven in green, red and blue with a woven patterns on the cross border. The Charan women wear a red *odhani* and *jimmi*, an unstitched skirt, which is woven with a black border, a speciality of the villages around Surendranagar.

The weavers of south Gujarat in the Chhota Udaipur area weave a highly decorative loin cloth for the Rathwa community, which has the front flap elaborately patterned. They also weave a white cotton *chaddar* with a plain border which is used as an upper cloth by the older men for special occasions.

Wool Weaving

Woollen weaves are associated with semi-nomadic people who move with their sheep, their herds of cattle and their camels and use the wool of their sheep to weave their needs. Saurashtra and Kutch have a tradition of weaving woollen shawls worn by the women as their *odhanis*, ornamented with tie-and-dye, gold bands and embroidery. In Saurashtra the Bharwad and the Rabari communities wear the intricately woven *jimmis* with inlaid designs, reminiscent of the patterns woven by the Baluchis on their Kilims. Men carry a woollen *dhabla* on their shoulders, woven with extra weft patterns or inlay techniques. Generally the *dhabla* is white with coloured patterns; priests however wear dark maroon ones which distinguishes them from others.

Silk Weaving

The tradition of weaving brocaded silk is an ancient one and some of the oldest brocaded textiles can be associated with the weaving centres of Gujarat. Many hangings scattered in museums throughout the world, probably fragments of the same piece, with a pattern of riders on a horse, were woven in Gujarat, in heavy silk, with an extra

Gold checked cotton *gharchola*, Gujarat

The tie and dyed *gharchola* in red is traditionally used in the marriage ceremony in Gujarat. The gold checked *odhni* was originally woven in Porbander with the pattern tied in Kutch and later dyed the brilliant red in Jamnagar. (Collection: Gujarat Handicrafts & Handloom Dev. Corpn.)

weft design in twill weave. This hanging is perhaps the earliest woven piece ascribed to Gujarat and has been dated by different authorities from the 12th to the 16th century.

The most important centres for silk weaving in Gujarat were Surat, Ahmedabad, Jamnagar, Patan and Mandvi. One of the common silk weaves woven all over the country was the satin weave known as *gajji* and *atlash*. This was an important material for making garments, as well as for decorating the home. The soft *gajji* and *atlash* were also used for making fine quality tie-and-dye half sarees, *odhanis;* long shirts, *abaṣ* as well as for skirts and clothes for children. The material was printed, tie-dyed and embroidered with silk or gold. The garments were made specially for the urban population, and for the families of the number of principalities which were to be found all over Gujarat.

Ahmedabad had workshops which specialised in weaving brocaded silks and velvets. The *ashawali* sarees of Ahmedabad were known for their intricate design in gold and silk thread. During the Sultanate period, Ahmedabad had large factories where brocades were woven. According to tradi-

tion the areas of Ahmedabad and Surat produced very fine gold brocade. The *nakshabands,* the pattern makers, who had migrated from Central Asia, had settled in Ahmedabad, before moving to north India. These *nakshabands* made a range of patterns and the *ashawali* sarees came to be famous in western India.

Later they simulated the designs of the Paithani *pallus* and border, but not the technique. In the 19th century, copies of the curvilinear *kalgas* of Baluchar and the outlined framed patterns of miniatures were also woven here.

Surat has been known as a centre for production of fine quality gold thread, *zari.* It also produced a variety of brocaded sarees and yardage. Today it continues to produce gold thread and a range of borders. Richly ornamented *odhanis* and skirt pieces with a one-sided border worked in gold, were a speciality of Jamnagar. Unfortunately this style of weaving is no longer in practice.

The silk *tanchoi* saree and yardage material said to have been introduced into Surat by Chinese weavers was continued by the Parsi community. Another tradition attributes its introduction to a Parsi family named Choi, who had learnt the technique in China. The name *tanchoi* was apparently

Prayer durrie from Rajasthan

A finely woven jail durrie used as a prayer mat. (Collection Caveh Munshi)

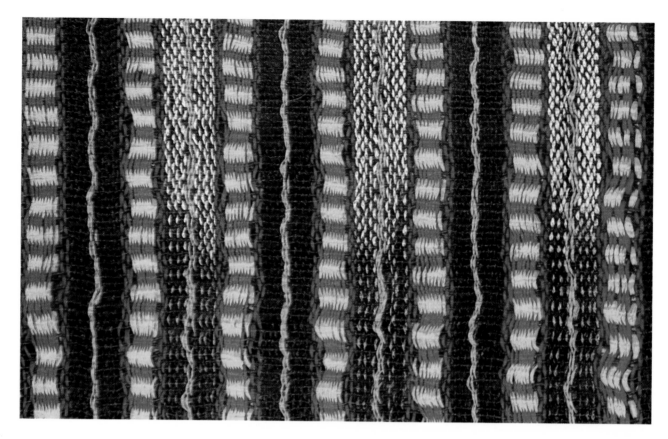

Silk and cotton *mashru* with ikat

Detail of a silk and cotton *mashru* woven with a striped extra warp pattern and an ikat warp. Though traditional, it is contemporary in design.

Opposite Page

Ashavali saree, Ahmedabad, Gujarat, contemporary

Richly brocaded *ashavali* sarees were woven in a twill weave to bring out the richness of the gold thread. This saree carries diagonal borders on the body, with the pattern inlaid into the gold stripe in green, purple and pink known as *meenakari kam*, since it simulates the effect of enamelling on gold. The border has a broad central band and smaller borders on each side.

derived from *tran choi* i.e. three Choi brothers who introduced the technique. As this tradition was dying the only master weaver of *tanchoi* in Surat was persuaded to run a training centre with the help of the Parsi community. The cost of the production was however so high that it was difficult to find a market. Banaras, meanwhile, using the *nakshabandi* technique, began to produce *tanchoi* in a range of patterns including a style with *zari* thread. The Surat *tanchoi* centre was unable to compete and was closed down. However the technique continues in Banaras.

Twenty years ago an attempt was again made by the All India Handicrafts Board to revive the brocade weaving traditions in Ridrol and Surat. At the time, 10 looms were being used at Ridrol, producing silk sarees and yardage material in *gajji* with gold *ashrafi butis* for consumption in the rural areas of Gujarat. They also produced fascinating textiles for the worship of Shrinathji, Krishna in the Pushti Marg tradition. These were *toranas* for family shrines, small woven *pichhvais* showing Shrinathji surrounded by cows and the *gaumukhi,* mittens used for covering the hand as devotees prayed with the rosary. The basic background colour was deep red with patterns worked in gold and silver, blue, green and yellow silk. Today only one loom is working and an attempt is being made to revive the industry.

Printed cotton Massoria-Kota saree, Rajasthan contemporary

The sarees of Kaithon village near Kota are known as Massoria or Kota sarees. These are of very fine cotton, woven with variations in picks and yarn counts that create a net-like effect. The gold thread checks emphasise the lightness of the fabric.

Mashru, a mixed fabric woven with a combination of cotton and silk was associated with the Muslim community. According to Islamic tradition, devout Muslims were not supposed to wear silk next to the skin. Thus *mashru* which was silk faced and had cotton at the back, was woven with a silk warp and cotton weft. The silk thus came to the surface while cotton touched the skin and it gave the effect of a satin weave, though with a far less consumption of silk. *Mashru* was woven all over India and may have been derived from the weaving traditions of the Tiraz factories of the Caliphates, in the countries having Islamic influences. These manufactures were also introduced into India during the Sultanate period.

Mashru continues to be woven even today and comes in a number of patterns. There is the all-over-dotted effect created by raising the white weft thread to produce a grid-like pattern. There are striped designs, further elaborated by introducing an extra warp woven pattern. Ikat patterns are also introduced by the tying and dyeing of the warp thread thus creating yet another dimension in the striped *mashru* patterns.

Today Patan and Mandvi are the only centres where *mashru* is woven. In the regions of Saurashtra and Kutch it is sold in large quantities to tribal women who stitch from it their *kanjari*, backless blouse, and the skirts and *chola* of the young unmarried girls. This is a recent phenomenon, and the women choose *mashru*, with woven designs, as a replacement for the richly embroidered garments, which were earlier prepared by them for their own and their children's use.

Resist Technique

The widest range of textiles in India's north-western region can be found in the resist technique. They range from the highly complicated *patola*, the double ikat of Patan, to the single *ikat* of Rajkot, the *bandhani* of Saurashtra and Kutch and the Rajasthani tie and dye of Shekhawati, Jhun Jhunu and Sikar. They also include the *lahariya* and *mothra* of Udaipur, Jaipur and Jodhpur, and

Khurjin, **donkey bag, Kutch**

The attractive double bag has a cotton warp and a weft base cloth, with the woven pattern worked in wool. It carries the same name as that used in Iranian Baluchistan, Sistan, and Pakistani Baluchistan. Similar geo-climatic conditions and shared traditions create a commonality of design and techniques. The motif of a caravan of camels is a typical scene of the desert area which has been recreated in this stylized woven pattern, in the villages of Dinara, located in Pachham, Kutch.

the resist or reserve techniques of printing on cotton and silk.

The *patola* combines the art of tying and dyeing of the warp and weft threads and their weaving together by placing the weft threads carefully against their corresponding colours. Besides Patan, the double ikat is woven only in Bali. Patan however produced a range of intricate patterns with precision. The *patolas* woven here were exported out of the country until the late 19th century, with different styles woven to the demands of different consumers. Though the old export markets have been lost, as has the major national demand, Patan continues to produce *patolas* for the Gujarat market where they are still a part of the ceremonial and ritual practices associated with marriage and childbirth. Though attempts have been made to copy the designs and techniques elsewhere, the complete mastery in handling the design by the remaining three families in Patan is unmatched. The *nari-kunjar*, lady and elephant pattern, and the *ratan chowk*, jewelled square pattern, are the speciality of the area.

Surat was also known to be one of the centres producing *patolas*. These were essentially woven for the Bora community. The saree known as *cheera* was produced with geometrical patterns and avoided the use of patterns such as *nari-kunjar, popat vel* and other patterns evolved with the use of animal, bird and human forms, banned to Islamic users. One of the weavers working with a Salvi family of Patan was employed by the Khadi and Village Industries for organising a training centre in Rajkot and thus *patola* weaving was introduced there. Today Rajkot has a number of weavers who weave single ikat *patolas* for sale in Gujarat itself.

The tie-and-dye fabrics known as *bandhani* are perhaps the finest produced in India. The most intricate and fine quality of *bandhani* is from Jamnagar, Bhuj and Mandvi in Kutch, Jodhpur, Jaipur and Sikar in Rajasthan. An interesting example of the tie and dye saree of Gujarat is the *gharcholu* worn by a bride at the wedding. The cotton for the *gharcholu* in fine counts, is woven with gold checks in Porbandar or Khambhat. The gold checks enclose a small motif woven with the *jamdani* or inlay technique. Then the saree or *odhani* is folded four times and tied into tiny knots and dyed white, yellow and green, while the background is dyed a brilliant red. The Khatris of Jamnagar bring the saree to Kutch, known for its very fine and intricate tying of knots. The final dyeing in red is carried out in Jamnagar, since the water of Jamnagar is supposed to produce the most

brilliant red colour. This practice is prevalent even today and the Khatris of Jamnagar can be seen in Bhuj with bundles of their *gharcholas* tied in Kutch and taken back to Jamnagar for the final dyeing. However the finest work is in the *chanderkhani* or *khombi odhani* made by the Khatris of Kutch for use by their own women. These *odhanis* are quite distinctive and stand out as some of the finest.

The tiniest knot however is tied in the village of Ramnagar, in Sikar district of Shekhawati. Brilliant colours, fine patterns and a totally different colour palette distinguish the Rajasthani tie-and-dye from that of Gujarat. The intricate technique of *laheria*, the diagonal, zigzag patterns or crossed patterns of *mothra* on turbans are specially of Rajasthan.

The oldest known printed fabrics from India were from Gujarat. They were resist-dyed and printed cottons found at Fostat. The fragments were first dated from the 13th to the 17th century. Recent excavations at a Red sea port, Quseir al Qadim, have shown that these fabrics must have been widely distributed, since a large number of fragments have been found. Analysis of the fragments showed that indigo printed textiles were of coarser cloth, while madder dyed fabrics were on a finer fabric. This may be because the indigo materials were first painted with resist and then dyed while the madder patterns were block-printed with mordants and then dyed.

Agnes Geijer, in her book on oriental textiles, mentions the widespread use of the Indian printed and painted cottons throughout Europe. The textiles however came to be identified as Fustian cotton and until recently they were taken to be Islamic textiles. Possibly the cotton was distributed to Europe from Fostat and hence acquired this name.

The *ajrak*, resist printed cotton, is produced in Anjar, Dhamadka and Khavda in Kutch and is similar to that of Sindh (now in Pakistan), known for its finer quality. The most complex *ajrak* is the double-printed kind, specially that printed with vegetable dyes. Today Mohammedbhai of Dhamadka has revived vegetable dyeing and makes the finest *ajrak* in the area, be it Kutch or Sindh. For traditional use, two pieces of printed cloth are stitched together to prepare a rectangular piece which is used by the men as a *lungi*, as a turban, as well as an upper cloth. *Ajrak* continues to be used by the *maldharis* and the *Baluchis* from Iranian Baluchistan upto the border of Rajasthan and in most parts of Kutch. The patterns are similar to those found in the fragments from the Red sea ports as well as well as Fostat. Dhamadka village today has been transformed into a large production centre for the urban market — yardage material, sarees, table and bed linen are produced alongside with the requirements of the local market.

The *Mata ni Pachhedi*, a combination of printing and *kalamkari*, is made by the Vaghris for ritual purposes. Wooden blocks print the outline of the border and patterns, while the central figure of the Mother Goddess in her many manifestations, is drawn by a pen by the master craftsman. The Vaghari who produces the cloth is often also the priest who dedicates the cloth to the Mother Goddess.

Pethapur in Gujarat remains famous for its block making. Wooden blocks with intricate patterns, using four colours, are prepared even today. Traditionally, Pethapur was known for the mud resist prints, known as *sodagiri* prints, made for export to the Far East. *Sodagiri* prints were also prepared in Ahmedabad.

The Persianised printed patterns, produced for export in the 17th century, are not seen any more in Gujarat. What remains are designs favoured by locals and still in use today. The Persian influence has been absorbed in the traditional design.

The printed material produced in the region on coarse cloth came from a number of centres and was distributed all over the region. The coarse resist printed *khaddar* used by the tribal communities were very similar in Gujarat and Rajasthan and were comparable to those done in parts of Madhya Pradesh such as Jawad near Ratlam. The *nandra* print from Jawad and from the twin villages Tarapur and Umedpur was printed earlier with the use of indigo. It also used the mud resist technique and carried the pattern of a flowering shrub, with the stems and leaves worked in sage green and the round berries in red. Even today the Rathwas and Bhils of Chhota Udaipur and Jhabua wear full skirts of that cloth along with the *lugdi*, a half saree printed in deep red, with a spotted pattern in deep maroon and black dotted borders and cross borders with a *buta* design.

Sanganer, Bagroo, Barmer, Chittorgarh, Pipar City and Jodhpur in Rajasthan had distinct patterns printed for the use of the local inhabitants. Sanganer being close to Jaipur was influenced by the fine quality of printing and sophisticated motifs derived from Persian and Mughal traditions, while the other centres produced patterns linked to the tradition of Gujarat, especially of Deesa, Surendranagar and Rajkot.

Today this area retains the traditions essentially in the rich colours of the printed fabrics, of the tie-and-dye, of the woven woollen patterns and the richly embroidered fabrics of the peasantry and the nomads, for they compensate for the stark arid conditions of their environments.

FOOTNOTES

1. Gulati A. N. and Turner A. J., *Note On The Early History Of Cotton*, Bombay Act, 1928.

2. Dhamija Jasleen, *Folk Arts and Crafts of India*, National Book Trust, New Delhi, 1970.

Northern India

The rich Gangetic valley fed by the rivers Ganga and Yamuna had a cultural tradition which was highly developed from ancient times. It attracted migrating people from Central Asia where life was much harsher. To the north lay Punjab, the land of five rivers, its rich and fertile land open to migrations and raids from adventurous armies. When the high passes of the mountains opened after the winter, bands of adventurers raided the land, often seeking better lands and moving down into the rich land of Punjab. The richness of the land corresponded to the imagery of the people of Central Asia, where the powers of Ahura-Mazda were expressed as "where the running waters gush from springs, plants sprout from the soil, winds blow the clouds and man comes to birth ... and governs the courses of the sun, moon and

stars." The migrants brought with them not only their hardy spirit but also the nomadic skills of weaving ornamented textiles and decorative hangings.

Punjab absorbed the cultural traditions of the people who passed through it. To survive, people worked hard, tilling the earth and enjoying the fruits of their labour. Until the beginning of the century they were open to raids and the phrase "*Khada pita lahe da. Te baki Ahmed Shahe da*", "whatever you eat and drink is yours, everything else belongs to Ahmed Shah Abdali of Afghanistan," was heard everywhere.

The folk traditions of Punjab were rich and vibrant and the cities developed a culture of their own. The important textile techniques however were developed in the Gangetic plains, where life was more settled.

Varanasi, a popular place of pilgrimage, was the most important centre for fine quality cotton weaves. Buddhist tradition talks of Buddha's body being wrapped in cotton from Varanasi.[1] Pali lit-

Kulu shawl, contemporary

The traditionally *pattu*, woollen shawl, is woven in Manali by women for their personal use. The cross border at the end of the shawl, woven in the slit tapestry technique, carries stylized geometric motifs. The border of red and black is also woven with the tapestry technique but is interlocked.

A Gudma blanket from Kumaon, contemporary

The moutainous areas of Kumaon in Uttar Pradesh produce fine quality wool which is woven into shawls known as *pankhi* and thick blankets such as the fleecy *gudma* and heavy *thulma*.

Opposite Page

A Vaishnav brocaded shawl, Varanasi, 19th century

This gold brocaded shawl with Bengali script woven into it was used for *pujas* by affluent Vaishnav householders. (Collection: C.L. Bharany).

erature also talks of it as being an important weaving centre and textiles with the place names *kasikuttama, kasiya varanaseyyaka* are mentioned frequently.[2] Later records however deal mostly with textiles from coastal areas visited by travellers, and Varanasi is not mentioned. The present day master-weavers talk of having come from Central Asia during the 12th century, and one of the families traces its origin to Bokhara.[3] It is strange therefore that the *Ain-i-Akbari* does not mention Varanasi as a centre for weaving, while many an important centre is mentioned. Ralph Fitch (1583-91) talks of Varanasi as a thriving centre for cotton textiles. But, two hundred years later, Manucci mentions that it exported the finest quality gold and silver brocades all over the world. Today Varanasi dominates the field of silk weaving and brocading. The finest cloths in the country are being woven here and the weavers are capable of reproducing any technique or design.

Silk weaving was carried out only in a few other centres. Bhagalpur in Bihar was developed into a centre for silk weaving, and produced material ranging from fine quality spun silk, to heavy raw silk used till 1960 as waste material to be woven into rough silk shawls worn by peasants. Punjab had a few other centres where silk *lungis* were woven.

Cotton weaving was carried out all over the country and even today Maunathbhajan in Azamgarh district, Ghaziabad and its environs has a large concentration of looms. The finest cotton however was woven in the *jamdani* technique in Tanda, with delicate patterns of white on white for shoulder scarves, *odhanis* and for the traditional *angarkhas* worn by the men. The extra weft design was woven with fine cotton of the same count as the warp and weft so as to form a part of the fabric itself.

Bihar wove a number of cotton sarees and *dhotis* for everyday use. Their speciality was the tribal sarees with rich cross borders, specially worn by the Santhals and Oraons.

The *khes* weaving, a complicated compound weave with a double set of warp threads, is today a speciality of Haryana. This technique was practised all over Punjab in undivided India, the finest being from Multan, now in Pakistan.

Amritsar was known for its weaving of Kashmir shawls. These were introduced into Punjab by weavers who had migrated from Kashmir because of the high taxation on the *jamewar* shawls imposed by the British during the 19th century. Until 1960, *jamewar* shawls were woven with intricate patterns, using the system of *tālim* which was a tradition developed in Kashmir.

The art of printing and dyeing was another important technique in the region. Parts of Haryana, which lie adjacent to Rajasthan, produced tie-and-dye *odhanis* used by Jat women. The patterns and the colouring were very similar to those of Shekhawati in Rajasthan. Gurgaon and the villages around used to make bright red, yellow and deep maroon tie-and-dye *odhanis*. Another interesting form of tie-and-dye was found in the northern part of Bihar bordering Nepal. Sursand also produced tie-and-dye sarees with bold patterns on the *pallu* and borders.

Hand block printing was carried out all over north India. Block printing extended from Samba in Jammu to Jullundar, Gurgaon, Delhi, U.P. and Bihar. Farookabad developed into a commercial printing centre from the late 19th century when it produced cotton printed material for export. The tree of life motif printed on curtains, bed covers, etc. was a speciality of this centre. Printers simulated the painted *kalamkari* tree of life design which used to be made on the Coromandel coast. Large blocks carved in wood were prepared for printing the designs. The printed curtains made from the use of multiple blocks were generally prepared to print a surface of 3.1/2 to 6 feet, so as to cover a door frame. Farookabad had its own

block makers and they produced fine blocks for printing in 3 to 6 colours.

Tanda and Kanoj had a tradition of block printing which was often done on handspun and handwoven cotton, using the resist print technique. The outline was printed with a linear pattern, while the fill-in block known as *datta* had small holes which were filled with felt so that the block absorbed the dye. The printed surface was richly dyed and had a tonal quality with a graphic effect. Over-printing, the use of a combination of blocks and a range of variations were produced by printers who worked only during the summer months. Printed fabrics were exported to Nepal and Tibet and were often used for lining the Tankhas, ritual banners, as well as for lining of garments used in the Himalayan areas. The poorer people used the printed cloth as padded garments while the richer used it for lining. This technique and style of printing existed also in Central Asia, in a village near Herat in Afghanistan, as well as in Bojnurd in Khorasan, north Iran.

North India also has a range of very fine embroidery such as the *chikankari* of Uttar Pradesh, *bagh* of Punjab and the *chope* of Haryana. The white on white embroidery, *chikan*, was used for making the white muslin *angarkhas*, *kurtas* and caps used by the men during the summer. This fine embroidery combined with applique began as an art pursued by the women of affluent houses. According to tradition the intricate and fine stitchery was developed in the *harem*, where the women competed with each other in producing fine quality embroidery. Lucknow and Rampur have the reputation for producing the finest applique

Opposite Page

Square brocaded silk and gold
***rumal*, 19th century**

These *rumals* were used by women as *odhanis* or as a rich folded scarf carried with a sword by scions of royal families on special occasions. This *rumal* has a diagonal pattern and an elaborate *kalga* at each end.

Shikargah brocade, Varanasi, contemporary

This heavy brocaded silk carries curvilinear stems, leaves and flowers within which are distributed a range of animals: ponderous elephants, rampant lions, fleeing deer and prancing horses. The mastery of the designs and *naksha bandha* can be seen in the manner in which the repeat has been disguised.

work of white on white, used for preparing mosquito nets and curtains.

The tradition of commercial applique work was developed for making tents and canopies using as motifs stylised shrubs, the tree of life, and even animals and birds. Canopies and *kanats* for use in smaller towns and temples were based on folk drawings and paintings of the area, and showed elephants, horse riders, soldiers and even people at work.

Bihar too has a fine range of embroidery with large scale production of applique, white on a red background for canopies, *kanat,* etc. The excellent applique of Darbhanga was quite distinctive. In the rural area, women prepared blouses, and long, intricately patterned pillow covers, where different textures and colours combined to create a rich effect. The quilted *sujani* were not as refined as the *kanthas* of Bengal but had a distinctive quality. They were similar in composition to the paintings of Mithila, now famous as Madhubani paintings.

Wool weaving is carried out throughout the Himalayan area. The most important centre is Kashmir which, from ancient times, has been famous for its wool weaving. Besides the *kani* shawl, more popularly known as *jamewar,* Kashmir wove plain woollen fabrics. The most famous of them was the *shahtoosh,* woven from the soft wool of the high altitude goats. The plain *pashmina* shawl, known historically as *dhusa,* continues to be woven even today and can be distinguished by a finely woven border attached to it. The *kani* shawl, of a much lesser refinement than those woven earlier, continues to be woven in the village of Kanihama.

The hill areas of Himachal Pradesh — Kinaur, Lahul, Spiti and Kulu — weave the long checked or plain shawls with solid borders in contrasting colours, interlocked with the main body with the use of three shuttles. The end borders carry geometric patterns woven with non-continuous weft threads in the interlocking technique. Large shawls known as *pattu* are worn by the women as a single piece attire. Woollen tweed of a local wool known as *patti* is woven into yardage which is used by the men.

The Kumaon, Garhwal and the upper ranges of Uttar Pradesh weave a type of thick tweed, and a long *pashmina* shawl known as *pankhi.* Their speciality however is the soft, double, long-haired blanket known as *gudma* and the thickly woven long-haired blanket known as *thulma.* The long hair is teased out of the woven fabric by using a comb.

Pattis, pattus and local tweeds are woven all over the hilly regions. Recently a number of centres have also tried to blend different wools so as to weave a range of tweeds for sale to the urban clientele.

FOOTNOTES

1. Dr. Anand Krishna, Vijay Krishna *"Banaras Brocades",* Craft Museum, New Delhi 1966.

2. Dr. Moti Chandra, *Prachi na Bharatiya Vesha Bhusha,* (Hindi) 1980

3. Mr. Ali Hasan of Messrs. Kaloo Hafiz of Varanasi, one of the finest *naksha bandhas* was the informant.

Eastern India

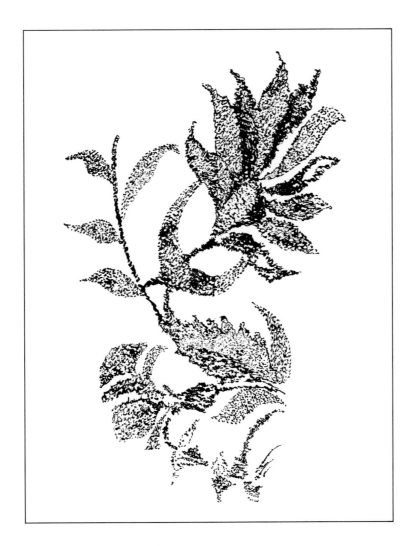

While discussing the textiles of Eastern India, one talks usually of the fine woven muslins, the *jamdani, kantha, baluchari, tangail* and *bandhas,* but rarely of the rich and varied range of tribal weaves, and the fabrics woven for people's personal use. The north eastern region of India has an amazing variety of weaves which range from the sophisticated and distinctive silk of Assam, introduced by the Bodo tribe who migrated from Central Asia, to the intricately woven loin loom weaves of the hill tribes and the different communities which inhabit Nagaland, Mizoram, Arunachal Pradesh, Manipur and Tripura.

Bengal was known from the earliest times as an exporter of fine cottons. A highly developed urban

Kabui Naga Strong, Manipur

Kabui Naga women weave these sarongs for themselves and for their men's use. They create a range of textures with the use of different types of yarn and by combining weaving, embroidery and tassels of golden grass.

civilization and trade flourished in the area two thousand years ago.[1] Mention of the flourishing port town of Tamralipti is found in early Buddhist, Jain and Hindu texts. Greek and Roman records mention the fine muslins of Bengal, and the *Periplus of the Erythraean Sea* mentions the port town of Gange at the mouth of the river. Orissa too had a rich tradition of brocaded silk, fine cotton and intricately woven *bandhas*.

In the north-eastern tribal belt there is a distinct difference between the work of the hill tribes and that carried out by the plains people. The hill tribes weave essentially with the use of the back strap or loin loom, used only by the women; in the plains, both men and women use a frame loom. The only exception are the hill Garos, who also weave on the frame loom.[2] However, except in Manipur, the highly organised commercial weaving is carried out generally by the men.

Nagaland, Manipur, Tripura, Mizoram and Arunachal Pradesh are the most important centres for back strap weaving which uses the body to give the tension to the warp. The loom comprises of a

series of bamboo sticks which separate the continuous warp threads, thus creating the two sheds for weaving. One of the sticks is attached to the strap which attaches the warp to the body; the other end of the continuous warp is tied to a wall, a tree, or to two stakes driven into the ground. By pressing her feet against a piece of wood or a wall, the weaver creates the tension in the warp. A forward movement loosens the tension and enables her to lift one of the heddles, thus raising alternate warp threads. The wooden beater is inserted in between the warp threads, forming the shed through which the weft is inserted. A backward movement creates the tension. The second shed is now created by lowering the heddle, moving the second bamboo closer and adding another weft thread into the shed. Since the warp is often circular, it can be pulled closer to the weaver as the weaving progresses. The warp threads are closely placed together, creating a weave.

The women weave the sarongs and shawls woven for their own use, as well as for the men. Since the body is used for creating the tension, the weaving is strenuous and women are unable to weave con-

Cotton shawl, Gopalpur

Cotton shawls are from Gopalpur, Assam, woven on the loin loom, and worn by the women over their *mekhala*. The patterns are woven with thick cotton and in contrasting colours so as to create a rich effect.

Woven sampler, Riang tribe, Tripura

Young Riang girls preserve the traditional designs by weaving the motifs used by their tribe. In the process they also learn to weave.

Riah, **breast cloth, Tripura, contemporary**

A boldly patterned breast cloth from Tripura uses brilliant colours. It is worn by young girls on festive occasions.

tinuously for too long a period. The fact that the warp is attached to the body, limits the width of the cloth to a maximum of 50-60 cms. Pieces must be stitched together to make the complete cloth. The woven jackets worn by the Mishimies are woven in two pieces and put together. The Lotha Naga shawl is woven in nine parts and stitched together to make up a piece. The Lushai shawl or the complex Apatani priest's shawl is also pieced together.

A number of fabrics have stripes which are worked by the introduction of colour variations in the warp. An extra weft is introduced in some of the stripes to create a variation in the movement of the linear pattern as well as to create a dimensional effect. The patterns of the Mishimies, Apatanis, Wanchos and the Kengah have elaborate extra weft patterns. Though the environment provides the inspiration in the highly stylised weaving of the tribes, the motifs used express a range of symbolic meanings which vary in different tribes. A geometric pattern stands for the eye of the yak in one tribe while another sees it as the sun. A spiral is seen as a snake or a hook. A lozenge with tendrils is seen as a temple in one tribe, while in another it is a bird.

The narrow width which concentrates the attention of the weaver, the closeness of the warp threads to the weaver, as well as the close link of the weaving process with the body's rhythm, all lend themselves to the weaving of intricate and delicate patterns. Some of the finest weaves can be seen in the woven sarongs of the Idu Mishimies, in the Lushia wedding sarongs, in the richly patterned *riha*, breast cloths, of Tripura and in the ritual shawls used by the Apatani *shaman.*[3]

The traditions of weaving are so much a part of the life of the women that a mystique has developed around the weaving of patterns and the use

Galong tribal weavers

Women, using a loin loom, weave all their personal needs in north-east India. Here, Galong girls are weaving the striped cloth used by them for their sarongs.

of colours. Amongst the Tiperas of Tripura, legends are both sung and told of woven patterns which suddenly came to life, or of a poor orphan girl who married the prince because of her skill in designing and weaving. And one of the worst punishments that a ruler could inflict on a group was to forbid the use of colours in their weaving.

Assam too has a very important tradition of weaving. Until recently every household used to weave its own requirements of cloth and the women were experts not only with the loin loom, but also with the frame loom. The Bodo tribe which originally migrated from Central Asia brought the art of weaving and silk reeling with them. The Bihu festival of Assam with its special Bihu dance owes its origin to the Bodos. It is customary even today to offer to the elders of the family a woven scarf, *gamcha,* woven by the young women, in white cotton, with a patterned border worked in red. Intricate patterns used to be woven by the women to honour the elders in their family and women vied with one another to create novel combinations and designs. Old patterns were preserved by the families by being woven as samplers, with bamboo sticks added in place of the weft so as to preserve them over generations. The silk *mekhala,*

Idu Mishimie jacket, Arunachal Pradesh, contemporary

This simple strip of cloth is woven on the loin loom by women. The patterns are worked in with white and coloured threads twined on thin bamboo needles. The strips are stitched together to create a jacket.

Opposite Page

Baluchar saree, 19th century

This traditional silk brocaded saree from Bengal has an elaborate *pallu* and a long cross border. It carries *kalgas* in the centre and outlines of a miniature around it with flowing silken brocaded borders. The body carries a delicate all over *buti.* (Collection: Crafts Museum).

Following Page

Tangkhul Naga shawl, Manipur, contemporary

Thick shawls are woven on the loin loom by women for men, using mercerised cotton for the warp and the weft. The closely woven fabric carries a bold and harmonious combination of colours. At the ends of the shawl are finely woven jewel-like motifs

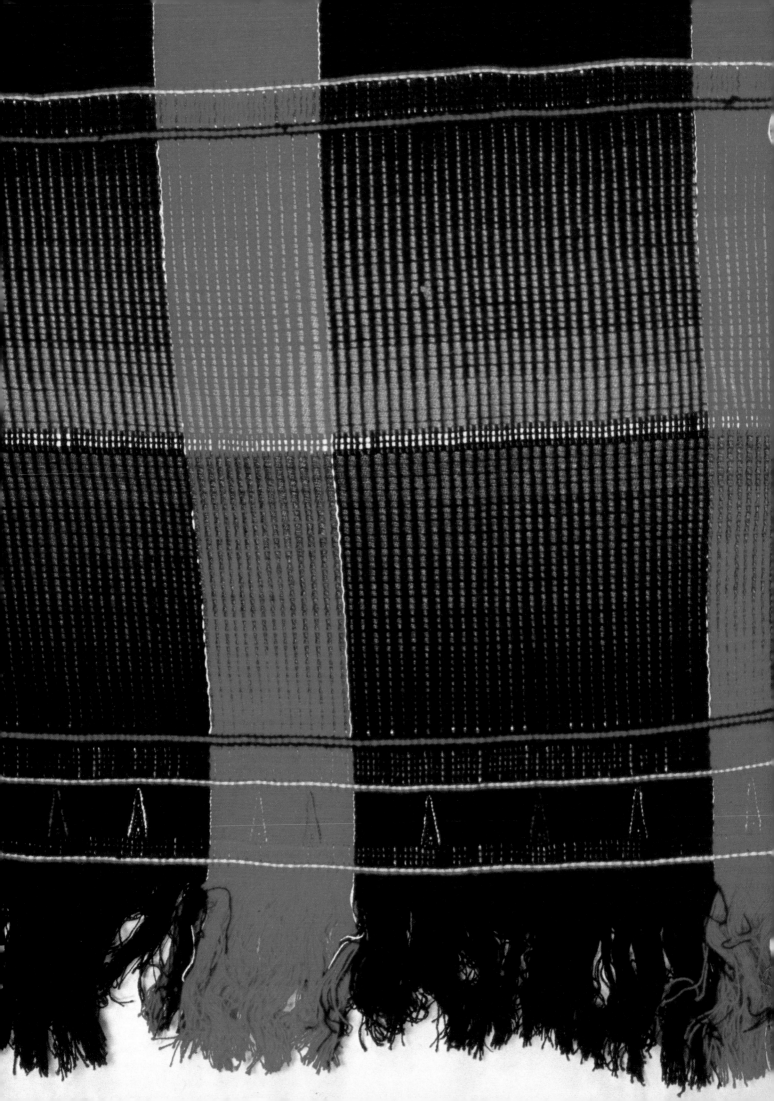

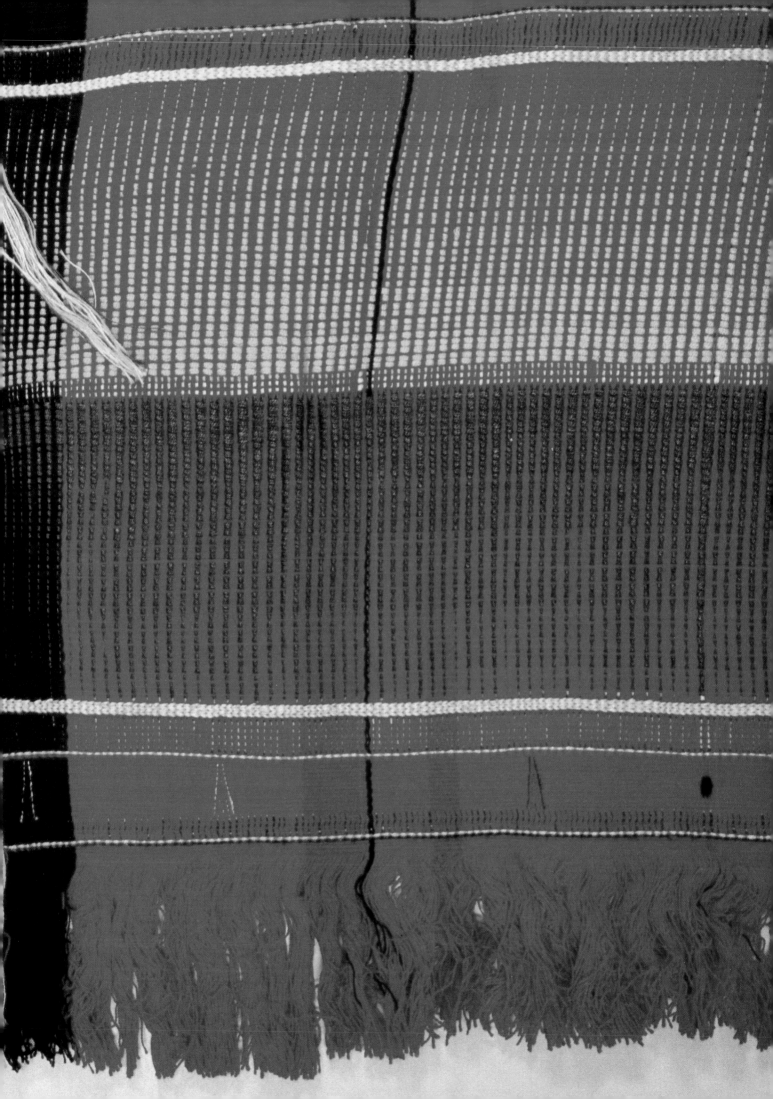

sarong, traditionally worn by the women of Assam, is woven from the golden coloured *moga* silk which is a speciality of Assam. Sualkouchi remains one of the most important *moga* silk centres of Assam. Rich brocaded patterns are woven on the *moga* silk with thick extra weft patterns worked in black, red or in natural white. A finely woven *chadar,* matching with the *moga* silk *mekhala,* is an essential part of the wedding ceremonial or festival dress of the people.

Bengal has been known from ancient times for its fine cotton. *Mal-mal,* known as muslin in Europe, was exported from Bengal and was known as gangetic muslin in the Greek and Roman records. It was described as being transparent, and as light as the winds — *nebula venti,* woven winds. Travellers visiting Bengal from China and the Arab countries talk of the rich merchants of Bengal, whose most important item of export was textiles. Ancient records talk of trade links, not only with the Far East and the Arab world, but also with Ethiopia.

The finest woven cottons of Bengal belonged to the *jamdani* or the Daccai weaves. The cotton sarees had extra weft weaving which was non-continuous. The woven designs ranged in quality from the fine *jamdani,* woven in the same shade and count as the weft yarn, to create a shadowy effect, to bold patterns in multi-colours with a thick twisted cotton yarn. This fine quality was mostly created as yardage material for garments. Sarees were woven with a range of designs with different coloured weft threads of the thicker count and with a range of colours. The *jamdani* weaves of Dacca were extremely valuable and formed a part of the annual tribute paid by Dacca to Aurangzeb (1658-1707). Besides meeting the demands of the court, the traders had contacts in many parts of the country and speciality goods were woven for different markets. Closely worked *jamdani* patterns were woven for export to Khatmandu where it was used for making caps worn by the well-to-do Nepalese. The material was considered so precious that the caps were covered by a thin muslin cloth, through which the pattern was visible. The court of Tripura received special Daccai *mekhlas* worn by the women for special occasions. Till recent times, each saree was packed in specially made lacquered boxes similar to those used for carrying the annual tribute sent to the Emperor Aurangzeb. Gold and silk were also woven into materials to meet the demands of other regions.

The production of fine quality muslin reached its peak in the 18th century to meet orders of the East India Company. With the introduction of machine-made cloth by the end of the 18th century, both in Europe and in the Indian market, the weavers' market was adversely affected and many of them were thrown out of employment. It was common to hear people say that the thumbs of the weavers were cut off, a phrase that has often been taken literally — it actually meant that their only means of livelihood was lost because of the influx of cheap industrial cloth; and the weaver, who had a delicate physique and was unable to do any type of manual work, was completely impoverished.

Silk weaving was known from ancient times and used in the weaving of ritual cloth, as well as combined with cotton to vary colour and texture. Later with the introduction of mulberry silk, a number of silk weaving centres developed in Bengal and in Orissa. Every town and several villages had their silk looms, where weavers drawn from the traditional weaving castes of Tanti and Kayasthas carried out the weaving.

Murshidabad was the centre for silk weaves and the most famous product was the Baluchari saree, originally woven in the small village of Baluchar. The fine twisted silk warp had heavy silk as the weft, often in contrasting colours such as red and black, and yellow and purple, creating an effect of light and shade. The patterns were woven with untwisted silk, giving a rich woven effect. The most dramatic portion of the saree was the *pallu,* end portion; which was made up of a series of long curvilinear *kalgas,* mango motifs surrounded by framed outlines of miniatures, showing a *sahib* with a lady seated on a chair, a woman riding a horse, a steamer with passengers, etc. This art died with the death of Drabraj, the last weaver at the end of the 19th century.

The Jaggi caste produced the cheapest cloth, woven from a mixture of cotton and jute which was used by the poorest.[4] Amongst the Jaggis, men and women worked side by side sharing all the work, unlike in other communities, where the men sat on the loom and wove the cloth, while the the women did the winding and twisting of cotton.

The finest silk and cotton were always woven for the rulers with only the second quality made available to the trading companies for export. The Portuguese were the first traders to have a strong influence on the textile trade. They controlled the weavers through brokers, by advancing large loans. The weavers were heavily indebted and practically bonded to the company, and consequently earned poor wages. A lullaby sung even today in many parts of Bengal indicates the plight of the

Ganga-Jamuna cotton saree, Tangail, contemporary

Bengal has a range of cotton weaving centres where the tradition is of weaving richly patterned sarees with heavy borders contrasting with a finely textured body. This saree has a blue-black body with patterns woven in the *jamdani* technique. The dramatic contrast in colour and the combination of a white pattern on a blue-black body makes it a contemporary piece, made for the changing tastes of today.

Preparation of *bandha* warp for dyeing, Orissa

Young weavers tie the warp threads stretched on the frame to create the design of the *bandha* saree in Ragardi village, Orissa. The frame has the pattern drawn on the stretched warp threads with powdered coal dust. The wall decorations which represent a mythical mountain and mounds of rice are worked in geometric units, as is the warp.

poor: *Aye ghoom jaye ghoom Borgi alou deshe Bulbuli teh dhan khaye jaye Kaj nah debo keshe.* Sleep comes and sleep goes, the Portuguese have come to our land. The nightingale eats away the grain, how will I pay my taxes?

Despite the adverse effect of the introduction of mill-made cloth, sarees and *dhotis,* the traditional saree centres continued to weave. The number of weavers however shrank, but the skills remained. Each centre produced its special weave and even today the tradition continues. The *tangail,* the *dhanekhale,* the *shantipuri* and Bengali *tantair* cotton sarees are simple and yet have a range of borders. Today the *tangail* sarees are making elaborate *pallu* designs using the *jamdani* technique. Generally the sarees are white but now a range of colours has been introduced; and they are available from 60 to 120 counts. The introduction of *moga* silk in the body, in the form of checks or lines, and in the border, adds to the subtle richness of the sarees.

Murshidabad continues to weave the *garad* silk saree in natural colour *tussar* silk with a broad red border, an essential part of a woman's trousseau and worn on special ritual occasions. The Baluchari tradition has also been revived and today Murshidabad produces a range of these patterns.

Orissa has been weaving a range of cotton and silk sarees. The most important tradition has been the weaving of the *bandha,* warp and weft tie-dye technique for making sarees in cotton and silk, and the weaving of extra warp border designs and extra weft *pallus.* The silk tie-and -dye sarees of Naupatna carried a rich *bandha* pattern on the body, extra warp woven patterns on the border and rich multi-coloured designs in an extra weft on the *pallu.* The *bandha* patterns on the silk sarees were generally of single ikat. In the Sambalpur area where cotton *bandhas* were made, the body carried single ikat patterns on the warp while the *pallu* carried designs in stripes in single weft ikat. The lively cotton sarees known as *Vachitrapuri* carried the same combination, except in the case of the square checkerboard pattern which was done in double ikat. Here yellow *tussar* silk was woven into a patterned extra warp design of fish and lotus and checks in silk were also woven into the body.

The silk sarees with a rich extra weft *pallu,* but without *bandhas,* were also some of the finest. Unfortunately the *bandha* technique dominates all the centres and woven patterns have become rare. The extra weft cotton sarees, in thick counts, woven for the tribal women are also fast disappearing.

The *bandha* technique has become so popular that centres where *bandhas* are tied and dyed are preparing borders in single warp ikat and selling them to the centres which did not know the *bandha* technique. These borders have been introduced in some of the centres in Bengal and Bengal cotton sarees with staple *bandha* borders brought in from Orissa are now available for sale.

The dominance of certain techniques, following changes in fashion, has led to a concentration on one or two of them, and it is hoped that the other techniques will not be lost in the process.

FOOTNOTES

1. Robert Skelton, Bengal: The Historical Background from *Arts of Bengal.* Catalogue Trustees of Whitechapel Art Gallery, London, 1979.
2. Aditi Shirali, *Textile and Bamboo Crafts of the North Eastern Region.* National Institute of Design, Bombay, 1983

3. Verrier Elwin. The *Art of the North East Frontier of India,* North East Frontier Agency, Shillong, 1959.
4. Veronica Murphy, *Textiles from Arts of Bengal.* Catalogue, Whitechapel Art Gallery, London, 1979.

Southern India Weaves

The woven textiles of southern India have retained their traditional designs and techniques, for external influences were not as dominant there as in the north. An export trade catered to different markets creating a range of products to meet the varying demands of different countries. This however did not affect the design and the techniques of the goods produced for the local market. Even the influence of the alien tradition of a ruling elite did not spread to the woven traditions, except perhaps in the introduction of new products such as *himroo* and in *kalamkari* designs. Woven designs, especially those of sarees, retained their traditional patterns and colour combinations; for instance, though the Golconda *kalamkari* had a very strong Persian influence, the weav-

Kanchipuram saree, Tamilnadu

A heavy silk saree, with contrasting colours typical of the silk sarees woven in Tamilnadu.

Opposite Page

Silk processing, Tamilnadu

The weaver on the roof top is drying freshly dyed silk for sarees.

ving centres around continued to weave checks and the extra warp patterns that were the traditional techniques of the area.

The distinctive characteristic of the cotton and silk textiles of southern India is that the woven designs are an integrated part of the woven fabric, rather than an addition to the fabric, as in the case of extra weft weaving. The *jamdani* or inlay technique was used in the cotton weaves of Venkatagiri known for their fine quality weaving. Even in the silk extra weft patterns, the *malli moghu* was woven in with the inlay technique. Checks and stripes were worked as variations in colour and texture. The most famous of these were the Cornad sarees which combined silk and cotton, creating textural and colour variations. *Veldari,* the creeper, pattern of the Kanchipuram silk saree was woven with the use of extra warp and the border carried extra warp patterns of the *rudraksh,* mango, guinea or sovereign and *patta.*

The most interesting technique which was possibly developed in the Tamilnadu area is the weaving of solid borders known as *korvai* with the use of three shuttles. The two side shuttles carry colours for the border, which are of the same

Preparation of the warp, Tamilnadu

In a long street traditionally found in all weaving communities, the warp of a saree is being prepared by the weaver's family.

material and colour as the border warp and the centre shuttle carries the material and colour of the body of the saree. First the shuttle on the right is thrown by hand through the shed created in the border; the thread is intertwined with the weft of the body and placed on the woven section. The second shuttle is thrown right across, to the other border where the thread of the third shuttle is intertwined with the body weft and thrown across the border. The shed is closed and the operation is repeated. In this way, the borders are woven with a non-continuous weft and interlocked together, creating the solid colour borders of the saree. The solid *mundhi-pallu* matching with the border is created by cutting the warp thread and

adding another warp by twisting the new set of warp threads with the original warp of the body.

The main body warp and *pallu* warp are then woven together with the weft of the pallu thread for approximately 1¹/₂″ to 2″ before actually cutting the body warp. This process is known as *petni*. This complicated technique of weaving was used for weaving traditional sarees both in cotton and in silk. In Andhra Pradesh, especially Gadwal and Wanaparti, the technique combines the silk border and *pallu* with a cotton body. The technique of extra weft weaving was used only in the rich gold brocaded sarees made for weddings or for offering to the temple. The extra weft patterns were generally woven on the *pallu* of the saree and sometimes all over the body.

Tamilnadu has a range of cotton sarees such as the Nagercoil sarees of coarse counts with brilliant checks and contrasting border and *pallu,* the Coimbatore and Salem cottons as well as the fine, gold bordered Madurai cottons.

Pure silk sarees were an essential part of the life of the Brahmin community. Ritual observations required that the housewife should wear only silk sarees, since silk was the only material considered pure. It was she who performed the *puja* to the

Kanchipuram cotton saree

Richly woven cotton sarees based on traditional silk patterns are being woven in Kanchipuram. This saree has contrasting borders and carries an extra warp pattern in stripes on the body.

149

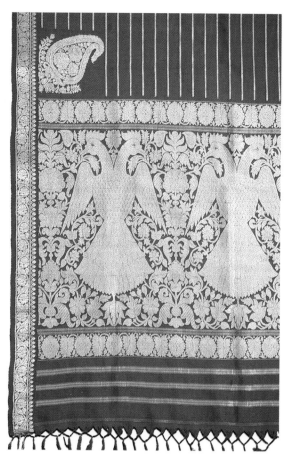

household deity and prepared the food for the family. Even the housewife of a poor Brahmin household would be expected to dress in silk and often had only two sarees, wearing one and washing the other.

Sarees were bought during the *Deepavali* festival and the whole family participated in the yearly visit of the family weaver to the house. Family members pored over the patterns and colours, the type of gold thread to be used and the weight of the sarees, for sarees traditionally were never bought off a shelf. Weavers came from the weaving centres of Thanjavur, Kumbhakonam, Kanchipuram and Dharamavaram, bringing samples of new designs, colours and different qualities of silk. Families of weavers worked over generations with large joint families and since each design had to be woven in a set of three (the warp of three sarees had to be prepared at a time), the family had to work with the weaver to develop variations within the limitation of a single warp.

The finest known examples of the Kerala looms are the *karalakudi* sarees, woven in off-white or unbleached cotton with a gold woven border and *pallu.* The region has hardly any silk weaving centres and the concentration is on the weaving of cotton in white or off-white.

**Silk and gold brocaded saree,
Tanjore, Tamilnadu**

The purple silk saree has a rich gold border and gold stripes woven into the body with the use of extra warp threads. The *pallu* is woven with gold threads worked into an all-over pattern with a dominant motif rarely seen on textiles, that of the double-headed eagles known in Karnataka as Gandhaberunda. The double-headed eagle can also be seen in some old temple jewellery made for the deity.

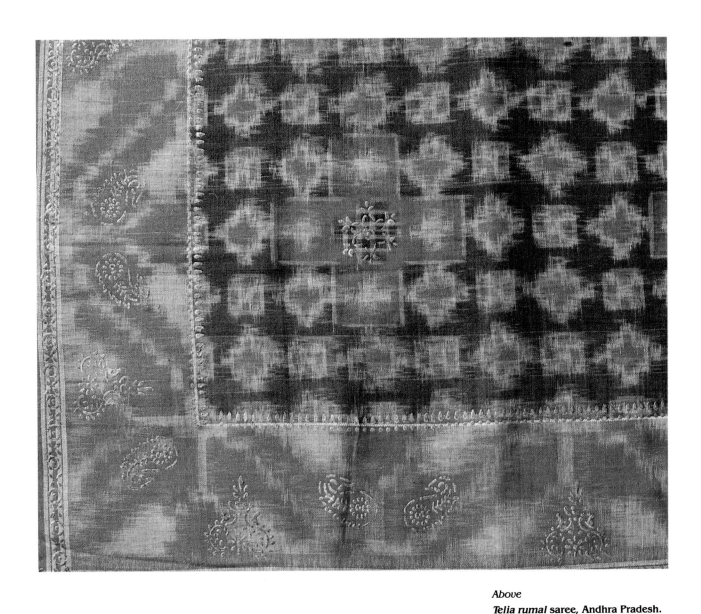

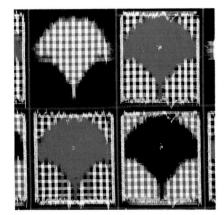

Above

Telia rumal saree, Andhra Pradesh.

Telia rumal weavers sometimes used gold in some of the long pieces, and in some rare cases combined it with embroidery as well. Here the weavers wove a saree that was later printed with goldwork *khardi* to create the effect of a gold weave.

Below

Cotton Cloth in *telia rumal* pattern from Pochampalli, contemporary

Detail of fabric using the traditional Chirala checkered double-ikat technique, in which the solid single coloured motif is enclosed within a square. This type of patterning was typical of the earlier *rumals* produced in Chirala, which were meant for export to the Middle East, the Gulf and Iran. The original colouring was maroon and white with possibly a touch of black. The checkered pattern was used only in maroon and white. Here the technique has been greatly refined and the checked pattern is extremely fine.

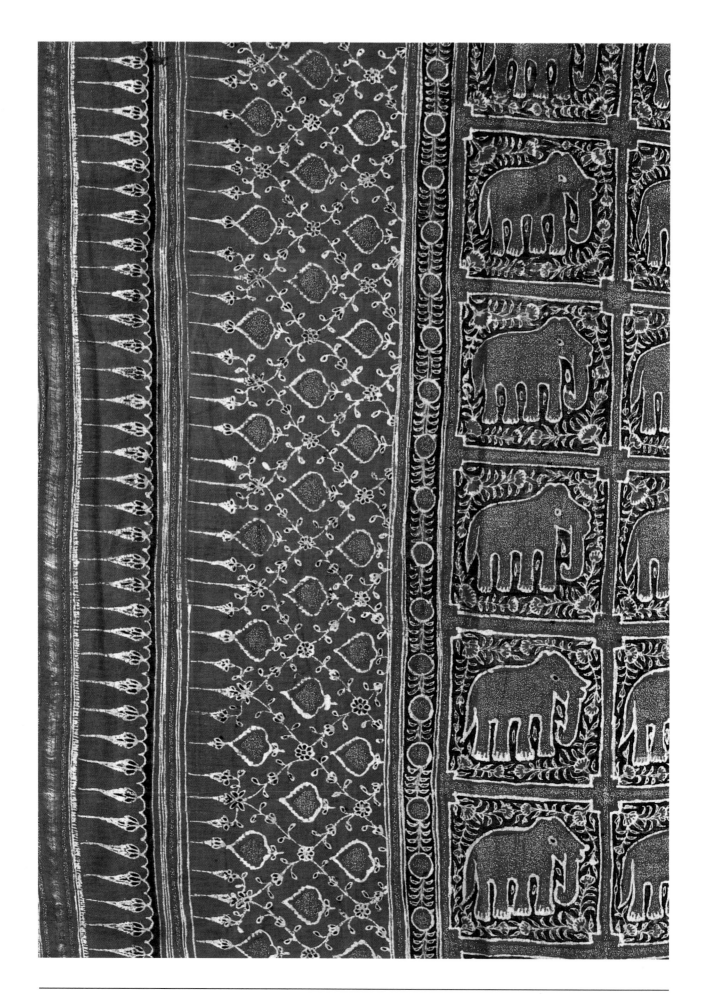

Andhra Pradesh was known for its very fine cotton weaves and Ganjam district has woven these from ancient times. The skill was later transferred to the weaving of *khadi*. Velamma and Pattusali wove very special fine *khadi* for the use of those who had taken to only wearing *khadi* as a part of their involvement with the independence movement and the philosophy of self-reliance, *swadeshi*.

Today there is an amazing range of techniques in Andhra including the finely woven silk of Arni, Puddakottai, Armur, Narayanpett, Siddipet, Sangareddy, Peddapuram, Wanaparti, Gadwal and Ponduru. Sangareddy and Puddakottai wove sarees similar to those of Tamilnadu, while the Narayanpett sarees of silk and cotton were typical of the Maharashtrian style. Armoor used to weave silk sarees with extra weft *butis* of a star or a single flower on the body, and a gold *patta* border. The heavy gold *pallu* had gold thread as the weft and extra weft patterns woven with silver thread in the centre. Borders on four sides were woven in extra weft with silk yarn. The cottons used were brilliant and contrasted with the gold base of the *pallu*. Above the *pallu*, merging into the body, were woven large paisley patterns which created the transition between the richness of the *pallu* and the delicacy of the patterns woven on the body.

Opposite Page

Kodalikaruppar brocaded and printed saree, Tamilnadu

A speciality of the Tanjore area, made for the royal family of Tanjore, this saree combined finely woven cotton with motifs worked with *jamdani* weave in gold thread. With the woven designs as the focal point, the outlines and details were worked in with natural dyes in the *kalamkari* technique. This technique became extinct during the beginning of the century and was revived through the Vishwakarma exhibition, by the Weavers' Service Çentre, Madras.

Poothkulli, Nilgiris, Tamilnadu

The *poothkulli* is a long cloth woven in cotton in two pieces, with woven stripes in red and black, by the Kotas. Within the stripes the Toda women embroider motifs that simulate the weaving technique. The patterns are similar to some of the ancient Ionian patterns. The *poothkulli* is a traditional garment worn by the Todas and is also used for their funerals.

Kanchipuram silk and gold saree, Tamilnadu

The silk saree with contrasting border and *pallu* worked in gold thread carries *zari* stripes on a black ground. Sarees of this kind are usually worn by older women.

Paithani *pallus* have been famous from ancient times. These were woven with a weft of gold thread with patterns worked in silk with the interlocked tapestry techniques. This was essentially a technique of the Deccan and extended upto Chanderi. The older examples of the pattern carry, besides the *pallu*, borders also woven with the *paithani* technique. The sarees were made in cotton and were nine yards long, worn in the *sakacha* or Maharashtrian style. For formal occasions and for the upper caste women to wear outside the home, an elaborately worked *shalu*, a four metre by one-and-a-half metre shawl would cover the wearer from head to toe.

Wanaparti and Hyderabad also had a few weavers knowledgeable in the *paithani* technique. Molkalmuru in Karnataka used the *paithani* technique until the fifties but with a different style of motifs. It was obviously a technique which was highly prized since a number of centres like Armoor, Gadwal and even Surat and Ahmedabad imitated the *pallus* during the beginning of the century.

Changing fashions and Western influences amongst the affluent families and the princely states, found the ladies of the household taking

154

to wearing imported chiffon and georgette sarees; demand for the *paithanis* died down. The weavers began to produce *pallus* to be attached to the chiffon sarees, and small place-mats for the English tourists who visited the Ajanta caves. The designs were thus based on the paintings of lotus flowers, leaves and birds found on the ceiling of the Ajanta caves.

The technique of *ikat* was known in the area from very early times. Research in the origin of the technique indicates that it possibly originated in the Deccan and was carried to Patan. The technique is used in the border of sarees woven in many centres, spread all over the Deccan. The Molkalmuru sarees of Karnataka carry ikat patterns on the body and the border, as does *mashru* woven in Hyderabad.

Telia rumals with ikat patterns, in maroon, white and black were traditionally worn by the men in Andhra Pradesh. They had multiple uses, being worn as a *lungi*, as a turban, as well as a scarf to be thrown on the shoulder — similar to the manner in which *ajrakh* is used in Kutch. The cloth was initially woven in Chirala and was introduced into Pochampalli at the beginning of this century. *Telia rumals* were exported to the Gulf countries, to Africa and to Iran, with the weavers creating patterns suited for different markets. The close contact with Iran led to the development of a brisk trade with the Persian market. In the 60s the All India Handicrafts Board assisted the weavers of Pochampalli to start weaving sarees. Silk weaving was also introduced by training two weavers in Banaras. Pochampalli, a small impoverished village, slowly captured the market for ikat sarees and today the whole of Nalgonda district works on ikat weaves which can compare with the very best in single ikat warp weaving. Pochampalli is copying the *patola* of Patan but it lacks the vitality and beauty of the original.

Certain styles of textiles were developed in the southern states which were especially distinctive. One such was the *himroo,* a mixture of cotton and silk, woven with a warp of cotton and weft of silk. Extra weft patterns were introduced with a silk weft. The cloth, like *mashru,* was used by the Muslim community. Hyderabad and Aurangabad were the important centres of production.

The Kodalikuruppur sarees were developed for the Thanjavur royal family. Fine cotton sarees were woven with gold *jamdani* patterns of stars, lines, wide borders, a delicate tree of life pattern on the *pallu* and roundels all over the body. The gold woven pattern was the core and was enclosed by intricate all-over patterns in maroon and black, worked in the *kalamkari* technique. This technique has recently been revived by the Weavers Service Centre in Madras for the Vishwakarma exhibition. The woven pieces were as fine as the original pieces to be found only in museums.

Sungardhi sarees are woven and tie-dyed in Madurai for the use of communities of Saurashtries settled in Tamilnadu. Some of these were weaver communities having migrated originally from Gujarat and are known as Saurashtries. The finest silk weaving is done by the Pattunulkar who belong to this community. The weavers are called *saliyar,* a word derived from the Sanskrit word *salika,* the weaver, and similar to *salvi,* the family name of the Patan *patola* weavers.

The *kalamkari* tradition in Andhra has a strong tradition of temple cloths, used as a part of the temple ritual, relating the episodes from the Ramayana and Mahabharata. These cloths are also used for decorating *rathas*, chariots, used in processions organised by the temple on special occasions. The centres preparing temple cloths today are in Madras and Kalahasti, while the decorations for the *rathas* are prepared at Chikanayakapetta. Golconda used to produce elaborate hangings and square *rumals* made with designs derived from miniatures but does not do so any more.

The *kalamkari* work of the Coromandel coast was for piecegoods exported to the Far East, essentially to be bartered as trade goods in exchange for spices. Masulipatnam is the only centre which survives today. The style of Masulipatnam is closely linked with the *kalamkari* of Ispahan, Iran, which imported quantities of *kalamkari* from Masulipatnam. Persian craftsmen had been brought to Masulipatnam at the turn of the century and they introduced their techniques and patterns; soon it became difficult to distinguish the Indian *kalamkaris* from the Persian. Later the Indian craftsmen surpassed the Ispahani workers affecting their market adversely.

Rich variations in textiles continue to be woven in southern India despite the influence of films which have brought in pale pastel colours (locally called 'geva colours') as against the brilliant luminous colours which are traditional. Attempts have also been made to weave Banarasi patterns and to weave skirt border sarees. Tradition however is too strong to be lost, and there is today a resurgence of traditional, elaborately woven patterns based on old designs, both in silk and cotton, in all the centres of southern India.

The Handloom Sector of the Textile Industry: An Overview

V.K. Agnihotri

The handloom industry in India is today the largest economic activity in the informal sector, after agriculture. There are roughly 3.8 million handlooms in India, the largest number in the world, engaged in the production of natural fibre fabrics like cotton, silk and woollens, and in man-made and mixed fibre fabrics. The industry is an integral part of rural life and about 10 million people depend on these looms, fully or partially, for their livelihood.

The industry has a long tradition of excellent craftsmanship, forming a part of the country's cultural heritage — "a pulse beat of Indian cultural

The author is the Development Commissioner (Handlooms) and Chairman, ACASH.

life"[1] The weavers are the "link in an unbroken tradition which embraces both producers and consumers within a socio-religious community."[2] In a climate where the preservation of ancient heritages in considered vital, "the fine textile craftsmen of this country are national treasures, and should be so recognised."[3]

Since ancient times, agriculture and handlooms have existed side by side, an integral part of India's agrarian economy, maintaining the balance in the economic life of the country. It is imperative therefore to appreciate the importance of handlooms for maintaining the critical balance of the country's agrarian economy. Unlike natural wealth, which can be regenerated, it would be impossible to revive the handloom industry, if, due to a lack of appreciation of its crucial role, policy formulations were made which would affect its healthy growth.

Handlooms are an important component of the policy of self-sufficiency which is one of the goals of India's planned economy since Independence. Community and area development programmes and, lately, the "cluster approach" adopted by the Government for accelerating rural development, aim at creating self-sufficiency among the rural population of the country. For a long time to come, the basic minimum clothing requirements of the rural population will have to be met by the cloth produced locally on handlooms.

Unemployment and underemployment continue to be a major problem faced by the Indian economy. Several programmes have been initiated to generate additional employment in rural areas. The handloom sector, which employs a large number of people, has to be sustained through programmes which ensure that people employed in the handloom industry continue to derive their sustenance from it. It is unthinkable to provide alternative employment to the approximately 10 million people currently engaged in the handloom sector, for the socio-economic costs of doing so would be too great.

Recently there has been a remarkable growth in the handloom industry primarily as a result of the initiative of the weaving community. "The unique skill of the weaver, his comprehension of colour, texture and function, the weaver's capacity for rapid adaptation and for production of small yardage in a variety of designs"[4] has been the industry's greatest strength. Handloom cloth has become an important foreign exchange earner on account of its ability to meet the needs of fashion markets, producing even a hundred metres of fabric in a particular design or colour combination to meet the individual taste of the consumer. It is this "exclusiveness" of handloom that gives it an edge over cloth produced by the other sectors.

It is necessary to continue research on improving the quality and productivity of handlooms. Studies have shown that minor modifications in machines and processes can increase productivity by upto 50%.

The industry however is traditional and introduction of change is not only a matter of imparting skills, but of changing attitudes; many schemes started with enthusiasm and excellent intentions have not yielded expected results because of the weavers' resistance to change.

A view is sometimes expressed that, in the interest of standardisation and economy of production, handlooms should be gradually replaced by powerlooms or automatic looms. Powerlooms have, in fact mushroomed outside the handloom sector to such an extent that it has adversely effected the latter. A World Bank study has pointed out that the spectacular growth rate of the powerloom industry has been largely due to the fact that the market wage in the powerloom sector is far below that in the mill sector and not so different from that in the handlooms. The World Bank study further points out that the choice facing Indian authorities has been one of a large increase in employment at a low wage as against smaller additions to employment at a higher wage. Therefore, there is a case for encouraging the small sector in order to change the pattern of earnings in favour of low wage workers. This argument would, of course, apply even more strongly in favour of encouraging handlooms.[5]

The importance of the handloom sector in the nation's economy has been recognised by the government at the policy planning level, since Independence. Successive Five Year Plans have encouraged and supported the handloom industry. The outlays in the Central sector's Five Year Plans has gone up from an allocation of Rs.11.10 crores, during the first plan, to Rs.168 crores for the Seventh Plan. This has been further augmented by

Opposite Page

Cotton Maheshwari sarees, Madhya Pradesh, contemporary

The cotton looms of Maheshwar, an important pilgrim centre on the banks of the river Narmada, have a reputation for weaving very fine cotton, and silk and cotton combined sarees. They are woven with subtle coloured checks, a gold *patti*, mat, or a *rudraksh* border.

allocations in the plans of individual State Governments totalling around Rs.500 crores during the Seventh Plan period. As a result of these measures, the number of handlooms has gradually gone up from about 28 lakhs in 1951 to about 38 lakhs today. The production output from handlooms has increased from about 500 million metres in the early fifties to about 3700 million metres in 1985-86, a seven-fold increase in about three decades. Today the handloom sector accounts for nearly 30% of the total textile production in the country.

In successive Textile Policy statements of 1978, 1981 and 1985, handlooms have been given primary importance. The 1978 Textile Policy listed a number of steps to enable the handloom sector to fulfil the role assigned to it in the industrial employment policies of the government. One of the objectives of the 1981 Textile Policy statement was to achieve the maximum possible growth of the handlooms sector to fulfil the role assigned to it in the industrial employment policies of the government. One of the objectives of the 1981 Textile Policy statement was to achieve maximum possible growth of handlooms in the decentralised sector, for generating employment and raising the standard of living of small weavers. It emphasised the revival of dormant looms, as well as their modernisation.

The Textile Policy statement of 1985 recognised the distinct and unique role of the handloom sector and proposed a number of measures for the preservation and growth of this sector as one of the priority areas in the country's development programme. One of the most important of these is the introduction of technical innovations in the looms used by the weavers, so as to increase the productivity and improve the quality of the product. The transfer of technology from the research institutions to the actual weavers working in the field has been emphasised. The diversification of production so as to increase the range of fabrics and thus have access to larger markets is another important part of the programme. The weaving of Janata cloth for the poorer sector of the population will also, to a large extent, be carried out through handlooms.

Parliament has passed a new legislation entitled: "The Handlooms (Reservation of Articles for Production) Act, 1985". On the basis of the recommendation of an Advisory Committee, 22 items have been reserved under this legislation. The government has also decided to set up an effective machinery for the implementation of this legislation. Three Regional Enforcement Offices have been created so far in Delhi, Pune and Coimbatore.

Other supportive measures have been undertaken by the government, in addition to an active programme of supply of materials, worksheds, common facilities, etc. to be carried out through cooperatives and State Corporations. Special fiscal measures have been introduced to remove the cost handicap of handlooms vis-a-vis powerlooms. The existing marketing structure is being strengthened and an intensive programme for publicity and promotion has been launched to expand local and export markets. A census of handlooms is being carried out to broaden the data base. This would help in better planning and programming of the development programmes.

The formulations regarding the handloom sector in the new textile policy are based on the experience of the implementation of earlier handloom development programmes. The sub-group on handlooms, set up in 1983 to formulate policy for the Seventh Five Year Plan, had made recommendations pertaining to the gaps in the existing programmes, as well as new schemes to be taken up for the harmonious and integrated growth of the handloom sector during the Seventh Plan period. It stressed the need for strengthening the machinery for implementation, for monitoring and for the continuous evaluating of development programmes. It also recommended training and upgrading of the technical, managerial and administrative skills of personnel employed in the development and marketing of the sector.

With these measures introduced in the Seventh Plan, the handloom sector is expected to be greatly strengthened and many of the inadequacies that have existed in the system are expected to be overcome.

FOOTNOTES

1. Pupul Jayakar, A Handloom Prilgrimage, The India Magazine, December 1984 .

2. Ibid

3. Ibid

4. Ibid

5. Dipak Mazumdar: World Bank Staff Working Papers, No.645 — The Issue of Small Versus Large in the Indian Textile Industry (An Analytical and Historical Survey), 1984.

Glossary

abrawan — running water, trade name of muslin; Persian

acharo — top cloth of printing table covering in western India.

addhi — light muslin

adguvāsā — shoulder cloth for men

adhyaka — supervisor of weaving workshop, Mauryan period

agani — fire

ajrakh / azrakh — resist-printed fabric from Kutch and Sind

aksi — reflection, embroidery or weave visible on one side

aksu — a garment

aksāvana — garment with lace trimming

alankar — ornament

algodan — cotton in Spanish; derived from Arabic

alkatifa / alquatifa — velvet or looped woven cloth; Arabic

al-khamliyat — velvet; Arabic

alpona — ritual floor patterns in Bengal

alquaton — cotton; Arabic

alunah — pulling out of hair from sheep

amir — noble; Persian

amlikar — embroidered shawl

anānās — pineapple

anchal / pallu — upper end of the saree

angarkha / angarkhi — stitched upper garment for men

anjan — kohl

apave — weave back

apasraya — a garment

aribel — diagonal creeper pattern

aripana — ritual floor patterns

asavali / ashawali — silk sarees woven in Ahmedabad & Surat

asali-tus — underhair of mountain goat

ashrafi — gold coin

asil / asul — real

astarana — a garment

asule-jo pur — outline block, used for *azrakh* in Sind and Kutch

āto — flour

atlash — satin

āvika — wool; Sanskrit

avirmalha — sheep with small pendants on its throat.

babur khunr — gum of *Mimoza arabica*; used in printing

badam — almond

bagh — garden-an all over darn stitch embroidery from Punjab

bahi — account book

bahi-khata — account and record book

bala-pash / bala-posh — coverlet

Baluchari — silk brocaded saree of Baluchar, Bengal.

banda / bandha — ikat of Orissa

bandhani — tie-and-dye fabric

bandhu	— to tie	*charquab*	— coat; Persian
baqual	— importer of wool in Kashmir	*charu / charun*	— copper pot for dyeing
barāsi	— men's garment	*chati*	— clay pot
barge beed	— willow leaves, Persian	*cheera / chira*	— silk
bayton	— rectangular embroidered Bengal quilt	*chikan kari*	— white on white embroidery
be-puri	— double-sided; Persian	*chipp / chhipa*	— printers
bhagti marg	— path of devotion	*chipri*	— reed mat placed on dye container for dipping printing block
bhathi	— fireplace	*chiraha*	— turbans
bhuk	— handfull; Sindhi	*chitra*	— drawing, design
bigha	— measurment of agricultural land	*chitra virali*	— figured muslin
bogcheh	— cloth for tying clothes; Persian	*choli*	— blouse
boteh / buta / buti	— plant pattern	*chope*	— holbein stitch embroidery of Punjab, Haryana and Rajasthan.
boteh-kaj	— slanting shrub pattern; Persian	*cina patta*	— Chinese silk
boteh-reez	— small shrub pattern; Persian	*chint*	— variegated or sprinkled, derived from the Sanskrit *chitra*, i.e. chintz
bukram / bogranum / boccranum	— stiff cloth for lining derived from the place name Bokhara.	*cit-citary*	— printed cloth; Turkish
		citares	— printed cloth; Rumanian
		cuna / chuna	— lime
camri	— piece of cloth or paper to cut the printing block, used in north-west India.	*daccai*	— fine cotton saree with inlaid patterns
candātaka	— short skirt for women		
carbasina	— cotton; Latin	*dandio / dhandio*	— sticks
cat	— processing of printed cloth on sandy river bed	*darbhā / kusa*	— a kin of plant used for manufacturing textiles
chadar / chaddar	— wrap, shawl	*daree*	— non-pile carpet
chador	— veil	*degri*	— copper pot
chahar ghadi	— square shawl	*dha*	— to do the weft
chameli	— jasmine	*dhabla*	— blanket; Gujarati
chanderkhani	— moonlight pattern in tie-and-dye	*dharkala / dharkee*	— patchwork quilt from Kutch

dhoti	— unstitched lower cloth worn by men	*gharchola / gharcholu*	— auspicious red checked tie-and-dye saree used during marriage ceremony in Gujarat
dhussa-dursa-dursha	— men's shawl in Kashmir and northern India	*ghur*	— molasses
doshali amli	— embroidered shawl	*girha*	— measurement of cloth
dou-gul	— two flowers; Persian	*gopi*	— female devotee of Lord Krishna
dou-shala	— double shawl or long shawl		
dou-ruh	— double faced; Persian	*govyacha*	— garment with lace trimming
dou-rukh	— double sided; Persian	*grantha*	— a treatise or book
dou-ranga	— double coloured; Persian	*grivāh*	— neck
drapi	— a garment	*guduma*	— woollen blanket
dukula	— fine quality of bark cloth	*guduri*	— quilt made from worn cloth
dupatta	— long scarf draped over Salwaar and loose shirt worn by women	*gulenar*	— crimson, colour of pomegranate flower; Persian
dvaradeya	— gate tax	*gule parwane*	— butterfly flower; Persian
		guna	— virtues
ek puri	— one sided		
eka	— one	*haft rangi*	— seven-coloured; Persian
		haram	— unlawful
		hashieh / hashia	— border; Persian
gajji	— satin	*hasya*	— laughter
galaband	— scarf	*himroo*	— mixed cotton and silk cloth with extra weft patterns
galicha / galicho	— carpet	*hira kas*	— ferrous sulphate
ganga-yamuna	— gold and silver, two coloured		
garud	— natural colour silk	*ikat*	— tie-and-dye yarn woven to make a pattern
gaumukhi	— cow-faced; cover for the hand and the rosary	*izarband*	— belt or band for trousers
genda	— marigold		
ghar	— layers of cloth laid on printing table	*jal*	— net
gharo kakar	— red cloud	*jala*	— thread Jacquard

jaldar	— net pattern	**kattun (gurma)**	— cotton
jama	— upper coat	**kauseya**	— Chinese silk
jamevar	— woven woollen Kashmir shawl with an all-over pattern	**kesa**	— pieced cloak worn by Buddhist priests in Japan; Japanese
jamdani	— inlaid pattern of extra weft, without floats	**khadi**	— handspun and handwoven cotton cloth
jānu	— knee; Persian	**khand sanghatya**	— multiple pieces joined together
jari-zari	— gold thread	**kharita-khalita**	— bag, purse, envelope
jhul	— elephant cover	**khazz**	— plushy velvet
jimmi	— unstitched skirt worn in parts of Gujaat	**kheva**	— threads used in making the thread — jacquard in Varanasi
julaha	— weaver		
		khilet	— robes of honour
kabar-posh	— shroud	**khurjin**	— donkey bag
kajjari asp	— horse cover	**kim khab / kinkhab**	— gold brocade
kajjari phil	— elephant cover		
kalabatun	— gold thread	**kiungridar**	— serrated border
kalamkari	— patterning of cloth with dyes and use of a pen	**korvai**	— solid border; Tamil
kalin	— carpet	**kos**	— measurement of distance
kamarband	— sash	**ksauma**	— linen
kambala	— blanket of wool	**kulpha**	— ankle
kantha	— quilted and embroidered old cloth; Bengali	**kunjar**	— elephant
kantha	— upper part of the chest	**Kurdi**	— from Kurdistan in Iran
kanat	— tent wall	**kusa**	— a kind of plant usd for manufacturing textiles
kani	— multiple weft patterned Kashmir shawl	**kusornāh**	— fibres of kusa plant
karkhana	— atelier, workshop	**lame**	— gold cloth, gold thread or gilted paper
karpasa	— cotton cloth		
kartana	— spinning	**langot**	— loincloth
Kasi	— Varanasi	**lata kritih**	— creeper design
kathivu-kathipba	— looped cloth or velvet; Arabic	**likhnam**	— drawing of pattern
		lungi	— sarong

lugdi	— half saree worn in north-western India.	*mundhi-pallu*	— contrasting colour cross border; Tamil
		muquim	— broker
majith	— red vegetable dye		
makhamal	— velvet	*nadiri*	— a style of Persian coat
makhi-buta	— fly-sized dots	*naksha*	— pattern. In brocade weaving of Varanasi, it means the making of a thread Jacquard.
makhmali-zarbaft	— velvet with gold woven patterns		
makhmali	— of velvet or like velvet	*naksha bandha*	— maker of the thread jacquard
mal-mal	— fine cotton cloth	*nandra*	— printed cloth
malli moghu	— jasmine buds; Tamil	*nari*	— woman
manga	— mango	*nari-kunjar*	— woman and elephant pattern in *patola* sarees
mar pech	— curved snake; Persian	*narikunjara*	— pattern of elephant formed from figures of women
mashru	— permitted, mixed cotton and silk cloth	*natai*	— reel or swift
Massoria	— fine net like cotton cloth of Kota, Rajasthan.	*nathai*	— thread used in making the thread Jacquard
masur buta	— lentil sized flower	*naqqash*	— design maker
Mata-ni-Pachedi	— painted and printed hanging of the mother goddess from Gujarat	*nawab*	— Muslim aristocrat, or ruler of a state
matandar	— central medallion	*nilambari*	— dark blue-black colour
meenakari	— inlaying of colours as in enamelling	*nirnij*	— a garment
		nivi	— loincloth
meheramat	— striped cloth, shawl; Persian		
mekhala	— sarong worn in Eastern India	*odhani*	— long scarf worn over skirt or half saree
meeti / mitti / mati	— earth, mud	*opasā*	— a garment
minā	— to enamel or blue colour	*ótavah*	— weft yarns
minā-badām	— blue almond	*otu*	— weft
moga	— golden coloured silk		
mogra	— double jasmine	*pachedi*	— long cotton *dhoti* with coloured cross border worn in Saurashtra
mohar	— Indian gold coin		
mothra	— checked tie-and-dye pattern or double *laheria*	*pāda*	— foot

paggia	— threads used in making the master pattern	**petni**	— twisting of new warp threads of the cross border with the warp threads of the body of a saree, in South India; Tamil
Paithani	— a form of weaving of non-continuous weft in interlocked tapestry technique	**phateh dozi**	— embroidery of Kerman; Persian
pandarā pāndya	— upper gament for men	**philkar**	— aluminium sulphate
pandva / pindavika	— woollen shawl worn for rituals	**phuldar**	— flowered
pankhi	— *pashmina* shawl from Uphill areas tie-and-dye	**phup / pusupa / pushpa**	— flower
panyala	— multiple coloured striped cloth from Rajasthan.	**phuli**	— flower
pallu	— cross border of saree or scarf	**pistani band**	— breast cloth; Persian
		piaeh	— base or feet
paramnaram	— exceedingly soft, name given by Akbar to Kashmir shawl	**plangi**	— tying and dyeing of fabrics
		poothkullie	— toga like cloth worn by the Todas
paridhāna	— a garment covering the trunk and thighs	**popat**	— parrot
paridhi	— the weaving implements / the loom	**pra-ve**	— weaving forth
parita	— swift, reed	**pranya tantūms tirāte**	— the one who extends the warp threads
paro	— stone for beating and washing cloth	**pravara / prāvārna**	— upper cloth
pashm-farosh	— retailer of wool	**purgar**	— wooden block-makers in Kutch and Sind
pashmina	— fine quality sheep wool	**purz dar**	— made up of pieces
pathia	— *azrak* printers low printing table	**pushpa-pattas**	— flowered cloth
patka	— sash		
patola (plural) patolo (singular)	— double-ikat of Patan, Gujarat	**qaba**	— coat
patta	— border, stripe	**qalghi**	— plume
patti	— mat design on borders	**qashida / kashida**	— embroidery
pattu	— woollen shawl, Kulu	**qatifa-yi-I-Purabi**	— cotton-velvet; eastern
pavāsta	— a garment covering the trunk		
pench	— superfine quality figured muslin.	**quba**	— an outer vest worn during Jehangir's reign
pesa	— embroidery		
pesa ka kara	— embroidery worker	**rach**	— spindle

rafoogar / *rafugar*	— repairer of shawls
rajayitri	— woman dyer
ralli	— quilt made from pieces of threadbare cloth carrying applique pattern
rangar	— dyer; painter of a prepaired pattern
ranga-tikat	— colour card
rasa chitra	— paintings associated with different emotions
ratha	— chariot
riah	— breast cloth; Tripura
rudhraksh	— auspicious seed used for making a rosary
rumal	— square scarf
safidalcha	— white
sakacha	— 9 yard saree worn with pleats tucked into the back.
saliyar	— weaver's caste in Southern India
salwar / *shalvar*	— loose pyjamas
salvi	— weavers of *patola* in Patan
śanah	— a kind of flax
saqlat	— scarlet broad cloth
sayaban	— awning
seh-gul	— three flowers, Persian
shabnam	— morning dew, name of a muslin
shakhe gavaz	— stag horn pattern; Persian
shal	— shawl; Persian
shale - termeh	— patterned shawl; Persian
shalu	— cotton or silk shawl worn by Maharashtrian women over the saree.
shal-hashiayadar	— shawl with borders

shal-phiri	— second quality shawl
sharad poornima	— autumnal full-moon
shahtoosh	— kind of wool, quality wool from the undercoat of mountain goats
shikam	— stomach
shikar gah	— hunting place; name of a hunting design
sir	— head
siras	— head
sodagiri	— printed cloth for trading
sofreh	— table-cloth; Persian
souzani	— stitched cloth, bath mat; Persian
śrnga	— horns of ram
stukā	— wool sleek haired wool producing sheep / carded
suchi	— wooden bobbin
suf	— wool; Persian
sungardhi	— tie-and-dye sarees of Madurai, Tamilnadu
suvasa urnavali	— valley of Sind known for its wool
swadeshi	— produced in the country. The Indian movement started by Mahatma Gandhi to boycott all foreign goods
tak posh	— shelf or niche cover; Persian
talim	— written instruction for Kashmiri shawl weaving
tan	— to prepare warp
tanchoi	— silk brocade originally woven in Surat
tanjeb	— fine figured muslin, or a coat made from it
tantair	— cotton
tantavah	— warp threads

tapai	— processing of a dye by sunning
tarah-guru	— master who reads out the design
tarahdar	— with designs
tarahadar guru	— master designer
tareh armeni	— Armenian pattern
tareh — farangi	— European pattern
tareh — rumi	— Turkish pattern
tarpyā	— upper garment of men made of whitish wool
tatā / tantu	— the warp
taviz	— amulet
termeh	— woollen material with non-continuous weft patterns woven in Iran.
thal	— net
thiyab makhmal	— velvet garments; Arabic
thulma	— thick blanket
tibri	— broken pot
tili	— straw
tilia rumal / telia rumal	— tie-and-dye scarves woven in Andhra
tilikar	— woven on the loom with small bobbins
tiraz	— factories originally belonging to the Caliphate to weave special fabrics. Later came to be known as royal ateliers.
toojins	— wooden bobbins
tritik	— stitch resist dyeing
tus	— woolly undercoat of high altitude goats
umah	— a kind of flax
upabarhana	— cushion for the throne
upadhāna	— a garment
upapaksā	— armpit
upasarya	— a garment
upastarana	— a garment
upastir	— a garment
urna	— a wool
urnavati	— sheep
usnisa	— men's upper garment of whitish wool, also turban.
ut-ji-gissi	— camel dung
utkrnatti	— the drawing up of heedle rods
Vaishnav	— followers of Vishnu
varatapani	— drawing on cloth with dyes.
vasas	— sacramental garment
vāsana	— a garment for consecration during sacrifice worn by men & women
vasovāya	— weaver
vasman	— a garment
vāstra	— fabric on the loom and a valuable object.
vastra haran	— depiction of Krishna stealing the *gopis'* clothes
vati	— small vessel
veldari	— creeper design
yantra	— ritual diagram

Captions

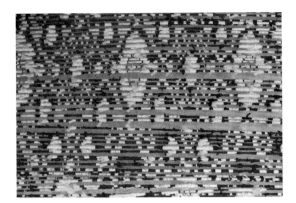

Warp of a Patan *patola*, Gujarat.

The tied and dyed warp threads are of a traditional *patola* saree from Patan. The basic outline of the design is created by tying the base colour of the warp threads. The colours are then dyed and tied until the entire pattern is created.

Raghardhi village, Orissa

Dyeing and weaving is part of the life of the *bandha* weavers of Orissa. They till the soil and grow their rice but their main occupation is the weaving silk and cotton *bandha* sarees.

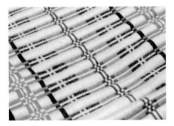

Woven quilt, Manipur, contemporary

The Manipuris have a tradition of weaving quilts with the use of cotton slivers introduced between closely laid parallel warp threads and then enclosed by weaving in weft threads. Variations in colours of the warp create a flowing linear pattern.

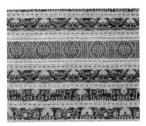

Bandha saree *pallu*, Sambalpur

The *bandha* in this saree is very refined. The outline of the design has been tied down first so as to create a clear linear pattern. (Collection: Crafts Museum).

Brocaded silk saree, Tanjore

The richly brocaded saree has an unusual *pallu* which merges into the body. The saree combines a range of techniques. The *pallu* is dyed a bright pink to match with the colour of the border, and the body is dyed purple after tyeing the dyed *pallu* warp threads. This results in the pink warp merging into the purple. The warp threads of the border are laid with an extra warp in *zari* to weave the border with the use of the dobby. The *pallu* is woven with extra wefts thrown across upto the border and then reversed. With the end of the pink warp the extra weft *pallu* comes to an end. The pattern is then woven in the *jamdani* or inlay technique where each motif has a separate bobbin. The diagonally placed *kalga* and the lotus flowers lend a symmetrical effect to a very classical pattern.

The body begins with stripes woven with an extra warp twisted with the silk warp threads in the same manner as used for making the *paithani* solid *pallu*. The stripe with a wavy pattern is so closely woven that it becomes a part of the fabric.

PHOTO CREDITS